GAME DEVELOPMENT ESSENTIALS:

GAME INTERFACE DESIGN

Kevin Saunders

Jeannie Novak

THOMSON

DELMAR LEARNING™

Australia   Canada   Mexico   Singapore   Spain   United Kingdom   United States

9-08

#70045889

THOMSON

TM

DELMAR LEARNING

Game Development Essentials: Game Interface Design
Kevin Saunders & Jeannie Novak

**Vice President, Technology
and Trades ABU:**
David Garza

Director of Learning Solutions:
Sandy Clark

Managing Editor:
Larry Main

Acquisitions Editor:
James Gish

Product Manager:
Sharon Chambliss

Marketing Director:
Deborah Yarnell

Marketing Manager:
Penelope Crosby

Director of Production:
Patty Stephan

Production Manager:
Andrew Crouth

Content Project Manager:
Nicole Stagg

Technology Project Manager:
Kevin Smith

Editorial Assistant:
Niamh Matthews

Cover: *World of Warcraft*® image provided courtesy of Blizzard Entertainment, Inc.

Library of Congress Cataloging-in-Publication Data:
Novak, Jeannie, 1966–
Game development essentials. Game interface design / Jeannie Novak.
p. cm.
ISBN 1-4180-1620-9
1. Computer games—Programming.
2. Computer games—Design.
3. User interfaces
(Computer systems) I. Title.
II. Title: Game interface design.
QA76.76.C672N68 2006
794.8'1526—dc22
              2006018192
ISBN: 1-4180-1620-9

NOTICE TO THE READER

CONTENTS

Chapter 2   Goals and Considerations: what are we trying to accomplish? 18

Chapter 3   Categorizing Interfaces: what are the options? 52

Chapter 6   Control Schemes: empowering the player 148

Chapter 7   Feedback Schemes: informing the player 176

Part III: Practice 211

Chapter 8 Process of Interface Design: how interfaces are created 212

Chapter 9 Prototype Interface Design: putting it all together 238

Introduction

Game Interface Design
creating the connection

The key difference between electronic games and other forms of entertainment is *interactivity*. With the help of game interfaces, players truly connect with the game and participate in the entertainment experience in unprecedented ways.

Traditionally, interfaces are often relegated to secondary importance in game development. Even within teams that recognize the significance of the interface, design and implementation are often assigned to less-experienced artists, designers, and programmers rather than specialized interface designers. However, game interface design is increasingly being recognized as an integral aspect of game design. It is now a known fact that players will become frustrated or confused if they don't get the feedback and control that are made possible by well-designed game interfaces. A thorough understanding of interface design and how it is related to gameplay is essential for a highly polished game.

In this book, you will learn: the role of interface design in developing great games; tricks of the trade for creating seamless and effective interfaces; the relationship between solid interface design and incredible gameplay; and techniques for making your games more entertaining through interface design. As one of the few books of its kind on the market, *Game Interface Design* is a much-needed, invaluable resource for students and game developers alike.

As the game industry continues to mature, game interface design will become increasingly important. We hope that this book provides you with a solid understanding of game interfaces and drives you to explore new and innovative ways of creating amazing experiences for your players.

Kevin Saunders
Santa Ana, CA

Jeannie Novak
Santa Monica, CA

About the *Game Development Essentials Series*

The *Game Development Essentials* series was created to fulfill a need: to provide students and creative professionals alike with a complete education in all aspects of the game industry. As more schools continue to launch game programs, the books in this series will become even more essential to game education and careers. Not limited to the education market, this series is also appropriate for the trade market and for those who have a general interest in the game industry. Books in the series contain several unique features. All are in full-color and contain hundreds of images—including original illustrations, diagrams, game screenshots, and photos of industry professionals. They also contain a great deal of profiles, tips and case studies from professionals in the industry who are actively developing games. Starting with an overview of all aspects of the industry—*Game Development Essentials: An Introduction* —additional books in this series focus on topics as varied as interface design, project management, artificial intelligence, gameplay, level design, audio, player communities, online games, mobile games, and game development history.

Jeannie Novak
Lead Author & Series Editor

About *Game Interface Design*

Game Interface Design provides an overview of the important yet often overlooked topic of user interface design for electronic games—including the history of game interface design, manual vs. visual interfaces, passive vs. active interfaces, platform-specific interface design, genre-specific interface design, control schemes, feedback schemes, process of interface design, and interface prototyping.

This book contains the following unique features:

- Key chapter questions that are clearly stated at the beginning of each chapter
- Coverage that surveys special topics in game interface design—including usability, accessibility, aesthetics, prototyping, and multiplayer considerations
- Thought-provoking review and study questions appearing at the end of each chapter that are suitable for students and professionals alike to help promote critical thinking and problem-solving skills
- A wealth of case studies, profiles, tips, and quotations from game industry officials
- An abundance of full-color images throughout that help illustrate the concepts and techniques discussed in the book
- A companion DVD that contains documentation, research, and both game and software demos

There are several general themes associated with this book that are emphasized throughout, including:

- Differences between games and other entertainment media (such as film)
- Usability and player control as primary aspects of game development
- Importance of accessibility when designing game interfaces
- Significance of the connection between gameplay and interface design

Who Should Read This Book?

This book is not limited to the education market. If you found this book on a shelf at the bookstore and picked it up out of curiosity, this book is also for you!

The audience for this book includes students, industry professionals, and the general interest consumer market. The style is informal and accessible, with a concentration on theory and practice—geared toward students, artists, and game designers.

Readers that might benefit from this book include:

- Interface designers from other media (such as web development) who are interested in migrating to the game industry
- Game designers and artists who are interested in honing their interface design skills
- College students in game development, interactive design, communication, graphic design, and emerging technologies programs
- Art, design and programming students who are taking introductory game development courses
- Professional students in college-level programs who are taking game development overview courses
- First-year game development students at universities

How Is This Book Organized?

This book consists of three parts—focusing on foundation, theory, and practice.

- Part I—Foundation (Ch 1–3): This part focuses on the history and basic principles of interface design—including descriptions of manual, visual, passive, actual, aesthetic, and accessible interfaces.
- Part II—Theory (Ch 4–7): This part focuses on interface design issues related to platforms, genres, feedback, and control.
- Part III— Practice (Ch 8–9): This part focuses on the interface design process, development cycle, prototyping, and interface design documentation (IDD) elements.

How to Use This Text

The sections that follow describe text elements found throughout the book and how they are intended to be used.

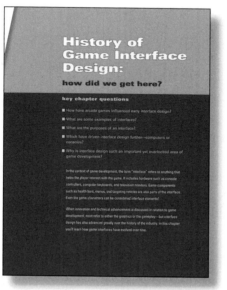

key chapter questions

Key chapter questions are learning objectives in the form of overview questions that start off each chapter. Readers should be able to answer the questions upon understanding the chapter material.

sidebars

Sidebars offer in-depth information from the authors on specific topics—accompanied by associated images.

notes

Notes contain thought-provoking ideas provided by the authors that are intended to help the readers think critically about the book's topics.

profiles

Profiles provide bios, photos and in-depth commentary from industry professionals and educators.

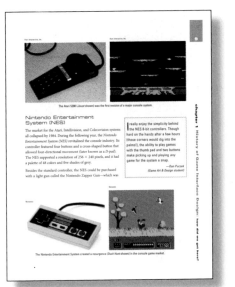

quotes

Quotes contain short, insightful thoughts from players, students, and industry observers.

case studies

Case studies contain anecdotes from industry professionals (accompanied by game screenshots) on their experiences developing specific game titles.

Game Interface Design: creating the connection **introduction**

tips

Tips provide advice and inspiration from industry professionals and educators, as well as practical techniques and tips of the trade.

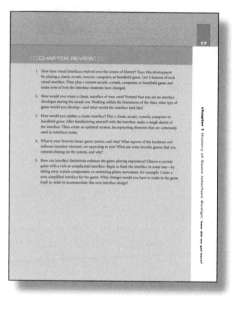

chapter review

A *chapter review* section at the end of each chapter contains a combination of questions and exercises, which allow readers to apply what they've learned. Annotations and answers are included in the instructor's guide, available separately (see next page).

About the Companion DVD

The companion DVD contains the following media:

- *Torque* game engine (Windows and Mac versions 1.4)
- Game design document (GDD) template (Chris Taylor/Gas Powered Games) and *Sub Hunter* GDD (Michael Black/Torn Space)
- Accessibility videos (*Cyberlink, Demor, Doom 3 [CC]*, and QuadControl demonstration by Robert Florio playing *The Matrix: Path of Neo*)
- One-switch games (which allow physically disabled players to use only one button as a controller; *Alice Amazed, Aurikon, Mini Golf: One Button Style, Orbit Racers, Penalty Shoot Out, Sentinella, Strange Attractors*, and *Dork*)
- Additional accessibility games (*Access Invaders, Driver, Win Pong, Doom 3 [CC]*, and *Terraformers*)
- Interface, accessibility and game design articles (from Harvey Smith/Witchboy's Cauldron and Barrie Ellis/One Switch Games)

- Game demos/trial versions from 2K Games (*Prey*), Blizzard (*Diablo II*), Ubisoft (*Heroes of Might & Magic V, Blazing Angels: Squadrons of WWII*), Stardock (*Galactic Civilizations II: Dread Lords*), Enemy Technology (*I of the Enemy: Ril'Cerat*), Star Mountain Studios (*Bergman, Weird Helmet, Frozen, Findella*), and GarageGames (*Dark Horizons: Lore Invasion, Gish, Marble Blast: Gold, Rocket Bowl Plus, Zap!, Tube Twist, Orbz, Think Tanks*)

About the Instructor's Guide

The instructor's guide (available separately on DVD) was developed to assist instructors in planning and implementing their instructional programs. It includes sample syllabi, test questions, assignments, projects, PowerPoint files, and other valuable instructional resources.

Order Number: 1-4180-1623-3

About the Authors

Kevin D. Saunders programmed his first game, a 'port' of Intellivision's *Astrosmash,* on a ZX81 at the age of six. His interest in programming (and games) continued through college, where he worked on developing artificial intelligence systems for natural language processing. His official career as a game designer evolved from his graduate research in environmental engineering. This research included lab experiments that required hourly monitoring over two- to three-day periods. These lengthy experiments gave Kevin the time to explore the world of online games and led to an opportunity to work on Nexon's *Nexus: The Kingdom of the Winds,* which launched in 1998 and became one of the world's earliest massively multiplayer online games (MMOGs). Kevin subsequently designed and produced *Shattered Galaxy,* the world's first massively multiplayer online real-time strategy (MMORTS) game and winner of the Best

Multiplayer Strategy Game of 2001 from GameSpot. Kevin has worked as a Game Designer at Electronic Arts (*Command & Conquer Generals: Zero Hour* and *The Lord of the Rings: The Battle for Middle-earth*). He is currently a lead designer at Obsidian Entertainment, where he has worked on *Star Wars: Knights of the Old Republic II: The Sith Lords* and *Neverwinter Nights 2.* Kevin's hobbies include volunteering at the Speech and Language Development Center—a school for physically, emotionally, and mentally challenged children. Kevin earned his Master of Engineering degree from Cornell University.

Photo credit: Luis Levy

Jeannie Novak is the founder of Indiespace—one of the first companies to promote and distribute interactive entertainment online—where she consults with creative professionals in the music, film and television industries to help them migrate to the game industry. In addition to being lead author and series editor of the *Game Development Essentials* series, Jeannie is the co-author of three pioneering books on the interactive entertainment industry—including *Creating Internet Entertainment.* Jeannie is a game instructor and course development expert at the Art Institute Online, UCLA Extension, Art Center College of Design, Academy of Entertainment and Technology at Santa Monica College, DeVry University, and Westwood College. Jeannie has developed or participated in game workshops and panels in association with the British Academy of Television Arts & Sciences (BAFTA), Macworld, Digital Hollywood, and iHollywood Forum. She is a member of the International Game Developers Association (IGDA) and has served on selection committees for the Academy of Interactive Arts & Sciences (AIAS). Jeannie was chosen as one of the 100 most influential people in high-technology by *MicroTimes* magazine—and she has been profiled by CNN, *Billboard Magazine,* Sundance Channel, *Daily Variety,* and the *Los Angeles Times.* She received an M.A. in Communication Management from the University of Southern California (USC), where she focused on games in online distance learning. She received a B.A. in Mass Communication from the University of California, Los Angeles (UCLA)—graduating summa cum laude and Phi Beta Kappa. When she isn't writing and teaching, Jeannie spends most of her time recording, performing and composing music. More information on the author can be found at http://jeannie.com and http://indiespace.com.

Acknowledgements

We would like to thank the following people for their hard work and dedication to this project:

Jim Gish (Acquisitions Editor, Thomson/ Delmar), for making this series happen.

Sharon Chambliss (Product Manager, Thomson/Delmar), for moving this project along and always maintaining a professional demeanor.

Tom Stover (Production Editor, Thomson/ Delmar), for his help during the production phase.

Nicole Stagg (Content Project Manager, Thomson/Delmar), for her consistent responsiveness during production crunch time.

Ralph Lagnado (Image Research & Permissions Specialist), for his endless commitment and superhuman efforts in researching, finding, tracking, and clearing the many images in this book.

Niamh Matthews (Editorial Assistant, Thomson/Delmar), for her ongoing assistance throughout the series.

Dave Welsh (Project Editor, Carlisle Publishing Services), for his hard work during the layout and compositing phase.

Marcus J. Albers (IT Support Specialist, Carlisle Publishing Services), for his helpful content suggestions during the production phase.

Ben Bourbon, for his clever and inspired illustrations.

Per Olin, for his organized and visually-pleasing diagrams.

Ian Robert Vasquez, for his aesthetic and functional interface designs.

Dung Chi Trinh, for his help in capturing game screenshots for the book and the cover.

Martin Thomas, for his assistance in finding the perfect cover screenshot.

Jason Bramble, for his dedicated and quick work in capturing and annotating several screenshots and diagrams.

David Koontz (Publisher, Chilton), for starting it all by introducing Jeannie Novak to Jim Gish.

A big thanks also goes out to all the many people who contributed their thoughts and ideas to this book:

Aaron Marks (On Your Mark Music Productions)

Aggressive Game Designs

Alan Dennis

Alan de Lespinasse (Moo Job Inc.)

Barrie Ellis (One Switch Games)

Bob Mitchell (Sony Online Entertainment)

Brandon A. West

Brent LaDue

Brian Mitsoda

Brian Young

Briar Lee Mitchell (Star Mountain Studios)

Chris Avellone (Obsidian Entertainment)

Chris Parker

Chris Taylor (Gas Powered Games)

Dan Cash

Dan Puczek

Daniel Kim

Danny Boyd (Apocalyptic Coders)

Darren T. Priddy

David Brin

David Perry (Shiny Entertainment)

Dr. Dimitris Grammenos (HCI Lab for FORTH)

Donny Miele

Drew Davidson (Carnegie Mellon University)

Dung Chi Trinh

Eric Walker (Ominous Development)

Feargus Urquhart

Frank Gilson (Wizards of the Coast)

Gordon Walton (Bioware)

Harvey Smith (Midway)

Howard Kinyon (Breakaway Games)

Ian Bean (Priory Woods School)

Ian Wall (Obsidian Entertainment)

Irwin Robert Vasquez

Jesper Sorensen (ncom.dk)

Jim Kitchen (Kitchen's Inc.)

Joe Maruschak (GarageGames)

John Ahlquist (Ahlquist Software)

John Comes (Gas Powered Games)

Jonathan Clark

Josh Sawyer

Dr. Leonard W. Lion

Leonardo Sala (Gomma Animedia)

Lisa Hathaway

Luis Levy (TreyArch/Activision)

Marc Sapitula

Marianne Krawczyk

Mark Temple (Enemy Technology)

Mark Terrano (Hidden Path Entertainment)

Matt Garretson

Michelle Hinn (DonationCoder.com; IGDA Accessibility SIG)

Michael Andersson (michi.nu)

Michael Black (Torn Space)

Michael Ortiz (ESC Studios)

Nicole Lazzaro (XEODesign, Inc.)

Nir Silva

Norman Hechavarria (Naked Poly)

Oscar Leal

Pug Fugly Games

Randy Wallace

R. Chase Mack

Reid Kimball (Games [CC])

Dr. Richard I. Dick

Richard Taylor (Obsidian Entertainment)

Richard Van Tol (AudioGames)

Robert Florio

Robert Stewart

Scott Lee

Shawna Olwen (Digital Simulation Labs)

Stieg Hedlund (Perpetual Entertainment)

Thomas Westin (Pin Interactive)

Tim Donley (Bottlerocket Entertainment)

Timothy Nixon (Straylight Studios)

Trevor Kayser

Troy Dunniway (Midway)

Trystan Coleman

Vincent Leyba

Welter Almeida

Thanks to the following people for their tremendous help with referrals and in securing permissions, images, and demos:

Ai Hasegawa & Hideki Hyoshimoto (Namco)

Alta Hartmann & Brian Jarrard (Bungie)

Andrew Green (Shiny Entertainment)

Andrew Junker (Brain Actuated Technologies)

Andreas Raht & Markus Heinsohn (Out of the Park Developments)

Anthony Roux, Emmanuel Darras & Thomas Bahon (Ankama)

Barrie Ellis (OneSwitch)

Brian Hupp (Electronic Arts)

Chris Glover (Eidos)

Dave Timoney & Marlene Williams (Gas Powered Games)

Chrissie Rios & Brennan Reilly (Midway)

Chu Tim Kin (Enlight Software)

David Berman (Interplay)

David Kwock & Joy Rogers (Blue Planet)

David Swofford & Janna Bureson (NCsoft)

Elene Campbell (inXile entertainment)

Emmanuel Olivier (MC2)

Erick Einsiedel & Teresa Cotesta (BioWare)

Erick Low & Jocelyn Portacio (Ubisoft)

Ferenc Nagy-Szakall (Stormregion)

Frederic Chesnais & Cecelia Hernandez (Atari)

Garth Chouteau & David K. Haas (PopCap Games)

Greg Deutsch, Mike Mantarro, Megan Korns & Danielle Kim (Activision)

Guillaume de Fondaumiere (Quantic Dream)

Henk B. Rogers (The Tetris Company)

Hilary Ross & Kate Ross (Wizards of the Coast)

In Joon Hwang & Sean Parry (Madcatz)

Iris Wong (Getty Images)

Janet Braulio (Nintendo)

Jay Moore & Benjamin Bradley (GarageGames)

Jeff Reese & Christina Cavallero (Sony)

Jessica Van Pernis & Sue Carrol (Apple)

Jill Coderman & Nina Walia (PBS)

JoAnn Bryden & Kathy Carpano (Hasbro)

Joe Adamoli (US Department of Homeland Security)

John Tam & Dean Ku (Red Octane)

Jonas Stewart (Silver Creek Entertainment)

Junichi Kobayashi (Jaleco)

Kelly Flock, David Greenspan & Linda Torres (THQ)

Ken Yankelevitz & Diane Yankelevitz (KYE)

Kristin Hatcher (Stardock)

Liz Buckley (Majesco)

Marissa Gonzalez (GolinHarris)

Mark Beaumont, Estella Lemus & Michiko Morita Wang (Capcom)

Mark Perfrement (Lionhead)

Mark Temple (Enemy Technology)

Melisa Glasberg (DeLyon-Hunt & Associates)

Michael Domaguing (Tecmo)

Michael Dornbrook (Harmonix Music Systems)

Michelle Hinn (DonationCoder.com; IGDA Accessibility SIG)

Nancy Figatner, Alicia Hatch, Craig Evans & Scott Callan (Microsoft)

Nicholas Lefevre, Marc Franklin, Claire Moore, Jason Enos & Naoki Okda (Konami)

Nokia

Paul W. Sams, Denise Lopez & Brie Messina (Blizzard)

Paul Crockett (2K Games)

Pete Hines (Bethesda)

Pro Sotos (Strategy First)

Rod Rigole, Lori Inman, Kevin Crook & Sylvia Whiteshield (Vivendi Universal Games)

Ruth Fankushen (BigStockPhotos.com)

Scott Lynch, Doug Lombardi & Jason Holtman (Valve)

Simon Jeffery, Robert Leffler, Dyna Lopez, Jana Rubenstein, Jeanette Manahan, Jennie Sue & Molly Musler (Sega)

Stacey Reiner (Ragdoll)

Stephen Martin & Dennis Shirk (Firaxis)

Steven A. Bercu (lime, llc)

Sue Carrol (Apple)

Suzanne MacGillivray (DreamCatcher Interactive)

Taito Corporation

Zicel Maymudes (Mattel)

We would also like to thank the following reviewers for their valuable suggestions and technical expertise:

Sean Brown, Westwood College

Stephen Webster, Vancouver Film School

Randy Sturgeon, Westwood College

Brian Windsor, The Ohio State University

Bradley S. Thompkins, Art Institute Online

Nancy Wood, Art Institute Online

Questions & Feedback

We welcome your questions and feedback. If you have suggestions that you think others would benefit from, please let us know and we will try to include them in the next edition.

You may contact the publisher at:

Delmar Learning
Executive Woods
5 Maxwell Drive
Clifton Park, NY 12065
800-998-7498

Or the series editor at:

Jeannie Novak
INDIESPACE
PO Box 5458
Santa Monica, CA 90409
jeannie@indiespace.com

DEDICATION

For my beloved Lauren, for her unending support. In loving memory of Miriam Saunders.

—Kevin

For Luis, the classic console king. Thank you for never breaking the connection.

—Jeannie

Part I:
Foundation

CHAPTER

History of Game Interface Design:

how did we get here?

key chapter questions

- How have arcade games influenced early interface design?
- What are some examples of interfaces?
- What are the purposes of an interface?
- Which have driven interface design further—computers or consoles?
- Why is interface design such an important yet overlooked area of game development?

In the context of game development, the term "interface" refers to anything that helps the player interact with the game. It includes hardware such as console controllers, computer keyboards, and television monitors. Game components such as health bars, menus, and targeting reticles are also parts of the interface. Even the game characters can be considered interface elements!

When innovation and technical advancement is discussed in relation to game development, most refer to either the graphics or the gameplay—but interface design has also advanced greatly over the history of the industry. In this chapter you'll learn how game interfaces have evolved over time.

Arcades

Electronic games were first introduced to the masses through *arcades*. Interfaces for arcade games were extremely simple, but they progressed rapidly over only a few years. One of the first arcade games, *Pong*, had only a dial for each of the two players. Turning a dial would move a player's paddle vertically on the screen. Horizontal movement was not possible.

Atari Interactive, Inc.

The first arcade game, *Pong*, had a very simple interface.

For many early games, most innovation was gameplay driven, with new interfaces arising to suit new types of play. *Space Invaders* used horizontal movement and also introduced the concept of firing a weapon (though it could not be aimed). The popular *Pac-Man* introduced the multi-directional joystick, allowing the player to navigate in four directions. Later, *Centipede*'s track ball allowed eight-directional movement—unlimited horizontal and limited vertical movement. Though the game was successful, the track ball didn't catch on as a popular arcade game interface.

::::: An Early Innovation

One of the first innovations in interface design was the high score screen. Arcades had become a social phenomenon— a "hangout" for teens who would focus hours of time mastering arcade games. Keeping track of high scores and allowing players to input their initials helped fuel the competition by giving concrete bragging rights to good players. Arcade games at the time did not have hard disks or other permanent storage options, however— so when machines were unplugged, those hard-earned high scores were lost.

NAMCO BANDAI Games America Inc.

The high score display (*Galaxian* shown) was an early interface element that helped drive the arcade game industry.

Taito Corporation   Atari Interactive, Inc.   NAMCO BANDAI Games America Inc.

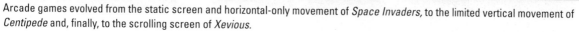

Arcade games evolved from the static screen and horizontal-only movement of *Space Invaders,* to the limited vertical movement of *Centipede* and, finally, to the scrolling screen of *Xevious.*

Controls for most arcade games included a joystick and buttons for one- or two-player mode. Depending upon the game, an action button such as "fire," "jump" or "punch" would also be used. Later, some games would include a second action button.

Interface improvements from arcade games were not limited to new hardware controls. *Xevious* introduced a scrolling screen, *Galaxian* a full-color monitor, and *Donkey Kong* the platforming elements of jumping and climbing.

Even as arcades grew in popularity, electronic games were also expanding further into players' homes. Consoles provided a gaming experience similar to that of the arcades, though their controls had to be consolidated into a single piece of hardware designed to handle a wide variety of games.

Consoles

Console systems are specialized hardware designed primarily for playing games. Typically, the games played on consoles are referred to as "video" games because they are often played using a traditional television. Though televisions have fixed graphical capabilities, the early consoles didn't achieve this quality—which could often make text difficult to read.

Atari Interactive, Inc.

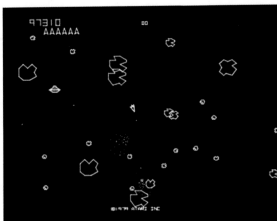

NAMCO BANDAI Games America Inc.

Nintendo

Though initially a severe limitation, graphic resolution quickly became sufficient to easily display text and numbers—shown in this progression from *Asteroids*, to *Pole Position*, to *Harvest Moon*.

In the early days of electronic games, screen resolution allowed for tremendous interface improvements. Early games had such poor resolution that even showing a few numbers onscreen took up a significant amount of real estate. By the mid-1980s, however, resolution had improved enough that displaying text and numbers was not a major limitation except for some text-intensive graphical games.

Special Effects

Advanced special effects have had great interface applications. Instead of using text or icons to give the player information on what is happening in the game, graphic effects can do so while maintaining the game's immersion. For example, if a monster catches on fire, graphic effects can be used to make it look like it is burning instead of having to indicate this through an immersion-breaking method such as floating text.

Early video game consoles were limited to 8, then 16 possible colors. Personal computers were sometimes even more restricted—with monochromatic (2-color, including black) monitors being common throughout the early 1980s. When computer systems with 8-bit color ($2^8 = 256$) came to market, color was no longer a significant limitation in terms of interface design. Interfaces generally shouldn't use subtle color variations, since players might have trouble noticing the distinction. Current systems typically use 16-bit (over 65,000) or "32-bit" (over 16 million) color. (While 32-bit color uses 32 bits of data, only 24 bits actually contain color information.)

Console controllers have also experienced an evolution, which may not be obvious at first. Though controller components have been standardized for the most part, the first consoles experimented with a wide variety of possible controls. Let's take a look at some of the major console systems throughout electronic game history.

Atari 2600

The first generation of consoles was a time of experimentation. The Atari systems of the late 1970s and early 1980s—such as the *Atari 2600*—used joysticks with a single button. All games were designed to be played with only the eight-directional movement and a single action, though combinations of holding a direction and pressing the button were also possible.

Atari Interactive, Inc.

Activision Publishing, Inc.

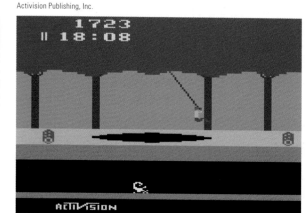

The Atari 2600 (*Pitfall* shown) used a one-button joystick.

Intellivision

The *Intellivision* had a more complicated controller. A disc was used for eight-directional movement, and four side buttons were typically action buttons. The Intellivision also had some games that benefited from a more complicated interface—such as math puzzles and role-playing games.

Used with permission from Mattel, Inc.
©2006 Mattel, Inc. All Rights Reserved.

Used with permission from Mattel, Inc.
©2006 Mattel, Inc. All Rights Reserved.

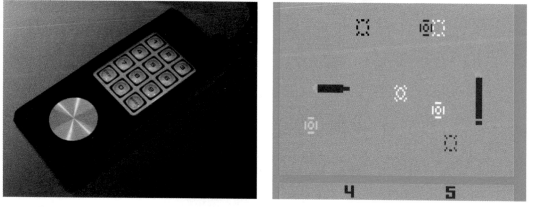

The Intellivision's (*Snafu* shown) controls were much more complicated than those of the Atari systems.

chapter 1 History of Game Interface Design: how did we get here?

For these types of games, the Intellivision controllers included a 12-button numeric keypad. The functions of these buttons varied from game to game, with each including plastic overlays that the player could slide over the controller. They were decorated to suit the particular game, and the function of each button was shown on the overlay. The Intellivision system brought other interface innovations. *Snafu* was the first console game that employed music and, along with a special piece of hardware called the Intellivoice, the system supported voice in a few specific games.

Colecovision

The *Colecovision,* the third of the first set of major console systems, had a controller similar to the Intellivision—with a 12-button numeric keypad and two side buttons. Instead of a disc, it used a variation of the joystick. Unlike the controllers of modern systems, these early designs were intended to be held in one hand and then operated with the other. The Colecovision supported superior resolution, at 256 × 192.

Hasbro, Inc.

Zaxxon is made available courtesy of Sega Corporation © Sega Corporation 2006

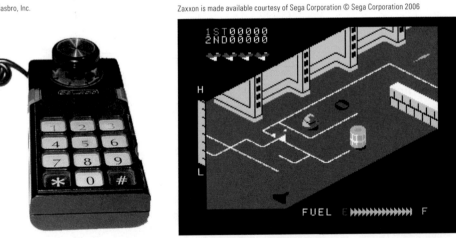

A strong competitor of the Intellivision and Atari 2600, the Colecovision (*Zaxxon* shown) had its own unique controller.

Atari 5200

In 1982, the *Atari 5200* was released. This system competed with the Intellivision and Colecovision systems. It allowed a resolution of 320 × 192 pixels, had four-channel sound, and also employed a more complicated controller—with a numeric keypad similar to that of a telephone. The system's controller—which would often break and had no automatic self-centering (i.e., did not return automatically to an upright and centered position)—proved to be a mistake, and the later 7800 system reverted to a simpler joystick.

Atari Interactive, Inc.

Atari Interactive, Inc.

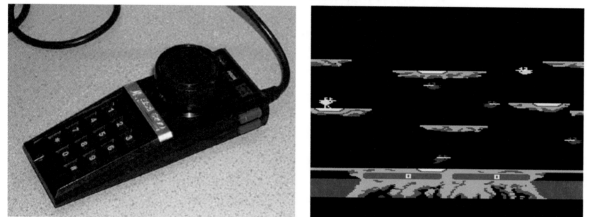

The Atari 5200 (*Joust* shown) was the first revision of a major console system.

Nintendo Entertainment System (NES)

The market for the Atari, Intellivision, and Colecovision systems all collapsed by 1984. During the following year, the *Nintendo Entertainment System (NES)* revitalized the console industry. Its controller featured four buttons and a cross-shaped button that allowed four-directional movement (later known as a *D-pad*). The NES supported a resolution of 256 × 240 pixels, and it had a palette of 48 colors and five shades of grey.

Besides the standard controller, the NES could be purchased with a light gun called the Nintendo Zapper Gun—which was

I really enjoy the simplicity behind the NES 8-bit controllers. Though hard on the hands after a few hours (those corners would dig into the palms!), the ability to play games with the thumb pad and two buttons make picking up and playing *any* game for the system a snap.

—*Dan Puczek*
(Game Art & Design student)

Nintendo

Nintendo

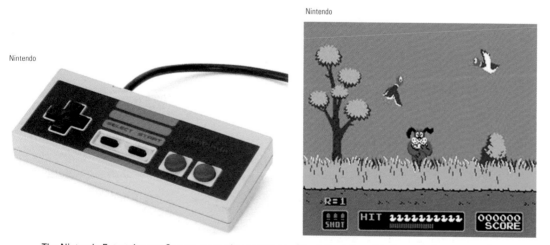

The Nintendo Entertainment System created a resurgence (*Duck Hunt* shown) in the console game market.

featured with the popular game *Duck Hunt.* In 1988, Nintendo released the Power Pad (developed by Bandai), which was a floor controller with 8 buttons on one side and 12 on the other. The Power Pad was used in games like *Dance Aerobics,* which was a predecessor to physical games such as *Dance Dance Revolution.*

Sega Genesis

Console technology continued to improve rapidly. The *Sega Genesis*—released in 1989—had 512 colors (64 onscreen), a resolution of 256 × 224, and six sound channels. The Genesis had an eight-directional D-pad and three action buttons. Another version of the controller—created especially for fighting games, but compatible with all Genesis games—contained six action buttons.

Genesis photo is made available courtesy of Sega Corporation
© Sega Corporation, 2006

NBA Live 1995 image is made available courtesy of Sega Corporation
© Sega Corporation, 2006

With the release of the Sega Genesis (six-button controller and *NBA Live 1995* shown), Nintendo's dominance of the console market was finally challenged.

> My favorite console controller is the SNES controller. It's easy, small, and practical. The only real improvements it could make to be up to par with today's crazy controller needs would be to have an extra button somewhere, a little more ergonomic on the body and the buttons. I remember having my thumb constantly blistered when *Mortal Kombat* came out!
>
> —Welter Almeida
> *(Game Art & Design student)*

Super Nintendo Entertainment System (SNES)

In 1991, the *Super Nintendo Entertainment System (SNES)* added four more buttons to the NES controller, supported 4096 colors (512 onscreen), and allowed resolutions as high as 512 × 448. It used two sound chips: three channels for sound effects and eight for the main chip.

Nintendo

Nintendo

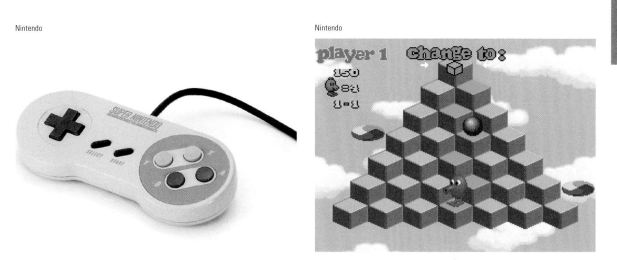

The Super Nintendo Entertainment System (*Q*bert 3* shown) was a major upgrade to the popular NES.

Sony PlayStation (PS)

Sony entered the console market in the United States in 1995 with the *PlayStation* (PS), which allowed resolutions up to 640 × 480 and 2^{24} (almost 1.7 million) colors. It used 512 KB for sound and 1 MB for video (compared to the SNES's 64 and 128 KB, respectively). The original PS controller had the same general buttons as the SNES, though the design was different. In 1998, a new controller, the DualShock, was released. It added two analog sticks and an additional set of two buttons (activated by pressing the analog sticks in)—and it was used by both the PS and its successor, the PlayStation 2.

Sony Computer Entertainment of America Inc.

Sony Computer Entertainment of America, Inc.

The PlayStation (*Cool Boarders 2001* shown) was Sony's first foray into the console market.

Before the Nintendo 64 arrived, most of the console controllers were very simplistic in design—usually preventing certain games from having deep combat systems due to lack of buttons. Lo and behold, here comes this strange, three pronged controller with an analog joystick in the middle. It took a little while to get used to the analog joystick—but for first-person shooters such as *GoldenEye* and *Perfect Dark*, the controller allowed for an uncanny amount of accuracy. The positioning of the "Z" button, normally used for firing weapons, was under the middle prong and actually made players feel like they were pulling a trigger. In my opinion, the Nintendo 64 controller feels the most natural.

—*Matt Garretson*
(Media Arts & Animation student)

The controller for the N64 is the most ergonomic controller I've ever used, and it's just right for a variety of hand sizes. The button placement is such that I can easily reach everything without tiring or cramping muscles under long periods of gameplay.

—*Lisa Hathaway*
(Game Development student)

Nintendo 64 (N64)

Nintendo's last console of the 1990s was the *Nintendo 64 (N64)*. Unlike the PS, which switched to the CD-ROM media format for its games, the N64—released in the United States in 1996—continued to use ROM cartridges. The fast load times allowed by the cartridges reduced loading screen delays when compared to the PS, but the greater storage capacity of the CD-ROM gave the PS an edge in texture memory and thus game appearance. The number of colors and graphical resolution was the same as for the PS.

Nintendo

Nintendo

A direct competitor to the PlayStation, the Nintendo 64 (*Super Mario 64* shown) continued to use cartridges instead of CD-ROMs.

The Nintendo 64's controller had seven buttons, a D-pad, two shoulder buttons, and an analog stick. A rumble pak accessory released in 1997 could vibrate the controller during gameplay.

Sega Dreamcast

The last major console released in the United States in the 1990s was the Sega Dreamcast. Its controller was very different in appearance than the N64, but featured the same components. It had improved sound and graphics (including a VGA output, which allowed for superior picture quality and resolution) capabilities compared to the Sony and Nintendo systems, and it used proprietary media similar to CD-ROMs that could hold over 50% more data. It was also the first system to have a built-in modem and Internet support for online gaming. Although considered exceptional when first released, the *Dreamcast* was overcome by *PlayStation 2* a year after it was released—and Sega ultimately exited from the hardware development industry.

> I really enjoy the Nintendo 64 controller. I can have full control over the buttons without having to stretch to hit them all. With it, I can even control the game with one hand if I need to. Instead of pausing the game, I can answer the phone and keep playing—just turn down the volume!
>
> —*Jonathan Clark*
> *(Game Development student)*

Dreamcast image is made available courtesy of Sega Corporation
© Sega Corporation, 2006

Crazy Taxi 2 image is made available courtesy of Sega Corporation
© Sega Corporation, 2006

The Sega Dreamcast (*Crazy Taxi 2* shown) was highly advanced, but it was unable to overcome the momentum gained by the PS.

::::: Animation in Dialogue

Like special effects, animation allows games to convey information to the player in more immersive ways. For example, a wounded character can limp or stumble, making it unnecessary to explain their injured state through numbers or icons.

Until the late 1990s, dialogue in electronic games was delivered through, at best, static pictures of characters. However, as animation technology improved, lip-synching became possible.

BioWare Corp.

Hmm... we will have to continue our discussion later, my student. It appears we have more pressing matters.

Lip-synching in *Jade Empire* helps increase the immersion of conversations.

More recently, facial expressions and animation have become possible, allowing speaking characters to appear more lifelike and convey information to players (such as emotion) that was previously unavailable.

The dramatic improvements in graphical power and steady advances in controller design have continued through to the modern systems. We'll discuss these in more detail in Chapter 4.

Early handheld games such as Mattel Electronics' *Auto Race* employed light-emitting diodes for their graphics.

Handhelds

Handheld electronic games date back to the 1970s. These early games used simple *light-emitting diodes (LEDs)* rather than actual displays. Controls and gameplay were extremely simple, often involving just one or two buttons. Games would have simple sound effects such as beeps. *Liquid crystal displays (LCDs)* were later developed. These allowed greater detail, though each image had to be pre-placed on the screen. Movement of images was faked by turning off an image in one location and turning on the same image in a nearby location.

Though several other devices emerged throughout the 1980s, handheld systems did not become popular until Nintendo's Game Boy arrived on the scene in 1989. The Game Boy was equipped with a small monochromatic screen, a D-pad, and four buttons. Sega competed in the United States with the Game Gear in 1991. Instead of the vertical design of the Game Boy, the Game Gear used a horizontal layout—with the D-pad and buttons to the side of the screen. The Game Gear also used a color display. Both of these systems were a great improvement over the early handhelds because they used game cartridges—allowing the same handheld to play a wide variety of games just like the consoles could. In 1995, Sega released the 16-bit Nomad—a portable version of the Genesis that could run any game in the Genesis library; by plugging in a second controller, two-player games were possible.

Nintendo's Game Boy and Sega's Game Gear were competing systems at the dawn of modern handheld technology.

Though several other systems were released through the 1990s, the controls of hand-helds changed very little from these two basic designs until some of the most recent systems—such as the N-gage, PSP, and DS (all of which are discussed in Chapter 4). Of course, graphics technology, battery life, and other design aspects also improved with time.

Computers

Since their arrival in homes in the late 1970s and early 1980s, personal *computers* were immediately used for games.

::::: Commodore 64

The *Commodore 64 (C64)* was the mainstay computer of the 1980s. It was manufactured from 1982 until 1993 with only cosmetic and price changes. The C64 featured 16 colors and three sound channels. As the most popular computer system for games in the 1980s, the C64 saw many interface innovations throughout its lifetime. For example, *Neuromancer,* released in 1988, included an opening song written by Devo. One of the words, "change," was actually intelligible.

Commodore Computers.

Interplay Entertainment Corp.

The Commodore 64 (*Neuromancer* shown) was a dominant household computer throughout the 1980s.

Home computers such as the C64 were partially responsible for the collapse of the console industry in the early 1980s. Over time, however, consoles have resurged—and currently personal computers comprise a mere 20% of the electronic game market.

Initially, the keyboard was the sole control mechanism for using a computer. Each game command was tied to a specific key on the keyboard. Even at this early stage, the importance of interface design was understood—with the most important command (usually *jump* or *fire,* depending on the game) often being bound to the prominent

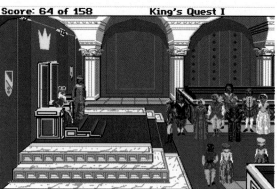

Some early games, such as those made by Infocom (*Zork* shown), used an interface entirely comprised of text.

King's Quest's interface combined both graphics and text.

spacebar. Most computers were equipped with ports to allow joysticks to be used as controllers.

Adventure games, which typically involved puzzle solving and exploration, used an entirely text interface. The player would type out simple phrases, typically consisting of a verb-noun combination such as "get knife" or "kill troll." Until the late 1980s, these games supplied only text to the player as feedback—no graphics! They eventually incorporated still images and then later full visual interfaces. Some games, such as the *King's Quest* series by Sierra, included both text input and the control of an onscreen character. Still, even when they were first introduced, most computer games employed graphics of some variety.

As console systems and arcades grew in popularity, computers were built with ports for joysticks and other specialized controllers. Generally, these joysticks had only one button—though some later versions used two.

The mouse was a major innovation in interface design. Though its origins can be traced back to the 1960s, the mouse didn't become a popular interface device until the 1990s. It has become the standard for all computers and is a key interface element in almost all computer games. Current computer games are often designed to be completely playable with only the mouse, if necessary—though keyboard shortcuts and controls are used by experienced players.

For desktop computers, hardware interface design has not changed in over a decade. Laptops have experimented with a couple of other types of controls, such as the touchpad. These designs are generally inferior to the mouse, but can be built directly into the laptop.

In this chapter, you learned the brief history of how game interfaces have evolved over time—including how arcade games drove initial advances in interface design, and how gameplay and interfaces are intimately related. In the next chapter, you will study the two primary goals of interfaces (feedback and control) and the four major considerations to keep in mind during interface design: functionality, usability, aesthetics, and accessibility.

:::CHAPTER REVIEW:::

1. How have visual interfaces evolved over the course of history? Trace this development by playing a classic arcade, console, computer, or handheld game. List 5 features of each visual interface. Then play a current arcade, console, computer, or handheld game and make note of how the interface elements have changed.

2. How would you create a classic interface of your own? Pretend that you are an interface developer during the arcade era. Working within the limitations of the time, what type of game would you develop—and what would the interface look like?

3. How would you update a classic interface? Play a classic arcade, console, computer or handheld game. After familiarizing yourself with the interface, make a rough sketch of the interface. Then create an updated version, incorporating elements that are commonly used in interfaces today.

4. What is your favorite classic game system, and why? What aspects of the hardware and software interface elements are appealing to you? What are some favorite games that you enjoyed playing on the system, and why?

5. How can interface limitations enhance the game-playing experience? Choose a current game with a rich or complicated interface. Begin to limit the interface in some way—by taking away certain components or restricting player movement, for example. Create a new, simplified interface for the game. What changes would you have to make to the game itself in order to accommodate this new interface design?

CHAPTER

Goals and Considerations:

what are we trying to accomplish?

key chapter questions

- What are the goals associated with game interface design?

- How can a balance between *aesthetics* and *functionality* be maintained?

- How are *usability* and *accessibility* related?

- How are *feedback* and *control* utilized in game interface design?

- How can *audio* enhance a game interface?

Though game interfaces have existed since the beginning of the electronic game industry, it's a field of study that has received little direct attention until fairly recently. To design better interfaces, one must understand what an interface is supposed to accomplish and what elements contribute to or detract from its effectiveness. Interfaces have two primary goals that drive most aspects of their design: feedback and control. These two objectives drive most aspects of interface design. To achieve these goals, four major considerations should be kept in mind: functionality, usability, aesthetics, and accessibility.

> **M**ost game interfaces are far too stylized and obscure.
>
> —*Gordon Walton*
> *(Studio Director, BioWare Austin)*

Goals of Game Interfaces

To design great *user interfaces* (referred to in this book as *game interfaces, player interfaces,* or simply *interfaces*) for games, you should first understand their role in game design. While you'll want to use interface conventions in your designs, applying such rules of thumb universally can be detrimental. Knowledge of the fundamental objectives of interfaces will allow you to determine which guidelines apply and which will not work in a specific instance.

Primary Goals

The main purpose of a game interface is to allow players to communicate with the software (game). Interfaces thus have two primary goals: feedback (receiving information from the game) and control (providing information to the game). All elements of a game interface should further at least one of these two goals.

Feedback

The interface is responsible for *feedback*—conveying to the player what is happening in the game. What obstacles are you facing? What is your score? How many lives do you have left? Without conveying to the player the *state* of the game, there is no game. Feedback is most often accomplished visually through a monitor, television,

:::::: Avoiding Conventional Design in *Think Tanks*

GarageGames

In *ThinkTanks,* we decided to forgo the health meter in favor of using smoke on the tanks to communicate damage level. I felt it was more intuitive and allowed one to become more connected with the object they were driving (a tank). Our beta testers complained about it constantly during testing. The final game has no health meter, and it may have probably hurt sales, but I think it is a better interface.

— *Joe Maruschak (Creative Director, GarageGames)*

or display. Feedback has two purposes in game design: indicating progress toward goals and teaching players new concepts (discussed in more detail in Chapter 7).

Progress

Players like to know how quickly they are making *progress* toward their goals, both short-term and long-term, in any game. Feedback allows the player to answer many questions, including:

- *Strategies:* Which strategies should I use?
- *Duration:* How much longer until I achieve my goal?
- *Success:* Am I winning?

Let's consider a few examples. The goal in a fighting game such as *Street Fighter* is to reduce your opponent's health to zero before your opponent can do the same to you. If your opponent is extremely low on health, you don't have to attempt a powerful attack because you can finish them off using a conservative method—such as an attack that deals little damage but doesn't expose you to a counter-attack. The game will likely be over soon—so even though your thumbs might be getting sore from using the controller, you're inspired to finish this part. You also feel good about how you've done (you've almost won!), and if you do end up losing, you feel the satisfaction of at least having put up a good fight—or the frustration of almost having won. Imagine how different the experience would be if you didn't know that your opponent was on the brink of defeat.

:::::: *Call of Duty 2:* Red Alert for Health

Activision Publishing, Inc.

Call of Duty 2 managed to create a first-person shooter (FPS) without giant health point numbers anywhere on the screen. The game instead displays health with visual and audio representations; when a player is severely hurt, the screen becomes red— and the character hunches over, breathing heavy and erratic. They pulled that off quite well. Not only is it a step forward in user interface design, but it's also much more engrossing to the player.

—*Ian Wall (Senior Artist, Obsidian Entertainment)*

21

chapter 2 Goals and Considerations: what are we trying to accomplish?

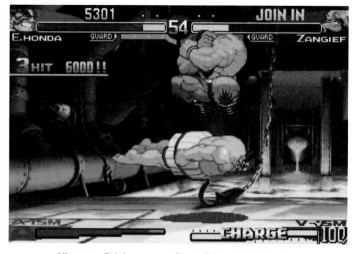

Like many fighting games, *Street Fighter Alpha 3* makes excellent use of the interface to show progress.

Note that in a good interface, even a simple piece of information, such as your opponent's health, is conveyed in many ways. The most obvious method is the length of the power bar at the top of the screen. It is visible at all times and large enough for you to read without taking your focus off the action. The information conveyed through the power bar's length is bolstered by its color. When the bar is green, your opponent is fully healed; when it is red, your opponent is close to death.

Multiple Interface Mechanisms

You have many tools at your disposal to provide feedback to the player. These include shapes, sizes, colors, sounds, and fonts. For more important information, such as changes to player health, combine several of these tools to ensure that players notice what you are trying to tell them.

Furthermore, the game provides information on when the state of your opponent's health changes. After you hit your foe, the character reacts to the blow. Particularly damaging hits are shown with more powerful graphic and audio effects. In addition, the amount of damage inflicted is not random; each time you complete the same move relative to your opponent's defense, you will inflict the same amount of damage. Over time, you can learn exactly how many of each type of hit is required to defeat a given opponent. All of these components combine to very clearly convey your progress toward completing your goal of defeating this opponent.

On the other extreme in terms of complexity is a turn-based strategy game such as *Civilization IV*. Whereas a game like *Soul Calibur 3* may take a few minutes to play, even a "short" game of *Civilization IV* will require several hours. Your goal is to conquer the game world through one of several different methods, such as eliminating all other civilizations, establishing the dominant culture, or being the first to launch a spaceship for colonization. Fortunately, the game breaks down these epic objectives into short-term goals—such as founding a new city, constructing a temple, or inventing the wheel.

In fact, the *Civilization* series is known for leading its players into taking "just one more turn"—which can keep them engrossed for many hours longer than they had planned. This excellent game design is made possible through what is essentially an

The gameplay of *Civilization III* is so complex that the main screen (top) must be replaced with secondary interfaces, such as the domestic advisor screen (bottom), for the player to have enough information.

interface feedback issue; by communicating to players just how close the next goal is to completion, the game drives them on.

For such a complicated game, the amount of feedback presented is staggering. The interface includes no fewer than 10 distinct screens for culture, military, foreign relations, espionage, trade, technology, score, and many other elements. These interfaces all serve to inform players about the states of their civilizations so that they can ascertain their progress toward both short- and long-term goals. For example, the technology screen shows what advance (such as the wheel or literature or gunpowder) a player is researching, how long it will take to learn it, and the relationship between all of the technologies (e.g., the development of writing comes before the development of literature). The game's main screen provides abbreviated information for all of the major goals—with the world map working like an aesthetically appealing menu system. Regardless of how simple or complex a game's interface is, it will almost always provide the players with information on their progress toward their goals.

Instructions

A good interface also uses feedback to help teach players the rules of the game. Players often do not read the game manual. By implicitly including the *instructions* in the interface itself, you can ease the learning curve of a game and allow it to appeal to a busier or more casual gamer. Let's consider an example of how this is done.

Nintendo

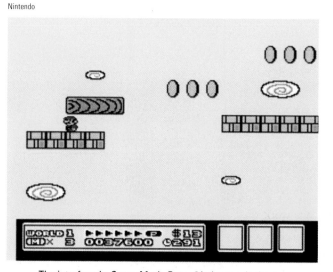

The interface in *Super Mario Bros. 3* helps teach players that they should collect coins.

One of the goals in *Super Mario Bros. 3* is to collect coins. In the game world itself, a player might see coins in various locations. When the player collides with one (collecting it), it vanishes with a graphical effect and a short, happy sound. This feedback immediately informs players that they've done something good. Near the top of the screen is a small coin icon with a number next to it. When a player collects a coin, the number increases by one. The icon is exactly the same as the coin graphic in the game world—so even if one is playing the game for the first time, it is easy to learn the game mechanic being used.

But what do the coins do? The game doesn't tell the player directly, but it does provide a clue. The number next to the coin icon has only two digits. This suggests that reaching 100 coins might cause something to happen. Indeed, 100 coins results in an extra life, which is depicted through another icon and number pair that is also always visible.

Teaching the player through the interface becomes substantially more difficult as the game becomes complicated, however. Returning to the example of the *Civilization* series, it's apparent that a game can become complicated enough that, without a tutorial, players will be unable to learn even the basics without considerable effort. Even so, *Civilization* makes good use of interface to ease the learning curve.

Firaxis Games, Inc.

Though too complicated to avoid having an involved tutorial, *Civilization IV* employs interface feedback to ease the game's learning curve.

For example, in *Civilization IV*, most goals—such as technology research, training units, and city growth—use progress bars that are labeled with both the goal and the amount of time remaining. *Mouseover* (placing the mouse cursor over a certain location) shows even more detailed information, such as exactly what factors are contributing to the happiness of a city's inhabitants.

Control

In addition to giving the player feedback, the interface must also allow the player to communicate with the game. Seeing the obstacles presented by the game isn't enough; players must also have a method of overcoming them. An interface provides players with *control* over what happens in the game. For example, analog sticks on most console controllers are interfaces that give players control over the game experience. Control is almost exclusively provided through manual interfaces, which are discussed in further detail in Chapters 3 and 4.

Note that feedback and control interface elements often work in tandem. If activating a control does not provide some sort of feedback, players will not be certain whether their commands were executed. For example, when the player clicks on a button in a menu, the button will graphically appear to be pressed and a sound effect will be played—providing the player with feedback. Similarly, pressing an action button might result in a character action such as jumping or shooting. (You'll learn the details of control scheme design in Chapter 6.)

Sony Computer Entertainment America Inc.

Not surprisingly, controllers (PlayStation 2 shown) allow players to control their game experience.

> **T**he interface to *Manhunt* is nearly perfect: there practically isn't one. For a suspense-thriller such as *Manhunt,* having a minimal interface allows you to get into the game up to your chin.
>
> —*R. Chase Mack*
> *(Game Art & Design Student)*

> **M**yst is my favorite visual interface because there isn't one. The gameplay was so tightly integrated into the environment that it let me forget I was playing a game.
>
> —*Nicole Lazzaro*
> *(Founder & President, XEODesign, Inc.)*

Secondary Goals

While feedback and control are critical components of any game's interface, well-designed interfaces can accomplish other objectives as well. Unlike an interface's primary goals, these secondary objectives apply more to games than to other types of software.

Immersion

A game is said to be "immersive" when players get lost within it, forgetting for a moment that they are playing a game. For most games, *immersion* is a desirable goal. It is thus sometimes said that the best interface is one that players don't notice. It is difficult for an interface to add to a game's immersion, but a poorly designed one will certainly detract from it. Ideally, the interface will convey information to the player in ways that are consistent with the game world. Numbers, text, icons, buttons, menus, and other similar interface components all serve to remind players that they are playing a game—which can break their immersion.

:::::: *King Kong*'s Invisible Interface

Peter Jackson's King Kong: The Official Game of the Movie, courtesy of Ubisoft.

King Kong has no interface at all, making it one of the best game interfaces out there. The game is simple enough that you don't really need an interface, and there are enough visual and audio cues to tell you when you're in trouble, how much ammo you have, and more.

—*Troy Dunniway (Lead Game Designer, Midway Los Angeles)*

Consider a role-playing game such as *Neverwinter Nights*. During combat, when an enemy is hit, numbers flash over the enemy's head to indicate how much damage has been inflicted. A more immersive method to convey this same information is through the magnitude and type of sound effect of the hit, the animation used in the swing, and the visual damage inflicted upon the opponent.

However, using methods such as these to maintain immersion comes at a price. First, it would require many more resources to develop all of the systems (sound, animation, visible wounding) required to achieve this effect. Second, the details are hidden from the player. For example, if one hit inflicts 20 points of damage and another inflicts 24, will players be able to recognize the difference based upon the speed of the animation their characters use? Probably not. *Neverwinter Nights* is based upon the pencil-and-paper role-playing game (RPG) *Dungeons & Dragons*® (*D&D*), which utilizes a number-heavy rules system. For all *D&D*-based games, displaying numbers is not only easier, but also more closely fits the desired experience and fulfills the expectations of the player market. In this case, immersion is not the primary objective. In a simpler RPG, however, a more immersive interface might be preferable. (RPGs and other game genres are discussed in more detail in Chapter 5.)

© Wizards of the Coast. Used with permission.

In *Neverwinter Nights,* numbers on the interface indicate how much damage is dealt by an attack.

27

chapter 2 Goals and Considerations: what are we trying to accomplish?

The best visual game interface I've seen is used in LucasArts' *Indiana Jones and the Infernal Machine.* This interface allows for full screen visuals with only a few icons along the bottom of screen. Players can access these icons by pressing the escape key.

—*Michael Ortiz*
(3D Animator, ESC Studios)

I enjoy the game interface for *Neverwinter Nights* (PC). The game can be complex—but once you get the hang of things, you basically have so much you can do the longer you stick with the game. When you right-click on a character, more options become available. You can choose to make a pose, taunt, cast a spell, attack physically, talk, and more.

—*Marc Sapitula*
(Game Art & Design Student)

I like the radial system in *Neverwinter Nights.* Being able to control your characters' actions and inventory with just the mouse makes the game fun and easy to play. While exploring different dungeons and fighting off hordes of monsters, this interface is essential in keeping your characters alive to progress forward on their journeys.

—*Brian Young*
(Game Development Student)

::::: *Anachronox:* Interface as Character

Eidos Interactive Ltd.

Grumpos takes 285 damage!

The interface in *Anachronox* is one of my favorites. The premise was that the interface was actually one of the characters in the game; as a result, it had its own personality and sassiness to it. This made it more interesting than conventional interfaces, since I was never quite sure what would happen when I clicked on a button.

—*Chris Avellone (Chief Creative Officer & Lead Designer, Obsidian Entertainment)*

*N*everwinter Nights has one of the most versatile interfaces I've come across. The number of features and information that is compacted into a single, main control panel is amazing. If I need to know character info, who's online, or what's in my inventory, then I have all of the information at the click of a button. Not only this, but the assignable quick slots come into play quite often when I don't have the time to go through menus to get to a spell or command. The use of descriptive icons with tool-tips makes it very easy to find what I'm looking for, and the overall style fits with the setting. Creating movable, resizable, and transparent windows has made it one of my favorite interfaces.

—*Lisa Hathaway (Game Development Student)*

Atmosphere

A less important but still interesting purpose of the interface is to contribute to the game's *atmosphere*. The nature of the interface is ideally consistent with the type of game being played. For example, though an analog stick and a steering wheel both give the player control, the latter adds to the atmosphere of a racing game. For a shooting game, a gun interface can both provide better control and add to the game's atmosphere.

Mad Catz, Inc.

A specialized interface, such as the Mad Catz Blaster (for Xbox), can complement a game's atmosphere.

Although an interface does not add to a game's immersive qualities, it should always add to the game's atmosphere. In *The Bard's Tale,* an RPG, the interface takes up over three-fourths of the available *screen real estate*—displaying names, numbers, and other information to the player at all times. Still, the hewn-stone look of the borders and the dark grey color scheme are well-suited to a game that is largely about dungeon exploration. This interface, while non-immersive, supports the atmosphere of the game—thus adding to the experience. *Wasteland,* a post-apocalyptic game that features very similar gameplay (and was developed by the same company), utilizes a different aesthetic, making the interface fit the game much better even though it is functionally the same as the one used for *The Bard's Tale.*

Interplay Entertainment Corp.

Electronic Arts Inc.

The Bard's Tale (top) and *Wasteland* (bottom) have functionally very similar interfaces that provide very different atmospheres.

One of my favorite manual interfaces is the gun controller. Games such as *Time Crisis, Resident Evil: Dead Aim, and House of the Dead* would not be the great games they are if it weren't for the gun controllers. Try and imagine killing a zombie or a terrorist with a directional pad and the X button; it just doesn't cut it.

—*Brandon A. West*
(Lifetime Gamer)

My favorite manual interface has to be the gun controller in Sega's *Ghost Squad* arcade shooter. Similar to most popular arcade shooter games, this manual interface is much more complete and immersive than any other gun controller interface I've used. The gun is very similar to a real-life submachine gun—complete with recoil vibration. The gun has three buttons/switches— a trigger, an "action" button towards the front grip, and a selector switch for firing modes (which can switch your weapon from semi-automatic, three-burst, and fully automatic).

—*Welter Almeida*
(Game Art & Design Student)

The Importance of Audio

Audio provides important feedback to players on the effect of their controls. For example, instead of using the headphones, the iPod has a small external speaker that clicks as the user scrolls through menu items. This increases its appeal and improves use. Audio is essential for flow and creating a heightened sense of immersion. Audio can also create emotions.

—*Nicole Lazzaro*
(Founder & President, XEODesign, Inc.)

Players' actions can be guided by audio so that they more readily immerse themselves into the world of the game and are able to act purposely within it.

—*Drew Davidson*
(Faculty, Entertainment Technology Center, Carnegie Mellon University)

Activision Publishing, Inc.

In a fast-paced action game such as *Call of Duty 2,* using too many visual effects could potentially distract the player.

Though achieving these secondary goals is not necessary to a solid, functional interface, their use can greatly influence how players feel about the game.

::::: Audio as an Interface Component

Audio is an important component of any good interface. Clever use of sound and music can greatly enhance a player's enjoyment of a game and can also improve the feedback provided by a game. During a game, the player is constantly bombarded with visual information because the screen is filled with graphic elements. While some of these elements provide feedback to the player, many others concentrate on providing atmosphere or achieving other goals. This inundation of visual information can make it easy for the player to miss important details.

Audio provides another avenue for the game to communicate with the player, and it's particularly useful for:

1. *Eliminating ambiguity:* Through tone and duration, sounds can clearly convey whether what has happened is good or bad for the player. Visual feedback is not always obvious in this regard.
2. *Providing feedback without interrupting the gameplay:* In the midst of intense action, visual feedback can be either too subtle to be noticed or so dramatic that it distracts players from action that requires their attention. Since sound is (correctly) generally not a core component of gameplay, it can be used to provide feedback without interrupting the player's experience.
3. *Reinforcing visual effects:* Combined with appropriate visual effects, audio can suggest the significance of an event that has just occurred. For example, in *Super Mario Bros. 3,* when the player obtains the 100th coin, a stronger sound effect is used to alert the player that getting that coin did something more than getting the previous 99 did. While visual feedback is also provided to the player (life count increases by one), the sound effect draws more attention to the event.
4. *Creating atmosphere:* Sound effects can be used to help immerse the player in the game even while providing feedback.

Despite the obvious value of audio, it is inadvisable to make it a required part of an interface. Players have many good reasons not to utilize audio in a game: to avoid waking sleeping siblings, parents, or children; to play their own music; or to conserve system resources (on a PC). Incorporate audio into your interfaces, but don't make it a necessity.

The Challenge of Audio in Game Interface Design

Audio plays a huge part in game interface design. Sound is all around us in everything that we do. Subtle echos and changes in pitch can tell us how big or small a room is. It permeates our lives and gives us a lot of information about the world we exist in, and to an extent that most people don't realize.

As an experiment, I one day wore earplugs so I could not hear anything and tried to go about my normal business. I knew I would have problems with talking, but I was surprised at how difficult it was to type. The reassuring sound of the keys on my laptop really gives me a lot of feedback in the act of typing. I had to look back in a room to make sure I actually did switch off the light when I did not hear the reassuring "click" of the light switch. It really drove it home for me how much we depend on sound and how little we realize it.

Getting an interface to feel natural is very hard because the sound has to play its part and not stand out. It has to work with the rest of the game to reinforce what is happening in the game and try not to take center stage. When done right, it is amazing. How to play with the game is communicated on an almost subliminal level to the player. It is something I want to explore much more.

The sound is always the hardest part for me. Getting the sound to feel just right and communicate to the player what it needs to communicate can be very difficult. I like to attempt to give separate important feedback for all interactions that affect the player—such as if they are hit by something, or if they hit something. I like to have sounds that will allow the player to differentiate between them (and ideally have the sound react to the force of the impact).

It is hard technically, and hard in production, as we usually outsource the sound and music. It is a very interesting aspect of the project for me as I have to explain, sometimes in great detail, exactly what it is I am trying to communicate to the player and how I want them to feel about it. It is often necessary to be there with the sound designer making weird noises with my mouth: "I want something that goes, pfft … cllinkkkk……ssssssss" and then explaining what is going on while he is looking at boxes on the screen with me saying… "the blue box is a vehicle, and the red one, that is an enemy.…"

It is also the part that pushes me the hardest to broaden my skill set. On the game I am currently working on I had to pull my dusty guitar out of the closet and attempt to remember how to play in order to get the idea of what sort of music I was looking for to my composer. It is a great memory for me, sitting there on my porch, cell phone on the ground, trying to coax something pleasing out of a guitar so I could get across what I wanted the music to be. I felt so totally inadequate and underskilled. It is moments like these that let me know I have a long way to go.

—Joe Maruschak
(Creative Director, GarageGames)

Aaron Marks on the Role of Audio in Game Interface Design

Aaron Marks
(President, On
Your Mark Music
Productions)

Practically falling into the game industry seven years ago, Aaron Marks has amassed music and sound design credits on touch-screen arcade games, class II video bingo/slot machines, computer games, console games—and over 70 online casino games. Aaron has also written for *Game Developer Magazine,* Gamasutra, and Music4Games.net. He is the author of *The Complete Guide to Game Audio,* an expansive book on all aspects of audio for video games. He is also a member of the advisory board for the Game Audio Network Guild (GANG)—and he continues his pursuit of the ultimate soundscape, creating music and sound for various projects.

Audio plays its biggest role in the design of in-game menus, feature access, and implementation of the activated features. Imagine scrolling through menus and clicking on-screen buttons in complete silence; the immersive effect the developers are striving for in the game will be shattered! Just because the player isn't involved in gameplay, it doesn't mean the game has to stop. Everything you hear, from the music to the sound effects, should keep a player 'in' the game, 'in' the reality created by the game makers—and players should hear the sounds they would expect if they were really there. I mean, you wouldn't use electronic beeps, jet engine, or laser beam sounds in a game based in World War I. While these sounds would be 'cool' on their own, the effect it would have on the game would leave players shaking their heads in bewilderment. A skilled sound designer or composer will ensure all of the sounds in the in-game interface are entertaining but most of all appropriate.

:::::: *God of War*'s Animated Interface

Sony Computer Entertainment of America

Sony's God of War has a great minimal interface. It's fairly flashy and context sensitive so that it's easy to understand. It's also animated, and shows you exactly what you need to do, which turns out to be a lot of fun and really adds to the game experience.

—*Troy Dunniway (Lead Game Designer, Midway Los Angeles)*

Considerations in Interface Design

Other factors that play a role in interface design include functionality, usability, aesthetics, and accessibility. Keep these considerations in mind as you try to achieve the goals of feedback and control in your interfaces.

Functionality

Functionality refers to an interface's ability to achieve its goals—primarily providing the player with feedback and control. Does the interface give the player all the feedback that is required? Does the interface allow players to control every element they would want control over? If not, then the interface is not functionally sound. An interface's functionality is defined by *what* it must do.

Functionality is relevant for both feedback and control elements. For example, in *Pac-Man,* the player must be able to move the Pac-Man character in four different directions (control) and be able to determine in which direction Pac-Man is currently moving (feedback). A four-directional joystick provides the control, and the graphic clearly provides feedback on the direction of travel.

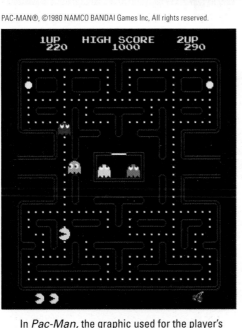

In *Pac-Man,* the graphic used for the player's character changes appearance to show the direction in which it is moving.

> The more recent games in *The Legend of Zelda* series contain scrolling "pause" screens and the use of controller button icons with item/action overlays. This is an excellent way to relay information in a compact fashion, all the while still allowing the player some customization.
>
> —Lisa Hathaway
> (Game Development student)

> The game interface for *The Legend of Zelda: Ocarina of Time* (Nintendo 64) was visually appealing and easy to remember when first playing the game.
>
> —Marc Sapitula
> (Game Art & Design Student)

The Legend of Zelda: Functional Interface Design

Nintendo

Functionally, my personal favorite interfaces would be in any of the *Zelda* games (*Ocarina of Time* shown above). Nintendo just made it so simple by using the color and shape associations of the controller buttons alongside each of the options that you were selecting. I think the menu interface found its ultimate incarnation in the Nintendo 64 version where they first implemented the cube-style menu. The four menu planes were pasted around the inside of a cube that you rotated around, which ended up being an elegant way of breaking down the increased complexity of the N64 title.

—*Timothy Nixon (Founder & Creative Director, Straylight Studios)*

Game Interfaces for Kids

Young children do not have the same conceptual abilities and manual dexterity as adults. Therefore, designing interfaces for young children requires some specific considerations. If you find yourself working on a game specifically intended for children, you should study child learning theory, such as Piaget's cognitive stages. Here are some brief examples of how interfaces should be different for children:

Public Broadcasting Service (PBS) and Ragdoll

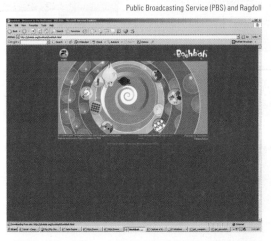

PBS and Ragdoll's website *Boohbah* (http://pbskids.org/boohbah/boohbah.html) contains games designed for children under age 3.

1. Children aged three or less usually cannot read, so any games designed for them should avoid the use of text. The website www.pbskids.org includes a program site called Boohbah, which is text-free.
2. When using a mouse or similar control hardware, a child's ability to select a specific spot on the screen is much less than that of an adult. Therefore, buttons should be larger and precise movements should be less critical.
3. Most children under six are unable to understand abstractions. Therefore, interfaces for these children should avoid the use of complex symbols.

Functionality is a non-negotiable aspect of any interface design. Without a fully functional interface, a game cannot be played.

Perfect Dark Zero: Now You See It—Now You Don't

Perfect Dark Zero also has a great minimal, context-sensitive interface that appears and disappears as you need it. In its basic form, it takes up very little screen and is unobtrusive. As you dual-wield additional weapons, use gadgets, or perform special tasks, the interface expands as needed but still stays very minimal and easy to understand.

—*Troy Dunniway (Lead Game Designer, Midway Los Angeles)*

Microsoft

Usability

The term *usability* generally refers to the user-friendliness of an interface. For a manual interface, can the player reach all of the buttons easily? In a visual interface, are menus easy to navigate? Are important actions easy to invoke? It is possible for an interface to be functionally sound but still be poorly designed because it is not sufficiently usable. An interface's usability is determined by *how* the interface achieves its functionality. Both usability and functionality are relevant concepts for both feedback and control elements.

Usability and Playability

In game development, you will occasionally hear the term *playability*—which refers to usability with respect to playing a game. These two terms can be used interchangeably.

One way in which an interface can lack usability is by forcing the player to take unnecessary steps in order to complete a task or achieve a goal. For example, if players must press a button every time they want to change Pac-Man's direction, the game becomes unnecessarily tedious. However, the interface is still functional because players can still complete the necessary action of changing direction. In *Civilization III,* conducting espionage and dealing with foreign relations are often done at the same time. However, no method of switching directly from one of these screens to the other is provided.

⁙⁙⁙How Important is Usability?

Firaxis Games

Firaxis Games

Though their functions are related, there is no direct method of switching between the foreign relations (top image) and espionage (bottom image) screens in *Civilization III*. These interfaces illustrate an important point. While it is clear that the design here is suboptimal, *Civilization III* is still an extremely successful game and is considered the front runner of all turn-based strategy games. While interface design is important, a "perfect" interface is not required for a successful game. How resistant a game is to interface problems depends in part on the type of game. Turn-based strategy games (discussed in Chapter 5) are typically quite complex and interface "heavy" (containing many interfaces that convey a wide array of information). Players of these types of games will tend to be more tolerant of minor problems. For an action game, however, interface design mistakes could be deadly—undermining the game pacing desired and frustrating the players.

© Wizards of the Coast. Used with permission.

Neverwinter Nights uses sound to add to the game's atmosphere.

⁙⁙⁙ Feedback Red Herrings

As a general rule, it is a bad idea to give the player misleading information. Sound can be an exception to this rule, however. In *Neverwinter Nights,* when they're in urban areas threatened by enemies, players can hear the distant cries of peasants. These peasants don't actually exist in the game; the sound misleads players into feeling a sense of urgency and despair, making them feel like they are actually in a distressed city. Note that providing false visual clues is potentially more damaging. For example, if sections of the city are burning, this also adds to the atmosphere. However, since players can see the flames, they initially want to interact with it—to put out the fire, for example. It is less confusing to hear sounds in the distance, especially if their sources can never be reached.

Though technically less important than functionality, usability in practice is just as necessary for a successful interface. One primary difference between the two is that an interface is either functional or it's not—but usability can vary along a spectrum. Very few, if any, game interfaces are perfect in terms of usability. In fact, by its nature, usability can vary depending on player preference.

Think Tanks: Combining Form and Function

GarageGames

The first step is always to understand, at the most basic level, the functionality required for an interface and implement it. It needs to work before you can start making it pretty. After it works to a basic level, you can start embellishing the functionality with art and make it look aesthetically pleasing. Sometimes this is a back-and-forth process, with art influencing design. For me, the goal is to make the visuals reinforce the design goal. We introduced an interesting effect in the Xbox version of *ThinkTanks* for the aiming of the tank weapon. What we implemented first was to have a series of rings that projected outward from the tank's barrel. When the tank 'locked' an enemy target, the whole series of rings would snap to point at the target. From a functional standpoint, it worked. One could tell when a target was locked, and when one was not locked, but it was very abrupt and a little confusing, and it was not pleasing. What we worked very hard on was the transition of the rings from an unlocked to locked position, and more importantly, from a locked to unlocked position. When unlocking, the targeting rings would deform to a point where unlocking was imminent, looking like a curving slinky. It would then 'pop' off the locked target in a spring like action. The effect was instantly understood by all of the testers. It felt like the locking of the targeting rings was under tension, and the effect in and of itself was both visually pleasing and informative.

—*Joe Maruschak (Creative Director, GarageGames)*

> It's more important to have a functional interface that you dress up aesthetically than to have an aesthetic interface that you have to try and make work functionally.
>
> —*Briar Lee Mitchell*
> *(Co-Founder, Star Mountain Studios)*

> Once the art style is defined for your product, extending that art style to the interface is crucial for a good interface. The player must feel like every button and every thing they see on the screen works in harmony with each other.
>
> —*John Comes*
> *(Lead Content Engineer, Gas Powered Games)*

Aesthetics

In interface design, form should follow function, but the *aesthetics* of an interface should not be ignored. While the onscreen action may change, the core interface does not. Look at game screenshots on websites or on the backs of game boxes. Note that most of these "screenshots" look cinematic and depict no interface at all! Part of the reason for this convention is to prevent the screenshots from looking too much alike. When advertising a game, you want the consumer to see dynamic, exciting examples of what the game is like. Showing a largely unchanging interface fails to achieve that goal and wastes limited advertising space. Also, it's widely believed (at least from a marketing standpoint) that including an interface in game marketing images can detract from the main in-game art.

Since the interface is always evident, it is especially important that it be attractive. A dull interface will undermine the best graphics and, in terms of total effort, it's much easier to make a beautiful interface than a beautiful game. That's not to say that designing an attractive interface is easy; it's not—especially because you first have to meet its functional needs. But the actual creation of the art assets used in a typical interface requires much less effort than developing the 3D models and animation sequences used in a game. Therefore, it is worthwhile to expend the energy to properly design an interface's aesthetics.

The aesthetics of an interface are affected by many factors, such as artistic style, color palette, and typography. Aesthetics affect interface elements associated with feedback—but not control.

Visual Style & Function

A visual style is first determined for the game experience overall. Then, the information is made to come across in the most immediate and understandable way. Finally, both form a framework for the user interface aesthetics. The visuals shouldn't drive the function, but they can certainly bend and influence it.

—*Stieg Hedlund (Lead Designer, Perpetual Entertainment)*

In these screenshots of *Dungeon Siege 2,* the top screenshot does not contain the interface, while the bottom screenshot does. Does the interface detract from the game's visual impact?

:::::: *Metroid Prime:* Setting the Tone

Nintendo

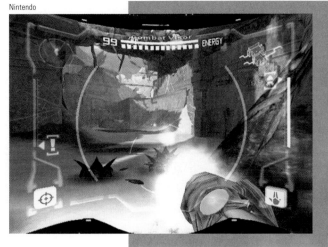

For visual style and pure aesthetic feel, *Metroid Prime* for the GameCube was really well executed. The background animations coupled with an eerie audio overture and simple yet stylistic layout made for a very tight presentation. It has this feel of traveling through an alien organism, and it immediately set the tone for the game.

—Timothy Nixon (Founder & Creative Director, Straylight Studios)

:::::: *World of Warcraft:* Balancing Aesthetics & Information Overload

World of Warcraft®, StarCraft®, Diablo®, and Warcraft® images provided courtesy of Blizzard Entertainment, Inc.

The interface for *World of Warcraft* somehow manages to communicate a barrage of information to the player quickly—in a way that doesn't make you want to tear your eyeballs out of your head. The depth of the interface is slowly revealed as you play (mostly when players fill up quick slots and gain new powers). It's heavily icon-driven; the aesthetics for the colors and fonts are good and blend well with the game world; and it's unobtrusive to such an extent that it never feels like it gets in the way of the action.

—Chris Avellone (Chief Creative Officer & Lead Designer, Obsidian Entertainment)

My absolute favorite game interface is used in *World of Warcraft.* The whole interface is completely customizable via an easy-to-learn scripting language, and it stays in context with the game's visual themes and textures. That means player-made interface add-ons look like they're still part of the *Warcraft* universe.

—Randy Wallace
(Game Art & Design Student)

Ian Wall on Interface Design Aesthetics

Ian Wall first started working with interface design in 1997 designing websites. His initial foray into digital artwork was with Photoshop 2.0.5 (before layers)! Over the years, Ian worked for various companies, did some freelance work, and eventually landed a job working as a web designer at Sony Online Entertainment. During his time at Sony in 2001, Ian designed graphical user interfaces for both *PlanetSide* and *EverQuest*. In 2003, he began doing 3D character artwork for *EverQuest*. He currently works at Obsidian Entertainment as a Senior Artist on *Neverwinter Nights 2*.

Ian Wall (Senior Artist, Obsidian Entertainment)

Strong graphic design and color theory are two major foundations for game interface design aesthetics. I try to keep my user interface designs slim—only using design elements as accents throughout rather than creating large graphical elements. Then I typically use texture, shape, contrast, size, and color break up areas as needed. Interface design is definitely a "less is more" realm of design. Concerning functionality, I try to break things down into flow charts and make all the paths throughout the interface as simple and minimal as possible. If going from point A to point B requires input from the player five different times along the way, I make sure that each of those points of input is necessary, makes sense to the player, and can't be combined or simplified or removed. There are areas of some interfaces that you might assume are fairly straightforward, but they can become extremely complicated for the player if they go unchecked.

Accessibility

Accessibility is similar to usability, but it applies specifically to players with special needs. People with physical or mental disabilities or impairments can have difficulties using interfaces. Currently, no regulations require accessibility to be implemented in computer software and hardware. It is the responsibility of the game industry itself to accommodate the needs of those with disabilities.

Addressing Accessibility

Addressing issues like red/green color blindness, deafness, mobility, and other impairments is important for the industry. In our work in consumer software outside of games, supporting those with disabilities (like curb cuts in sidewalks for wheel chairs) often ends up improving access for everybody.

—*Nicole Lazzaro (Founder & President, XEODesign, Inc.)*

There are many benefits to implementing accessibility in game interfaces. First, an accessible product—assuming it doesn't compromise its quality for the average player—will reach a larger audience. Since many games do not consider accessibility, the well-designed product will garner much attention and sales from those who benefit from it. Second, consideration of issues such as accessibility is viewed as socially responsible by modern society and aids a company in developing a positive reputation—which has many intangible benefits. Finally, through self-regulation, the game industry gains credibility with society—helping it to overcome the negative stigma games sometimes have.

Physical and mental disabilities include a wide variety of conditions and symptoms. It may not be practical to attempt to address all possible disabilities, but an awareness of common difficulties people might have can help guide your interface design. Accessibility affects interface elements associated with both feedback and control.

Michelle Hinn
(Vice President,
Game Division—
DonationCoder.
com; Chair, Game
Accessibility Special
Interest Group—
International Game
Developers Association
[IGDA])

Michelle Hinn on Accessibility and the "Right to Fun"

In addition to her involvement with DonationCoder.com and the International Game Developers Association (IGDA), Michelle Hinn is completing her doctorate at the University of Illinois, where she has been teaching courses on game design and adolescent psychology. She has a B.A. in Music Performance, a B.S. in Psychology, and an M.A. in Multimedia Design. Michelle worked at Microsoft Game Studios where she focused on piloting usability tests for Xbox multiplayer games. Michelle has also worked for Computer Sciences Corporation, the National Center for Supercomputing Applications (NCSA), and the University of Nevada at Reno. She is the co-editor of *Visions of Quality: How Evaluators Define, Understand, and Represent Program Quality* and is on the editorial board of the *Computers in Entertainment* magazine. Michelle is currently working on a Game Accessibility book with the IGDA.

In the game industry, we often talk about quality of life issues as employees—but we rarely stop and think about the positive impact of games on quality of life. Sure, we have government officials and groups that tell us that violent games are bad for us psychologically, but there are a lot of games out there that are good for us with regard to cognitive-spatial skills, collaboration, and more. There's a "right to fun" that I believe we all have; leisure activities can be healthy for us. Imagine if, as a game designer, you suddenly lost your sight, hearing, or mobility. Would you have a problem with not being able to enjoy playing a game—the leisure activity that ironically led you to work in the industry? Most likely you would. We are all aging—which brings about loss of sight, hearing, and mobility. In this industry, which is no longer composed of the "teenage boy" club, it will be interesting to see how an aging work force will address these concerns. We're already seeing some exciting things from companies such as Nintendo, with its *BrainAge* game series that may have some cognitive benefits for the aging brain.

I've been working to link groups together who are concerned with game accessibility, and I'm starting up some research here at the University of Illinois on game interface design with some college students with disabilities. The IGDA Game Accessibility SIG is working with funded groups such as game-accessibility.com (also SIG members) to start getting the word out about what the industry is doing "right" with game accessibility. Instead of approaching companies to say that their game is not accessible for the following 800 reasons, we let them know that they did five things right for gamers with mobility disabilities, for example. Even when game companies might happen to be doing some things that work well with certain assistive technologies (such as a head tracker), they often just don't know this because it was never brought to their attention that they might have players with disabilities. This is not a stab at the industry—but an indication of lack of awareness of what gamers with disabilities (who are extremely passionate about playing your games) have to do in order to *play*. It's quite sobering to realize that these players are hacking into hardware in order to play your game any way that they can. I think it shows us that even when our games go gold some gamers are still in the "design" phase, so to speak, figuring out how to make your completed project something that they can participate in and interact with.

Impaired Vision

Perhaps the most common disabilities relevant to interface design are those involving vision impairment.

Myopia

Myopia, or near-sightedness, affects approximately 25% of American adults. Though easily treated through glasses and contact lenses, it's important to recognize that many people using game interfaces do not have perfect vision.

SANS SERIF FONT
SERIF FONT

Arial is a sans serif font, while Times New Roman is a serif font.

Consider Color Blindness

Color blindness is an obvious disability that needs to be addressed in a game interface, as it affects 5–10% of the population. If you aren't thinking about this, you probably don't have a good design. Some hints: use more than color to cue the user and take care to pick distinct enough colors.

—Bob Mitchell
(Senior Programmer,
Sony Online Entertainment)

For most elements of games, the impact of myopia is minor—but the area to be especially careful about is text. Sans serif fonts (such as Verdana) and fonts with small serifs (such as Times New Roman) are believed to be easier to read in difficult conditions and are thus preferable choices. (*Serifs* are the cross strokes that appear on some letters.)

Having large, readable text is more important in games than in utility software for two reasons. First, console games often use standard televisions—which are less sharp than computer monitors. Second, in any real-time game, the player must be able to read the text quickly so that it does not interfere with playing the game.

Color Blindness

Color blindness is estimated to affect as many as 10% of male Americans to some degree. (Color blindness is considerably less common among women.) Most people with color blindness are still able to distinguish between many colors; however, in the most severe cases, color blindness can cause

The above images show a comparison between what a person who is not color-blind (left) and one who is color-blind (right) might see.

someone to see in only black and white. The most common form of color blindness is difficulty distinguishing red from green.

One simple guideline to address color blindness is to never use color contrast as the *only* method of conveying information. For example, a common convention is to use green to indicate full health, yellow to indicate a wounded character, and red to indicate a badly wounded one. However, instead of relying solely on color, a power bar is usually used—with a shorter bar indicating less health. While color plays a large role in depicting a character's health, a color-blind player can gauge health by the length of the bar.

Firaxis Games, Inc.

A special patch is available for *Alpha Centauri* that allows the game to use a "color-blindness friendly" color palette.

> I always consider ways of reinforcing or even building redundancy into game interfaces to allow for accessibility. Icons are good—but icons with tooltips, color coding, and associated sound effects are better.
>
> —*Stieg Hedlund*
> *(Lead Designer, Perpetual*
> *Entertainment)*

A more complete approach to accommodate color blindness is to use color palettes that are friendly to the common red-green blindness. This is generally not a practical solution for a default interface, but it could be provided as an option the player could choose. For example, Firaxis provides a color-blindness patch for *Alpha Centauri* that uses an alternate color scheme.

Making Your Interface Accessible

Interface accessibility for the disabled is extremely important. After all, games are for everyone. Unfortunately for a lot of game companies this is a lot of work, and it's not just the interface designer's responsibility to handle such matters. It's a company-wide commitment and requires input from all departments within a company. Some third-party companies are stepping up to help companies create more accessible games—for example, *Quake for the Blind,* which is a huge landmark for audio interfaces. That being said, there are some things you can do as a designer to help make your interface more accessible. One thing you can do is work with your programmers to make the interface scalable. This will allow people to increase or decrease the scale of the images displayed, so that people who are visually challenged can more easily read small text or recognize icons more readily due to their larger size. Another simple thing to do is to keep in mind the color blind. There are filters for Photoshop that you can download which can be used to color correct your images. This will allow you to see what your images would look like to someone who is red/green color blind. If your image is hard to see or read, then you can adjust it accordingly.

—Ian Wall
(Senior Artist, Obsidian Entertainment)

BioWare Corp.

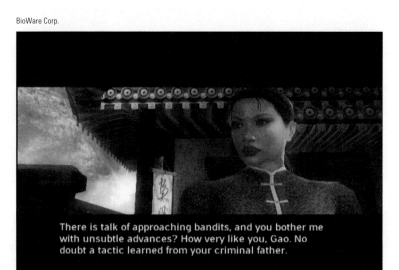

There is talk of approaching bandits, and you bother me with unsubtle advances? How very like you, Gao. No doubt a tactic learned from your criminal father.

Subtitles for games with voiceovers, such as *Jade Empire,* are preferred by some players—especially those who are hearing impaired.

Hearing Impairment

Designing your interfaces to accommodate hearing impairments is especially critical, since even non-deaf players will often be playing without sound or might be listening to their own music while they play the game. The best method of accommodating hearing impairments is similar to that for addressing color blindness. Any critical feedback to the player should not be done solely through sound or music. Use audio to enhance your interface, but do not make it a requirement.

Physical Disabilities

Physical disabilities can range from carpal tunnel syndrome to quadriplegic conditions. Specialized software and hardware have been designed to allow people to interface with a computer through other methods.

The importance of accessibility in interface design should not be overlooked. There has been some discussion among members of the International Game Developers Association (IGDA) about starting a game accessibility initiative similar to the web accessibility initiative that was introduced by the W3C (http://www.w3.org/WAI/).

Specialized Input Methods for the Disabled

Usually, the needs of the disabled are addressed through the use of specialized software or hardware input methods. In the case of voice recognition software, your interface must allow for hotkey activation and/or assignment to be accessible to that particular audience. Some people have looked at games purely based on sound to cater to a blind audience. There are also experiments taking place involving direct control from the nervous system—the initial results of which have allowed quadriplegics to play *Pong* with nearly 80% accuracy.

—*Timothy Nixon*
(Founder & Creative Director, Straylight Studios)

Production Advantages of Accessibility

Most of my experience with interface issues and the disabled usually come from compensating for color blindness in games (I've worked with a few color-blind designers in the past) and subtitle options for all of our games for the hearing-impaired. It's never been mandatory, but we've found that implementing for the disabled usually has production advantages (such as localization, cleaner interface aesthetics, variety of feedback). Of course, I seem to be becoming deaf as I grow older, so I'm appreciating subtitles more and more as time goes on.

—*Chris Avellone*
(Chief Creative Officer & Lead Designer, Obsidian Entertainment)

"Switch" Interfaces as Accessible Controllers

Some of the best-designed controllers are hacks by gamers with disabilities or people trying to create accessible controllers for a friend or a family member who has a disability. An example of this would be a "switch" interface (a one-button controller, essentially), that allows players to divide a controller in half if they have mobility limitations; instead of bringing both hands together to play, they can have controllers in each hand. See http://www.oneswitch.org.uk/ for more examples.

—*Michelle Hinn*
(Vice President, Game Division—DonationCoder.com; Chair, Game Accessibility Special Interest Group—[IGDA])

Robert Florio on Accessible Interfaces

Robert Florio (Artist & Student, Game Art & Design Program, Art Institute Online)

The QuadControl mouth stick is a well-designed manual interface that Robert uses regularly with games such as *The Matrix: Path of Neo, Psychonauts, and Devil May Cry 3.*

In 1996, when Robert Florio was only 14 years old, he injured his spinal cord while diving. After the accident, Robert decided to focus on pursuing his dream to be a game designer. Robert is a quadriplegic and creates all of his artwork with his mouth using a tool known as a mouth stick. Game accessibility to him means "finally gaining control over a world I no longer can interact with and reconnecting my senses to those actions." Robert is now 23 years old and lives in Maryland, working on obtaining his Bachelor of Arts degree in Game Art & Design from the Art Institute Online. He is learning to create his own games from home. Robert feels that many players who cannot physically function to play these games are at a disadvantage—and he hopes to bridge the gap by creating his own company and influencing the structure of games today. Robert can be found online at http://robertflorio.com

The most accessible games I've played allow the rearranging of all moves, special button selections, and combos of buttons in one—all in the game options menu. Making everything much more simple not only makes it easier for me to play, but it also simplifies games for others to enjoy. So many games on the market are becoming more complicated in design—especially with regard to the design of player interaction with the controller and the environment.

Game interfaces will eventually be even more interactive—with the senses implemented into the game control and environment. For example, I could use my mouth (by breathing in and out), chin, or bottom lip for certain functions. There could possibly be "mind control" through computer chips for those with complete quadriplegia. I would love to see the day where I could get a physical workout while playing a video game specifically tuned to my needs and functions as a quadriplegic.

Challenges and Rewards of Designing for Accessibility

Ideally, when I am thinking about a game, I strive to make everything intuitive. I try to use as many subtle visual and audio cues as possible to inform the player of what is going on. Ideally, both the visual and audio components should be able to stand on their own to inform the player, but this can be quite a challenge. I would be hard pressed to design a shooter for the blind. I am sure that it could be done—but it would be very difficult, and it would have to address the way that a blind person interfaces with the world.

I think about it, but I try not to go too overboard thinking about it. Game players with sensory disabilities have learned to cope with a world where interface is not designed for the most part to accommodate them. If the game world reflects the real world well enough, they can cope with it using the coping mechanisms that they have already acquired. I do try to the best of my ability to make sure that all feedback has both a visual and audio component, as I don't like to rely solely on audio as a feedback device (although at times it is the only option).

For those with disabilities that interfere with input (paralyzed), it can be quite difficult. I would relish the chance to design a game for the disabled . . . say, have an interface device that allows one to fly by controlling their breathing . . . unfortunately the economics of the industry don't really make that a probability. The hope is that the cost of creating specialized interface devices may decrease as technology improves. I can imagine, say, if cell phones had motion-sensing technology in them. If the software had an API that allowed this to be easily accessible, one could make the 'flying' game, make a module for a cell phone, and by having someone place the phone of the chest of the paralyzed individual, allow them to play the game by breath control.

Is it important? From a sales perspective, probably not. From a human perspective, most definitely so. Games and simulations are something that can be used to improve the quality of life for severely disabled people. If we can give those who are disabled the ability to interact with the world, socialize with others, and play in worlds where they are not held back in ways they may be in the 'real' world, we can make a real difference in their lives.

I would love to be able to somehow be a part of something that attempts to make the world more accessible to the disabled. As part of the legacy of life, this would be something far more important to me than making a ton of money.

—Joe Maruschak
(Creative Director, GarageGames)

In this chapter, you learned that the goals of an interface are to provide both control and feedback. You also learned of the importance of functionality, usability, aesthetics, and accessibility in interface design. In the next chapter, we will focus in more detail on the categorization of interfaces—including the distinctions between manual and visual, active and passive, and static and dynamic interfaces.

1. How can a game interface address accessibility issues? Choose a current game and discuss how you would modify it so that it addresses visual, audio, *and* motor disabilities.

2. How does audio enhance a game interface? Play an electronic game with and without audio, and make note of how audio is used as an interface element. How does the functionality of the game improve when audio is used?

3. What makes an interface usable? Play an electronic game for at least four hours. Do you feel that the game's "fun factor" is compromised by the interface? Why or why not? Make note of anything that seems "awkward" to you—such as the placement of interface elements and amount of time required to complete a task.

4. Does an interface always successfully address both primary and secondary goals? After playing an electronic game and familiarizing yourself with its interface, discuss whether or not the interface addresses these goals. Would you make any improvements to the interface?

5. How can an interface reach a successful balance between functionality and aesthetics? Choose an electronic game that has a highly functional but less aesthetic interface. Create a rough design in color that shows how you would improve upon the interface by modifying its aesthetic qualities.

CHAPTER

3

Categorizing Interfaces:

what are the options?

key chapter questions

- What are some examples of interfaces?
- What is the difference between *manual* and *visual* interfaces?
- What are different game *perspectives,* and how do they relate to interface design?
- What is the distinction between *static* and *dynamic* interfaces?
- How do *passive* and *active* interfaces differ from one another?

Several interface elements and types can be found in most if not all game platforms. This chapter focuses on elements and types of interfaces—such as manual, visual, active, passive, static, and dynamic.

As you've learned, the general trend in the industry is to reduce or minimize the interface. Minimizing the interface involves removing as many of these interface-only elements as possible without detracting from the gameplay. By definition, the interface is something undesirable, a necessary evil. It forces us to break the players' immersion to remind the players that they are taking part in a game.

This view of interface is easy to comprehend because it separates the interface from the game (specifically, the game's graphics). It is clear where the game ends and where the interface begins—making it easier to divide tasks, with interface designers responsible for developing these non-game elements. Further, viewing the interface as separate from the game allows us to apply traditional software interface design concepts (such as context-sensitive cursors and menu functionality) to game interface design.

Throughout this book, the term "interface" refers to this definition, with interface being considered separate from the game. However, this view of interface—which is common throughout the entire game industry—has some disadvantages. Let's consider more critically what an interface is and how else it might be defined.

Manual Interfaces: Grounding the Gameplay

Well-designed peripheral hardware exists that complements gameplay experiences. Dance platforms are one example; you play such a game by engaging in an actual form of dance through the manual interface. That helps to ground the gameplay, lending it a real connection to what it simulates.

—*Frank Gilson*
(Senior Developer for Online Games,
Wizards of the Coast)

Manual Interfaces

A *manual* interface is a hardware device such as a keyboard, mouse, or console controller. Manual interfaces provide control to the player. In the early history of computer games, companies experimented with numerous types of manual interfaces in an effort to improve the player's experience. Clear "winners" have appeared—and most manual interface elements currently used have been around for a decade or more.

Active feedback through a manual interface is currently very primitive and typically limited to vibration, which is included in the most current console systems (Xbox, GameCube, PlayStation 2, Xbox 360, PlayStation 3—and Wii). The controllers for these machines are equipped with *rumble* technology that causes the controller to "shake" when certain major in-game events occur—such as a player character taking damage from an enemy. Another form of feedback from controllers is more passive in nature, such as when a button creates a "click" sound or provides tactile resistance when pressed. The controls themselves are designed to inform the player when they have been activated so that the player trusts that the controller is working properly.

:::::*Burnout 3:* A Subtle Use of Rumble

Electronic Arts Inc.

Some not-so-exotic technology can be used to great effect on more mainstream games. In *Burnout 3,* the rumble on the console controller shakes just slightly as you pass very close to another car. The sensation is that of a 'whoosh' as you pass another vehicle— amazing implementation that really made me think, 'Woah, this is cool!' A manual interface feature does not need to be an earth-shattering departure to be effective.

—*Joe Maruschak (Creative Director,*
GarageGames)

:::::Analog and Digital Controls

Controls can be either digital or analog. Digital controls have only two settings (on or off), while analog controls have more than two. The power button on a stereo is an example of a digital control. When you press it, something happens; it doesn't matter how hard you press. The gas pedal of your car is an example of an analog control. As more pressure is applied to the gas pedal, the quantity of gas delivered to the engine increases.

The Xbox's "joysticks" are referred to as analog sticks. The left analog stick is often used for movement. Many games allow your character to walk when the analog stick is pressed slightly—but run when the stick is completely pressed in a certain direction. The D-pad also allows for movement, but this digital control cannot distinguish between the degree at which it's being pressed (light or hard). (Console controls will be discussed in more detail in Chapter 4.)

Microsoft

Console controllers, such as Xbox controller, contain both analog and digital controls.

Manual interfaces generally play minimal roles in providing atmosphere for the player. Some "exotic" manual interfaces, such as steering wheels or dance pads, can help reinforce the theme and feel of a game. However, manual interfaces are usually designed to be used by many types of games (and other applications, in the case of computers) and thus are too multipurpose to be designed to complement a game's atmosphere. Hardware is much more expensive to manufacture than software, making game-specific manual interfaces generally cost ineffective.

For the vast majority involved in game development, manual interfaces have platform-specific constraints. For example, Game Boy Advance (GBA) has one D-pad, two primary buttons, two secondary buttons, and two triggers. Any game designed for the GBA platform must confine its interface to these resources. The process of designing manual interfaces themselves is a highly specialized field and beyond the scope of this text, though a thorough understanding of how a manual interface affects game development is relevant to both software and hardware interface design.

Software manual interfaces are almost nonexistent, though it could be argued that touch screens, such as those used by many handhelds such as PDAs and the Nintendo DS, allow software-specific manual interfaces.

Manual interfaces specify what options games can use to provide control to the player. Obviously, when designing interfaces it is critical to consider the limitations of the manual interface players will use. The GBA, for example, has fewer controls than the GameCube—which makes more complicated interfaces (and thus games) less suitable, or at least more difficult to design.

Nintendo   Nintendo

The GameCube controller has more controls than the handheld GBA SP.

The reverse consideration is also important: Many games will not utilize all of the possibilities afforded by a platform's manual interface. For example, the computer game *Sid Meier's Pirates!* makes good use of the mouse but can be played without it.

Firaxis Games, Inc.

The computer game *Sid Meier's Pirates!* supports the mouse as a controller, but it can be played entirely with the keyboard if desired.

I really enjoyed the icon-driven interface *of Sid Meier's Pirates!* (2004). It ties the game world perfectly to the interface, never detracting the player's thoughts from anything but the 16th-century Caribbean. Bullfrog's *Dungeon Master 2* also provides some nice animation (and atmospheric music) during menu selection in the way of dangling chains. It's these little elements that continually feed the game into the player's mind—from seeing the box and screenshots in the store, to making menu selections and ultimately entering the game world itself at home. Every part of the gaming experience matters.

—Dan Puczek
(Game Art & Design Student)

When considering which portions of a manual interface to employ, you should keep standard conventions in mind so that players will not feel constrained by the control scheme. These conventions are very platform dependent and are explored in more detail in Chapter 4.

Visual Interfaces

Visual interfaces are generally involved in the feedback and atmosphere of the game interface. Visual interfaces are specifically related to software elements—not hardware.

Display

Throughout this book, the term *display* is used generically to mean any sort of display medium—such as a monitor, laptop screen, television, or cellular phone display.

Getty Images, Inc.

© Todd Taulman. Image from BigStockPhoto.com

© Albo Alessandro. Image from BigStockPhoto.com

Display can refer to a television (left), a laptop screen (middle), or even a cell phone display (right).

Besides screen size, visual hardware is generally categorized by four qualities: aspect ratio, color palette, resolution, and refresh rate.

Aspect Ratio

Aspect ratio refers to the proportions of the display screen. Standard televisions and monitors use an aspect ratio of 4:3, meaning that for every 4 centimeters wide the screen is, it is 3 centimeters high. Widescreen displays are becoming increasingly popular, since they use an aspect ratio of 16:9—the same proportion used in movie theaters. The widescreen aspect ratio is also fairly common for laptop computers. Cell phone displays tend to be vertically oriented instead.

Color Palettes

Color palettes for games also depend upon display hardware. Very early games were limited to monochrome displays, which had two colors. Current technology supports 16- or 32-bit color palettes, and color palette size is no longer a significant limitation.

Getty Images, Inc.

© Alex Melster. Image from BigStockPhoto.com

Console games should be designed to accommodate both traditional/full screen (left) and widescreen (right) televisions.

> A widescreen television is by far my favorite way to enjoy a good video game. There is nothing quite like having a game fully envelop your entire view! I'm all about the total experience, so add a quality surround sound system to the mix and you've got my perfect way to "live" the game.
>
> —Aaron Marks
> (President, On Your Mark Music Productions)

Resolution

Resolution describes the number of pixels that can be displayed at a time. It can vary considerably based upon the player's preferences and is expressed in terms of the length and width of the screen in number of pixels. The current minimum resolution commonly used is 640 × 480. High-definition televisions (HDTV) can provide much higher resolutions, with 852 × 480 or 1366 × 768 being common. Note that HDTVs are typically widescreen and also employ square pixels, like computer monitors—instead of the rectangular ones used in older televisions.

Console games should be designed to support the low resolution of standard televisions. Personal computer games will typically operate at higher resolutions, such as 800 × 600 or 1280 × 800. You should design your interface based upon the display resolution of your target audience, but it is highly desirable to support other resolutions as well. Though your target resolution has a great impact on interface design, resolution will typically be dictated by the graphics engine, not interface considerations.

Ignoring lower resolutions will mean that many players will be unable to play your game at all. Additionally, running a game at a higher resolution can require much more memory and processing power, resulting in reduced system performance. Even if a computer can support high resolutions, a game might best be run at reduced settings. On the other extreme, including options for higher resolutions is also desirable because players with more powerful systems will typically prefer to use the highest resolution possible. By comparison, the Atari 2600 employed a resolution of 160 × 192 and supported 128 colors.

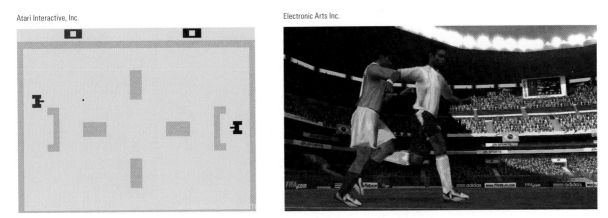

Atari Interactive, Inc.

Electronic Arts Inc.

The graphics from the Atari 2600 game *Combat II* and the PlayStation Portable (PSP) game *FIFA 06* illustrate how the graphics have developed from the first console systems to those of today.

Refresh Rate

Refresh rate is the frequency with which the display is updated. The higher the refresh rate, the less a screen will "flicker." The larger the display area, the higher the refresh rate should be. Typical refresh rates are 60-100 hertz (Hz), or frames per second. A game's *frame rate* is the number of frames of action that are displayed per second. Frame rate obviously cannot be greater than the display's refresh rate and is generally significantly lower because of processor limitations. While 60 frames per second (fps) is considered ideal, it can be difficult to attain and is often not a practical goal. In general, 30 fps is desirable, though frame rates as low as 10 fps can be acceptable for short periods of time. The issue of frame rate is important in game design, but it is generally not a consideration for interface design.

Perspective

Perspective (also known as "view") refers to the camera and basic control scheme the game employs. Perspective is one of the most important interface decisions, since it defines many elements of gameplay. It is also one of the first descriptors used to identify the game type. The major perspective options are discussed next, along with examples of each.

Two-Dimensional (2D)

Two-dimensional (2D) games provide a top-down view of an area. Objects are sometimes shown from above, but can also be represented in side views. The former provides a more realistic perspective, while the latter is often clearer because many objects lack detail when looked at from above.

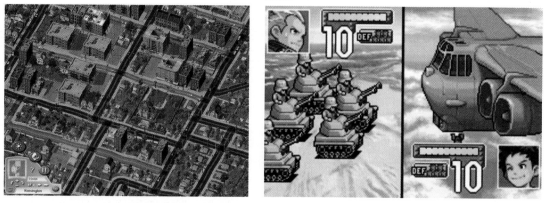

Sim City 4 utilizes a top-down view, while *Advance Wars* has a side view.

For the major consoles and computers, 2D games have become rare except for some budget titles. In terms of graphics in particular, 2D games are generally much easier to create, especially in terms of graphics; artists can create 2D sprites much faster than they can 3D models.

Diagrams by Per Olin

The 3D and 2D figures above are displaying the same information. Which one is easier to read?

Puzzle games like *Bejeweled* commonly use a clean and simple 2D perspective.

Even in most three-dimensional (3D) games, primary menu screens will be shown in 2D. Developers have several strong incentives to keep full-screen interfaces in 2D. First, as noted earlier, 2D graphics are much cheaper to create. Second, 2D is generally much cleaner for displaying information. Finally, the graphic quality of such interfaces is seen as much less important because it is not depicting a world.

The 2D perspective is still quite common in handheld and mobile games due to the technical limitations of those platforms. This perspective is also used for Flash games because Flash is ideal for 2D graphics. Finally, some types of games—such as puzzle games—will typically use a 2D perspective for the same reasons full-screen interfaces do.

Isometric

An *isometric* view, also sometimes called 2.5D, combines many of the advantages of 2D graphics with some of the appeal of 3D. The camera in an isometric game is above the world, looking down at an angle. The world acts completely in two dimensions, but the perspective provides the illusion of a 3D world. Some isometric games utilize sprites, while others might use pre-rendered or even real-time-rendered 3D models.

The four primary movement directions in an isometric game are the diagonal directions (top-left, top-right, bottom-left, bottom-right), though eight-directional games are also common. One limitation of an isometric view when compared to a 3D one is that the camera is fixed. Due to the way the graphics are represented, the player cannot change the camera's pitch. Rotating the view is made possible in some games, and the ability to zoom in and out is also fairly common. This latter feature is especially useful in strategy games because the player often wants to see the details early in the game and the bigger picture as their empire expands.

Diablo II uses an isometric perspective.

During action-packed moments in *Diablo II,* I can just glance at the interface out of the corner of my eye to see how well I'm doing in health. During the slower points in the game, I can get all the information I need on the game status/actions.

—*Darren T. Priddy*
(Game Art & Design Student)

The strategy game *Tropico* allows the player to zoom the camera in and out.

Everything you need to play *Diablo* is close by. The "belt" where you place your healing potion and other special potions is just below the game view port. You can change styles of attack by simply clicking again just below the view port without having to leave yourself open very much to attack. The health indicator is large and easy to see, as is your power meter.

—*Norman Hechavarria*
(CG Artist, Naked Poly)

The isometric perspective was once the norm for role-playing games (RPGs) and all types of strategy games (genres that will be discussed in Chapter 5), but it has been largely abandoned in modern games. Except for ease of implementation and lower demands on the player's game system, the isometric view has no advantage over a 3D view. As consoles and computers have become more powerful, this advantage has faded in importance and the isometric perspective has become essentially a poor man's 3D that is undesirable except for games created with very limited budgets or for handheld/mobile platforms.

Lady Vashj
This shattered world is called Outland, young prince. It is all that remains of Draenor, the former homeland of the orcish Horde.

Warcraft III utilizes a 3D perspective in a 2.5D gameplay space.

Red Faction, like all FPS games, utilizes a first-person perspective.

::::: **Perspective vs. Gameplay Space**

Note that a game's perspective does not always match the space in which the game is played. For example, recent real-time strategy (RTS) games, such as *Warcraft III* or *Rise of Nations,* use a 3D graphics engine but essentially play in a 2D space. Height does not have an impact on gameplay (though some units cannot attack flying units and others cannot attack ground units), and units cannot maneuver vertically.

The real-time strategy (RTS) game *Star Wars: Empire at War,* developed by Petroglyph Games, uses what they refer to as 2.5D gameplay. (RTS games will be discussed in more detail in Chapter 5.) Also utilizing a 3D engine, *Empire at War* allows limited, but not full, 3D movement by restricting vertical movement to layers. The result is the feeling of 3D space, but with less complexity than a fully 3D game such as *Homeworld.*

First-Person Point of View

The *first-person point of view (POV)* uses a 3D view that places the camera behind the eyes of the main character. For many first-person games, particularly first-person shooters (FPSs), players will see their arms or items they may be carrying. (FPS games will be discussed in Chapter 5.) This view has several primary advantages. It is considered the most immersive perspective because the player and character views are the same. Keeping the main character off-screen allows players to imagine that character in any way they wish—perhaps even as themselves! Besides improving immersion, this second aspect also reduces the required system resources since there's one less character model that must be shown onscreen at any given time.

Note that the first-person perspective does not require a 3D graphics engine. In fact, some of the oldest RPGs such as *Wizardry* and *Ultima I* employed a first-person view. These games were tile-based and restricted view to the four cardinal directions.

The primary disadvantage of a first-person perspective is that it can require greater player skill to master. For example, because players can only see a small section of the world in front of them, they might be attacked by unseen opponents with no idea of the direction of the threat. These types

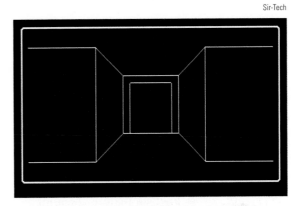
Sir-Tech

Wizardry I was one of the early games that utilized a first-person perspective.

of problems can be addressed through other aspects of the interface. For example, an icon could appear on the screen showing the direction of attackers. While solving this particular problem, solutions like this can reduce the level of immersion achieved by the first-person perspective.

Third-Person Point of View

The *third-person* POV also uses a 3D view but shows the player's character onscreen. The primary advantage of a third-person view over isometric perspective is higher graphical quality. Furthermore, in some third-person games, the camera can move around in the world freely to show more or less of the ground. Its primary disadvantage is that it requires a 3D graphics engine, which is much more difficult to create than a 2D one.

When compared to a first-person view, the third-person view requires more processing power and memory because one extra character is always onscreen. Also, it is considered less immersive because the player's view of the world isn't a natural one—especially since it's part of a first-person game. On the other hand, it allows players to see more of

Eidos Interactive Ltd.

Tomb Raider: Legend uses a third-person perspective.

the world at once; they can see what's on all sides of their characters. Being able to see everything around the player is important to the gameplay of some games, such as *Max Payne*. Additionally, the visual appearance and movement associated with game characters can improve character development and add more personality to the game.

Note that many third-person games do not allow free camera movement. In *God of War,* for example, the camera perspective is fixed for each area—with the camera moving as specified by the designers. This restriction both frees the player from having to worry about the camera and allows the designers to set what the player can and cannot see at any point in the game. By not relinquishing camera control to the player, objects can be hidden or emphasized and impressive vistas can be shown without worry that the player will find a camera angle that reveals too much of the world for the system to handle. Games that do not allow the player to control the location of the camera are said to be "fixed camera" games—which require much more "polishing" time at the end of a project, since poorly placed cameras can make a game very frustrating to play.

A third-person view can keep system requirements lower by restricting camera pitch. In a first-person view, the player can see off to the horizon. Without careful area design, this view can cause performance problems—since too many objects might be visible on the screen at once.

Sony Computer Entertainment America Inc.

God of War uses a fixed-camera, third-person perspective.

Hybrid Perspectives

Some games support multiple types of perspectives or use a hybrid view. Many games that employ a 3D graphics engine allow the players to switch between several views and even between first- and third-person views. For these games, the only difference between first- and third-person is the camera position—so if the gameplay supports both view types, it is desirable to allow players to use the mode with which they are most comfortable. Some third-person games, particularly those in which the player controls multiple characters, do not provide a first-person camera—since that view is not considered advantageous to gameplay. Multiple party members and choreographed combat sequences make a first-person perspective undesirable in *Star Wars: Knights of the Old Republic 2*. Yet for its "Turret" mini-game, it is able to utilize a first-person view.

A more unusual case is for a game such as *Black & White 2*. Technically, this game provides a first-person perspective. Players are seeing the world through the eyes of their characters, who are fledgling dieties. However, from a practical perspective, the game displays a third-person view. The camera can freely move throughout the game world, unlike in a traditional first-person perspective. Additionally, the player is often managing assets—buildings, people, and creatures—as one would in a third-person view.

Black and White 2 uses a hybrid first- and third-person perspective.

Static and Dynamic Interfaces

In Chapter 2, we noted that the goal of the interface is to provide the player with feedback and control. These are clearly desirable goals. For the most part, you want to give the players as much feedback and as much control as they can handle. Games are about interactivity—and these two elements are exactly what differentiate games from other forms of entertainment, such as movies.

With this in mind, consider another possible definition of a game interface—which consists of everything that conveys information to the player (feedback) or allows the player to send commands to the game (control). By this definition, all of a game's graphics are part of the interface!

Consider the arcade game *Asteroids*. The player's spaceship is depicted facing a certain direction. If the thrusters are applied, the ship will move in that direction; if the weapon is fired, the shot travels in the direction the ship is facing. If the spaceship was shown as a circle, this critical information would be lost. The players would have to use their memories and trial and error to determine in which direction to move or shoot when they activate the appropriate controls. It is clear from this example that the very graphics themselves are part of the interface.

I really love the simplicity of the interface in *Black & White* because it's nearly nonexistent. Players are left guessing the status of their pets and the condition of their standing with their worshippers. A game like this can have a ton of information fly at a player, but the interface reduces all that information to a minimal amount of cues for a player to pick up on.

—*Dung Chi Trinh*
(Game Development Student)

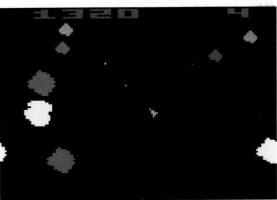

In *Asteroids,* many of the functions of an interface are handled by the game itself—not through special interface elements.

> I find that in-game interfaces are much more difficult to design than front-end interfaces. In-game interfaces must not only look good and be very functional, but they must feel good. Every player has a different definition of what feels good, so how do you design around that?
>
> —John Comes
> (Lead Content Engineer,
> Gas Powered Games)

In *World of Warcraft,* the armor and weapons being used by various characters convey vital information to the player. Again, we see game graphics contributing to the interface. (Still, with the many statistics and properties various equipment might have, the graphical representations alone are insufficient and the details can also be accessed by the player.)

We will refer to the interface-only elements as the *static* game interface (SGI) and those incorporated into the game as the *dynamic* game interface (DGI). The details of implementing each of these elements are very different and require distinct skill sets. For example, a programmer, 3D modeler, and texture artist are all required to make the armor for the *World of Warcraft* characters appear properly—while a programmer and perhaps a 2D artist would generally create the SGI.

Keep in mind that the principles of interface design apply equally to SGI and DGI design. When considering the entire game, it is critical to understand how these two forms of interface relate to and complement each other. To emphasize this point, we will occasionally explore the concept of a DGI in more depth throughout the book. Keep in mind, however, that it's common to use the generic term "interface" when referring to the SGI.

Active and Passive Interfaces

Interfaces can also be categorized as either active or passive. An *active* interface is one with which the player can interact. Therefore, active interfaces always offer some level of control—though they also often provide the player with feedback. Any menu system within a game is an active interface. Menu systems provide control, but little feedback. The inventory interface for *Neverwinter Nights 2* is an example of an active interface that incorporates both feedback and control. Players can see what equipment they are using as well as what they currently carry. Additionally, they can equip and unequip items, learn more about item properties, and transfer items between characters.

By contrast, a *passive* interface conveys information to the player but is not interactive and cannot be controlled by the player. The timer in *Burnout 3* is an example of a passive interface. It tells players how long they've been racing but does not allow for player control.

The inventory interface for *Neverwinter Nights 2* is an active interface that incorporates both feedback and control.

In this chapter, you learned about the various types of game interfaces and ways of describing them through the terms *active, passive, manual, visual, static,* and *dynamic.* You explored the various camera perspectives that are used in games. Finally, you learned how interfaces are composed of much more than buttons and displays. With this better understanding of what makes up an interface, let's take a more detailed look at game platforms and how they relate to interface design.

Electronic Arts Inc.

The countdown time in *Burnout 3* is an example of a passive interface. The player cannot interact with it, but it provides useful information.

:::CHAPTER REVIEW:::

1. What is your favorite visual interface for a game, and why? Describe the interface in terms of layout, content, and navigation. How does the interface enhance the game-playing experience?

2. How do active interfaces provide control to the player? Choose an electronic game and discuss how it utilizes an active interface design. What functions does the active interface provide? Critique the interface in terms of layout, content, and navigation.

3. How do passive interfaces provide feedback to the player? Choose an electronic game and discuss how it utilizes a passive interface design. What information does the passive interface provide? Critique the interface in terms of layout and content.

4. What is the difference between manual and visual interfaces? Choose an electronic game and take note of how the game utilizes both types of interfaces. What would you do in order to improve upon the game's manual and visual interface designs?

5. Come up with an original game idea and create a series of active and passive interfaces that could be utilized in your game. When will these two styles be necessary? What tasks will the player need to accomplish (active), and what information will the player need (passive)?

Part II:
Theory

CHAPTER

Platforms:

game hardware and manual interfaces

key chapter questions

■ What are the features of the major game platforms?

■ How do game platforms affect interface design?

■ What manual interfaces are associated with each game platform?

■ What visual interfaces are most appropriate for each game platform?

■ How will interfaces differ in the next generation of consoles?

Throughout your career in the game industry, you will likely develop for multiple *platforms*—hardware configurations such as arcades, personal computers (PCs), consoles (PlayStation, Xbox, GameCube), and handhelds (GameBoy, DS, PSP, mobile phones).

Platforms have several impacts on interface design. Though many components are similar, each platform has its own specific hardware—and, therefore, different controls.

Computer

Of all game platforms, the *computer* (or *PC)* is currently the most multipurpose. The keyboard and mouse manual interface must handle the widely varied needs of players, business executives, students, and Internet surfers. As a result, this manual interface combination is extremely versatile and powerful. The greatest challenge in designing a computer interface is not in accommodating the needs of the software, but in providing intuitive options for the player.

Operating Systems

An operating system (OS) is the software that runs behind the scenes, dictating how other software interacts with the system. Personal computers most commonly use Microsoft Windows as an operating system, though another OS called LINUX is also fairly common. Macintosh computers use a proprietary OS, though newer machines also support Windows. For the most part, a computer's operating system does not impact a game's interface design—though it certainly affects how any interface is implemented by programmers.

Computer Visual Interfaces

Many of the first personal computers were designed to use televisions for visual interface hardware. As long ago as the early 1980s, however, specialized displays (monitors) became the norm. Current monitors are capable of much higher resolution and graphical quality than traditional television sets.

Monitor

A computer's *monitor* is the key hardware component of its visual interface. As an interface tool, the monitor is currently almost exclusively used to provide feedback (though it could be argued that some monitors, such as that of the iMac, add to atmosphere as well). In modern computers, a device called a video card is used by the computer to interact with the monitor and present feedback to the player. The visual interface quality of a computer is primarily based upon these two components, with the video card usually being the limiting factor.

Monitors come in two main varieties: *cathode ray tubes (CRTs)* and *liquid crystal displays (LCDs)*. CRTs use technology similar to traditional television sets and are larger, heavier, and less expensive. LCDs—also called flat screens—are much lighter and less bulky, but they are more expensive. The visual quality of the two types of monitors differs somewhat, with players mixed on which type is better. Monitors have gradually increased in size, with the current range between about 15" and 24" (measured from one corner of the screen to the diagonally opposite corner).

© Andres Rodriguez. Image from BigStockPhoto.com

© Alessandro Bolis. Image from BigStockPhoto.com

The two primary monitor types are CRTs (left) and flat screens (right).

Computers can use two or more monitors simultaneously, which is a cost-effective way to increase desktop space. For games that fully support dual-monitor configurations, the player can run the game on one monitor while leaving the other available for chat, email, or other tasks. Since few home users employ this type of set-up, no games currently make full use of the dual-monitor configuration by running different elements of the game on each monitor.

Laptops have built-in, flat screen monitors. They use either standard or widescreen aspect ratios and, as one would expect, are typically smaller than desktop monitors. Larger screens require considerably more energy. Given limited laptop battery capacity, smaller laptop screens provide the dual advantage of less weight and longer battery life. Laptops can be set up to display on a monitor or television instead of, or simultaneously with, the laptop screen. This option can be especially useful for those performing demonstrations with a laptop.

The Image Bank/Getty Images

Laptops are designed to utilize other displays when needed.

Computer Manual Interfaces

While several unusual *manual* interfaces are available for computers, such as steering wheels or joysticks, the majority of computer games make use of two manual interfaces: a keyboard and a mouse.

Keyboard

The primary manual interface device for a computer is the *keyboard*, which is a descendent of the traditional typewriter. Though keyboards can vary slightly from system to system, they are largely standardized and include the following components:

© Elke Dennis. Image from BigStockPhoto.com

The keyboard is currently the most powerful manual interface.

- The 26 letter keys, 10 numeric keys, and 11 punctuation keys used in English. These keys typically produce the corresponding character.
- SHIFT, CTRL (control), and ALT keys, which often do nothing on their own, but, when pressed at the same time as another key, perform a new function. For example, the SHIFT key produces punctuation and uppercase letters.
- Function keys (typically F1 through F12), which perform some action. For example, F1 often opens a help menu for the selected application.
- An Enter key (also called Return or CR) that confirms the current action or moves the cursor to the next line.
- Assorted other keys such as Delete (deletes character following the cursor), Backspace (deletes character before the cursor), ESC (Escape, which cancels the current action), and TAB (moves the cursor forward depending upon the context in which it is pressed).
- A numeric keypad on the right side, to allow easy numeric data entry. Most of those keys' functionality is also mapped to other keys on the keyboard.

Carriage Return

Another term for Enter that you may come across is CR, which is an abbreviation for *carriage return.* On traditional typewriters, a device called the carriage slides from left to right across the sheet of paper. When the typist presses a key, a metal arm strikes the carriage's ink ribbon against the paper—causing the letter typed to appear on the paper. The carriage would then slide one space to the right. Upon reaching the end of a line, the typist would hit the carriage return key—which would "return" the carriage to the far left position, allowing the typist to continue typing on the next line.

With more than 70 keys in the typical keyboard, it is an incredibly complicated and powerful manual interface. This power can be dangerous for game design because it allows one to create interface schemes so complicated that a game can be hard to learn or play.

Photodisc Green/Getty Images

Ergonomic keyboards are designed to minimize strain on the typists' wrists.

Qwerty vs. Dvorak: Inefficiency Wins Out

Most keyboards use the Qwerty design, so named for the first six letters in the top left. Another variety, known as "Dvorak," allows experienced typists to type significantly faster by placing the most commonly used letters in the most easily reached locations. In fact, Qwerty keyboards were specifically designed to slow down typists so that their typewriters wouldn't jam! The Qwerty layout has become so common that it has stayed with us, despite its less friendly design. Keyboards in other countries, including France and Germany, typically use slightly different layouts.

In an effort to address carpal tunnel syndrome and other physical ailments, many readily available keyboards are ergonomically designed.

Mouse

The *mouse* has become almost as ubiquitous as the keyboard. Its primary purpose is to allow players to move a cursor around the display area, which allows them to select or otherwise interact with interface elements in an intuitive manner. The typical mouse has both a left and right mouse button. These are operated by the index and middle or ring finger, respectively. The left mouse button is used to select objects or take an action. The right mouse button often provides additional information.

© Alessandro Bolis. Image from BigStockPhoto.com

A typical computer mouse

A mouse can come in a variety of shapes and sizes, and could have additional buttons for added functionality—such as quick web browser navigation. The most common additional mouse feature is a mouse wheel, which is placed between the left and right mouse buttons. The mouse wheel is generally used to scroll through text

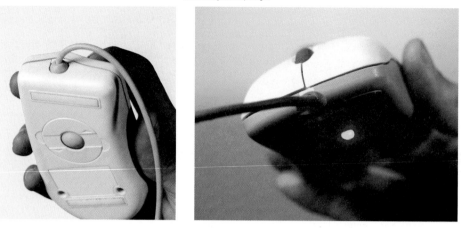

The bottoms of a ball mouse (left) and an optical mouse (right).

or zoom in and out. It can also serve as a third button. While you may want to support all mouse options, you should not assume that any player will have more than two mouse buttons available.

Several other mouse variations are available. An optical mouse requires additional electricity, but lasts longer—since it does not have moving parts to wear out. A wireless mouse has also become more common; although it requires no cord, its batteries must be replaced periodically.

Trackball

The *trackball* is a variation on the mouse; it's essentially an inverted mouse, where the player spins a ball while keeping the device itself stationary. Functionally, a trackball is very similar to a mouse. While much less popular than a mouse, the trackball is preferred by some players.

> The keyboard and trackball are my favorite controllers. The trackball gives me more precise control in first-person shooters—so much so that I have been accused of cheating (using AIM bots). The keyboard allows game designers to make more robust games. RPGs and games such as *Unreal Tournament 2004* make excellent use of the keyboard.
>
> —*Norman Hechavarria
> (CG Artist, Naked Poly)*

The trackball is an uncommon alternative to a mouse.

::::: Macintosh

For the purposes of this text, the term "PC" refers to both laptop and desktop systems that are Windows (and LINUX) compatible. An alternative computer platform is the Macintosh (Mac), which uses its own operating system (though recent Macs can also run Microsoft Windows). Unlike PCs, which are manufactured by a large variety of companies, all Macs are developed by Apple. The manual interface for a Mac is very similar to that of PCs, but there are a few important differences that Mac designers must consider. First, some Macs have a single mouse button and lack a wheel. Second, Macs have slightly different supplemental keys; they lack ALT and Windows keys and instead have Option and Apple keys. Since Macs have a relatively small percentage (about 5%) of the total computer market share, few games are created with the Mac as the primary platform. Instead, companies such as Aspyr port PC games to the Mac platform.

Several other interface types are available for computers. In general, games should not be optimized for use of these devices because few players will actually have them. Still, it is good to keep all relevant manual interfaces in mind when developing your game's control scheme. The players who have purchased these devices will appreciate that you're supporting them.

Mad Catz, Inc.

Joysticks, which were the norm for the older console systems of the 1980s, are still used with some action games.

Steering wheels can increase the immersion and playability of racing games.

chapter 4 Platforms: game hardware and manual interfaces

Computer Interface Guidelines

Computer interfaces should be designed for the majority. Know who your primary players are and provide a default interface that best suits their needs. Efforts to accommodate specialized needs in the default interface will result in a substandard interface for many of your players. Follow established conventions for the genre of the game you are designing. (Genres are discussed in more detail in Chapter 5.) For example, the WASD keys are commonly used for movement in role-playing games (RPGs)—with "w" providing forward movement, "a" and "d" respectively providing left and right movement, and "s" being used for reverse movement.

Customizable Controls

Allow players the option to *customize* all of their controls. You can then design for the majority without alienating others with specific preferences. Provide shortcuts for common customization choices to support the most common types of players. Some examples of customization schemes worth considering are discussed below.

Left-Handed Players

While right-handed players might prefer using the mouse and keys on the left side of the keyboard, *left-handed* players will be inconvenienced by this arrangement. Since they often use the mouse on the left side of the keyboard, left-handed players typically prefer keyboard commands on the right-hand side.

Compact Keyboards

The numeric keypad is excellent for movement, especially because its keys are aligned vertically, unlike the letter keys. However, not many laptops have a numeric keypad. Design your game's controls such that a *compact keyboard* option is possible.

Digital Vision/Getty Images · · · · · · · · · · · · · · · · · Blend Images/Getty Images

Keyboards can vary substantially in their number of keys. Compare the full-sized keyboard on the left with the laptop keyboard on the right.

Note that this advice violates the previously given rule that you should always design for the majority, since it is theoretically possible for a game to utilize the entire keyboard—making it simply unsuitable for a compact keyboard. However, given the richness of the keyboard and mouse interface, such an interface design would likely be too complex to be ideal anyway. If 50+ keys are necessary to navigate through your game, the design is probably flawed.

Mouse-Free

Many people use laptops without a mouse and find the touchpad clumsy to use for games. While not practical for all types of games, such as real-time strategy (RTS) games, provide a *mouse-free* option if possible. Again, the default configuration should employ a mouse, but a keyboard-only configuration option is desirable.

Reverse Mouse

Many hardcore players prefer a *reverse mouse* configuration for camera control. That is, pushing up on the mouse in any direction will tilt the camera in the opposite direction. So to look down, players would move the mouse away instead of toward them.

Computer and Console Technology

One important distinction between the computer and console platforms is how they advance in terms of technology. High-end computer technology will always exceed what the consoles are capable of. Consoles have to be made cheaply when compared to the multipurpose computer. Also, many computers are expandable. Manufacturers are constantly achieving advances in processor, video card, and memory technology. The hard-core player, who is more likely to spend more money on game equipment, can pick up the latest video card and install it—improving the playing experience. Consoles by contrast are standardized and, to date, are not designed to be expandable. The console manufacturers have two primary incentives to keep their systems standardized. First, a non-upgradable system is cheaper to manufacture. Second, if a system cannot be upgraded, then all players will be playing under the same conditions—reducing technical support and ensuring that all games for the system will work as designed for all players. A console life cycle is about three to five years, while advances for computer components are available every few months.

Duplicate Functionality

As a general rule, you should provide players with the one best way to accomplish any task. Multiple options can become confusing and result in a muddled interface. However, there are several cases in which *duplicating functionality* is preferable.

Mouse Wheel

Mouse wheels are becoming increasingly common, but are still not ubiquitous. Therefore, use the mouse wheel to provide additional, convenience-oriented functionality that can also be performed by some other portion of the interface. For example, a mouse wheel might allow easy scrolling through text in a role-playing game (RPG), but the numeric keypad and page up/down buttons accomplish the same task.

Conventional Interfaces

As mentioned earlier, it is unwise to require the player to use uncommon interfaces such as a steering wheel. Therefore, any support for these advanced manual interfaces is typically duplicate functionality.

Consoles

The term *console* refers to any dedicated game system from the Atari 2600 of the late 1970s to the Xbox 360 and PS3 of the mid-2000s. Typically the term "console" does not include handhelds—which are discussed in their own section later in this chapter. Though the computer game market is still strong, consoles account for the majority of game sales in the United States (approximately 80% according to the Entertainment Software Association)—and the console share of the market continues to grow. This increased market share is less about the decline of computer gaming and more about consoles becoming much more mainstream—in part due to the major marketing efforts by Microsoft and Sony as they compete for customers. In recent years, consoles have been moving toward becoming more general entertainment systems, with the ability to play DVDs and access the Internet.

> My favorite console controller is one that I do not need to struggle with. I want to interact with the game but not concentrate on the controller.
>
> —*Robert Stewart*
> *(Game Development student)*

In early 2005, the console market was dominated by the PlayStation 2 (Sony), the Xbox (Microsoft), and the GameCube (Nintendo). The PlayStation 2, in part because it was released a year before the other two systems, had the largest market share at the time—followed by the Xbox and then GameCube. It is an interesting time for game developers as the newest generation of consoles emerges after several years of minimal changes. Microsoft's Xbox360 was released in late 2005—and the remaining next-generation consoles are planned for release in late 2006 (Sony PlayStation 3 and Nintendo Wii).

Successful Console Controllers

Sony hit the ball out of the park with the PlayStation 2 (PS2) controller. The analog sticks, amount of buttons, the vibration and feel worked in a huge range of situations. There were controllers like the PS2 earlier but this was a major company making a huge investment. Sega had the bright idea to make the Dreamcast controller have an optional video display similar to what Nintendo did linking the GameBoy Advance (GBA) and the GameCube. In my opinion, it's a great move to have a visual display available to each player personally. I recently started playing with the Xbox 360 controller and really like the feel and layout. It seems to benefit from the latest generation of technology and ergonomics.

—Tim Donley
(Producer, Bottlerocket Entertainment)

The Sega-Microsoft Controller Connection

Some regard the "Japanese" Saturn controller as the best 2D controller *ever,* especially for fighting and driving games. It was an evolution of the six-button design from the second Genesis controller. The notorious 3D-control pad from the Saturn was sold along with *Nights into Dreams,* a major Sonic Team release that wowed gamers everywhere in 1996. Although the analog stick was Nintendo's invention (N64), Sega introduced the two analog triggers—later copied by both Xbox and Xbox 360. Also, Sega's design was a lot more ergonomic than other controllers, making clear that the paradigm of gamepads had changed mid-decade.

The connection between the Dreamcast controller and the 3D control pad is clear. Sega fully believed that the future controllers would consist of four buttons on the right (taking PlayStation's cue), a large-sized case, and a single analog on the left. The design had a problem, however: the cord protruded from the bottom instead of the top. This awkward choice, coupled with the size of the controller, gave Sega a bad rep among casual gamers. Hardcore gamers loved it, of course.

Sega influences in the original Xbox controller are visible: the controller is huge, it has four buttons on the right, and it has two analog triggers. Microsoft wanted to go after hardcore gamers in order to build a halo around the system.

Signaling another paradigm shift, the s-type controller (a smaller controller with a streamlined button layout developed originally for the Japanese market) was released. This was another Japan-exclusive controller, but many U.S. gamers revolted against Microsoft's original design and started importing it. Soon Microsoft realized its mistake and started selling the s-type officially in America. Later, every new Xbox console came with an s-type controller.

—Luis Levy
(Production Tester, Treyarch/Activision)

The newest next-gen crop of consoles includes the Xbox 360, PlayStation 3, and Wii.

Player Types by Platform

When considering interface design, it is tempting to think about who plays games on different consoles. For example, shouldn't the fact that Xbox players are not the same as computer players affect how an interface is designed? No—not directly. It's important to consider the target audience for the type (or "genre," discussed in Chapter 5) of game being made—not the platform for which you are creating it. A designer should target the audience of the game—not the audience of the game's platform. (When developing a game for multiple platforms, however, it *is* wise to consider each platform's customer base separately.)

Console Visual Interfaces

Consoles rely on a television set (or sometimes a computer monitor) as display hardware. Since consoles do not include their own visual hardware, the visual requirements of these systems are essentially identical to each other and also very similar to those of computers.

Console Manual Interfaces

All console systems employ a *controller* as their primary manual interface device. Controllers vary somewhat by platform but generally include the same components:

Drew Davidson on Well-Designed Manual Interfaces :::::

Drew Davidson is a professor, producer, and player of interactive media. He is a faculty member of the Entertainment Technology Center. Prior to this, Drew was the Academic Department Director for Game Art & Design and Interactive Media Design at the Art Institute of Pittsburgh and the Art Institute Online. Drew completed his Ph.D. in Communication Studies at the University of Texas at Austin. Prior to that, he received a B.A. and M.A. in Communications Studies at the University of North Carolina at Chapel Hill. Drew is primarily interested in stories across texts, comics, games and other media as well as conceptual interactive design, integrated narrative and interwoven media, collaborative design and development, applied media, and game logic. He has been a faculty member of Austin Community College, St. Edward's University, Southwest Texas University, and Indiana University of Pennsylvania—where he was Founding Director of the Applied Media & Simulation Games Center. Drew has written a book on narratives across media and is currently writing another on cross-media communication.

Drew Davidson, Ph.D. (Faculty, Entertainment Technology Center, Carnegie Mellon University)

I still find the original Sony PlayStation controller to be an ideal input device—easy to hold with a maximum amount of buttons well-placed for a wide variety of possibilities in terms of player input that can be translated into gameplay action. The dance pad for *Dance Dance Revolution* and the EyeToy for the PlayStation both serve as great examples of how players can get up off the couch and bounce around while playing video games. Finally, while I have only seen it, I'm excited about the potential to be had with the new controller for the Nintendo Wii. It seems to promise all kinds of interesting and innovative gameplay possibilities.

action buttons, analog sticks, D-pads, auxiliary buttons, and triggers. Controllers are intended to be held in two hands, and components are typically managed by the player's thumbs and index fingers. As their name suggests, controllers are typically used to give the player control. Small vibrators in many controllers allow them to provide feedback in some games—but, since the player's concentration is (and should be) focused on the display, the ability of a controller to provide feedback is limited. Typically, controller vibration is used sparingly—often to indicate when the player is close to death or when some major event has occurred.

::::: Precise and Sloppy Players

An innovative article by Mick West in the May 2005 issue of *Game Developer* discusses "sloppy" and "precise" player use of action buttons. According to the article, sloppy players place their thumbs in the center of the four buttons (on a PlayStation 2 or Xbox controller) and then rock their thumb to press the desired buttons. Precise players, on the other hand, move their entire thumb from button to button.

This distinction is important for interface design because the sloppy players will often have multiple buttons pressed simultaneously. The act of switching their thumbs from one action button to another typically results in the old and new buttons being pressed at the same time. Any control scheme should take this possibility into account so that the interface is not frustrating for either type of player.

Additionally, some players use an even more extremely precise method of pressing action buttons—using their index fingers instead of their thumbs to quickly press the action buttons needed. This method is most common for extreme action games, such as fighting games, where quick and accurate button pressing improves performance.

Diagrams by Per Olin

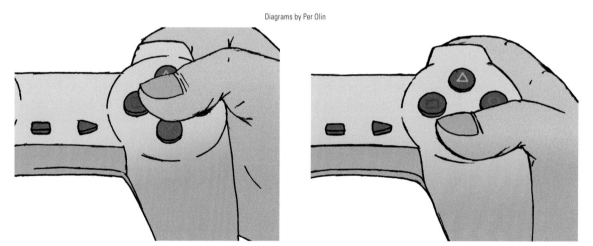

Sloppy (left) and precise (right) thumb placement.

Common Console Controller Components

Let's take a look at a few components that are common across all console controllers. These components include:

- action buttons
- analog sticks
- D-pad
- triggers
- auxiliary buttons (including start and select)

Action Buttons

All modern console platforms employ at least four *action* buttons—which are typically controlled with the right thumb and allow the player to perform a variety of events in the game, such as jumping or shooting. Action buttons result in an event (such as firing a gun) at the moment they are pressed. In some games, holding down an action button causes a more extreme event to occur. For example, a quick tap might cause a character to jump—while pressing and holding the same button would result in a higher, longer jump.

Analog Sticks

Analog sticks, or thumb sticks, became prominent in the previous round of consoles. These devices are joysticks that are intended to be manipulated by the player's thumb. Analog sticks are most often used for movement, aiming, or camera control. The PS3, Xbox 360, and GameCube each have two analog sticks. Often the primary analog stick (the leftmost one) is used for movement and the secondary one for camera control or aiming. The reason for this division of labor is that the left thumb is used solely for the analog stick, while the right thumb also has the responsibility of pressing action buttons.

An analog stick can also serve as a button; when pressed, some other event might occur. Caution should be exercised for this functionality, since it is easy for the player to accidentally press on the analog stick through play—especially when very involved in the game. Therefore, it is best used for more intense applications of the analog stick's primary objective. For example, in a racing game in which the analog stick controls direction and acceleration, pressing on it might activate turbo boosters.

As its name indicates, an analog stick is analog, not digital—meaning that how hard the player presses in a certain direction can result in a different outcome. For example, pressing forward lightly might cause a character to walk—while pressing hard results in a run.

D-Pad

The *D-pad* is a four- or sometimes eight-directional flat "button" typically used for movement or targeting. The term "D-pad" originated with the Sega Genesis, in which the D-pad was the fourth "button" along with action buttons labeled "A," "B," and "C." Functionally, D-pads are similar to analog sticks. They tend to be a bit less user-friendly, resulting in sore thumbs after extensive use. D-pads are frequently used for menu navigation.

Triggers

Triggers, also referred to as shoulder buttons, are located on the back of a controller and are designed to be "pulled" by the player's index fingers. Triggers typically handle secondary features that might be needed while also controlling the primary analog stick and either the secondary analog stick or action buttons.

Blocking or dodging maneuvers are often mapped to the triggers. In *Kingdom Hearts,* the triggers are used for camera control (an unusual choice)—allowing the player to be moving and attacking while also adjusting the camera angle.

Auxiliary Buttons

Other *auxiliary buttons*—such as Select, Start, and the Xbox's white and black buttons—provide additional functionality that is generally not critical to primary gameplay. These buttons are less prominently placed and are intentionally designed to be difficult to hit accidentally. They are typically used for controlling aspects of the game that are outside of the game itself—such as saving the game, adjusting sound and other options, and obtaining help information. Some more complicated games, such as *Advance Wars* for the GameBoy Advance, require the player to use these buttons more frequently—but this is generally not preferable.

Specific Console Controllers

While all current consoles employ the aforementioned components, it is important to understand the specific layouts of each system's controller.

Nintendo

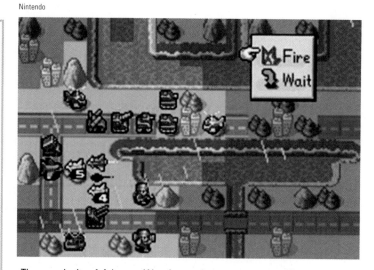

The complexity of *Advance Wars* forces the game to use auxiliary buttons for important gameplay functions.

After looking at different controllers over the years, I find that for ease of use (and lack of a clunky feel), the PS controllers have been the easiest for me. The buttons are fairly intuitive, the placement is good, and the addition of the shoulder buttons is useful. Notably, even Microsoft appears to have begun to move its controller into a similar design with the 360.

—*Howard Kinyon*
(Designer, Breakaway Games)

PlayStation 2 and 3

The *PlayStation 2* and *3* controllers consist of two analog sticks, one D-pad, four action buttons, four triggers (two on the left side and two on the right), Start and Select buttons, and an Analog button. The four action buttons are the □, △, ○, and ✕.

Sony Computer Entertainment of America Inc.

Annotations by Jason Bramble

The PlayStation 3 controller top view (top) and back view (bottom).

My favorite console controller has to be the PlayStation 1 or 2 controller. Whether it is the original (sans-analog) or the Dual Shock 2 with analog buttons and sticks, it just feels right. It conforms comfortably to the hands, and its layout is intuitive. It reminds me of the SNES, NES, and Genesis controllers—already familiar, and requiring no transition to learn. The real winning factor is that no button is awkward to press or requires strenuous motion to reach.

—*Randy Wallace*
(Game Art & Design Student)

Xbox and Xbox 360

The Xbox and Xbox 360 controllers consist of two analog sticks, one D-pad, four action buttons, two triggers, Start and Select buttons, and two auxiliary buttons (black and white). The four action buttons are the X, Y, A, and B. For the Xbox 360, the white and black buttons have been removed and two additional triggers have been added. The general controller layout is otherwise very similar.

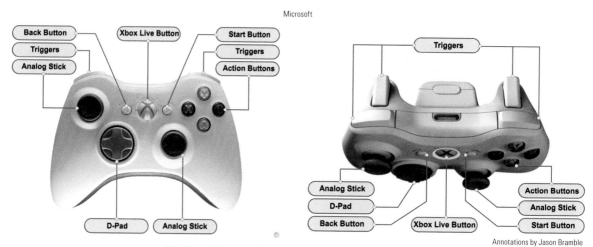

Microsoft

The Xbox 360 controller top view (left) and back view (right).

Annotations by Jason Bramble

My favorite controller has to be the original Xbox controller. It feels right in my hands, and the buttons are perfectly placed for me. I can reach all of them—even the black and white ones—with ease.

—Nir Silva
(Game Development student)

My favorite console controller is the Xbox 360 controller. Not only does it come standard with wireless, but the controller contours so perfectly to your hands that you don't even notice it's there. The "Xbox Guide button" can bring you right into the interface as well as turn the system off and on. You don't even have to leave the couch!

—Brent LaDue
(Game Art & Design Student)

GameCube

The *GameCube* controller consists of two analog sticks, one D-pad, four action buttons, two triggers, and Start and Select buttons. The four action buttons are the A, B, X, and Y buttons. Unlike the PlayStation 2 and Xbox 360 controllers, the standard GameCube controller has one primary action button (A) with the other three surrounding it.

My favorite console controller is the Nintendo GameCube controller. It fits snugly into my hands, especially since mine are small. All the buttons are in easy reach with my thumbs, the analog and the C-Stick are manageable, and my index fingers rest easily in the scooped-shoulder buttons, which prevent them from slipping during intense actions.

—*Vincent Leyba*
(Concept Art student)

Nintendo

Annotations by Jason Bramble

The GameCube controller top view (left) and back view (right).

Wii

The Nintendo *Wii* is being designed with a completely new set of game controllers. In addition to a "standard" controller, the Wii also uses remote and nunchuk controllers. Appearing much like a television remote control, the wireless and motion-sensitive Wii remote is held in one hand and includes easy access to a D-pad and A and B buttons. Sensors detect where the controller is aimed at the monitor or television screen, allowing the player to target different areas on the screen as if using a laser pointer. The remote can control anything from a sword to a paintbrush to a steering wheel. The Wii's nunchuk controller connects to the remote, allowing players to simultaneously control two elements at once with both the remote and nunchuk—such as a sword and shield in an RPG, and both running and throwing in a football game.

> I am looking forward to the Nintendo Wii controller. The possibilities of this controller are endless. The future of interface design will involve much more physical experience.
>
> —*Daniel Kim*
> *(Concept Artist)*

> The Wii controller holds a lot of potential for how we interact with games. You see games that allow you to interact through movement—such as fishing and baseball games—and the Wii is the next step up from those.
>
> *Lisa Hathaway*
> *(Game Development student)*

Nintendo

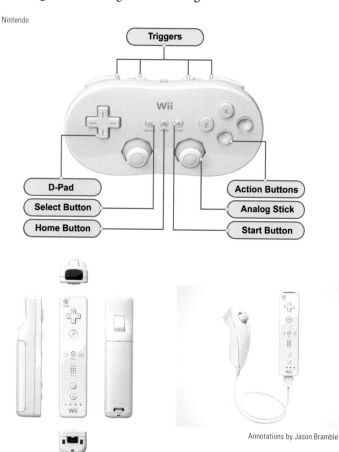

Annotations by Jason Bramble

The Nintendo Wii uses three innovative controllers—standard (top), remote (left), and nunchuk (right)—designed to reach more casual gamers and to allow new types of gameplay.

Handhelds

Handhelds can be described as miniature console systems. They are highly portable and include their own visual interface hardware. Games are typically stored on cartridges, which are platform-specific storage devices.

When compared to other storage media—such as floppy disks, CDs, and DVDs—cartridges have several advantages. They are very durable, making them good for travel and more suitable for the young audience targeted by most handheld systems. Since they are specific for each platform, they can be designed to hold exactly how much information the platform needs, allowing them to be optimized for size and cost. Additionally, their uniqueness makes piracy, or illegal copying of games, much more difficult; very few players have the equipment necessary to create new cartridges. The biggest disadvantage to using cartridges is their cost. While a DVD might cost about a dime in bulk, game cartridges cost at least several dollars—reducing the already slim profit margin for most electronic games.

Cell phones are typically not considered handhelds because gaming is a secondary function of the systems. Instead, cell phones belong to the "mobile" platform. Nokia's N-Gage system—which is a cell phone that also plays specific game cartridges—is an exception, since it is generally thought of as a gaming platform first.

Game Cartridges

Cartridges are specialized storage devices that are used almost exclusively in the game industry. Though their exact technology has changed over the decades, cartridges have been widely used since the late 1970s. Until the PlayStation, they were the storage medium of choice for console systems. Today, though having been replaced by CDs and DVDs for consoles, cartridges still dominate the handheld platform.

Nintendo   Nintendo   Nintendo

Nintendo

Nintendo Entertainment System (NES), Super Nintendo (SNES), Game Boy Advance (GBA), and Nintendo DS cartridges.

Handheld Visual Interfaces

Handhelds include built-in displays. The exact dimensions are platform specific—but, as one would expect from their emphasis on portability, their displays have substantially lower resolution than console or PC systems do. Combined with their weaker processors, handhelds are far behind consoles and PCs in terms of graphic quality—and display real estate must be used wisely. It is possible for some handheld systems to be connected to a TV or monitor, but all handheld games are still designed to work with the system's built-in display.

Handheld Manual Interfaces

Handheld devices, such as the Nintendo DS and the Sony PSP, typically function as console controllers. The visual interface (display) is built into the controller itself. Also, because handhelds are designed to be portable, they do not employ the bulkier manual interface options such as analog sticks—instead relying upon D-pads. Otherwise, handhelds typically employ action, auxiliary, and shoulder buttons—just as consoles do.

Some handhelds, such as the DS and tablet PCs, utilize touch screens that can be activated with a stylus. In these cases, the game system is able to recognize where the screen is pressed—allowing the player to press "buttons" on the screen and draw shapes with the stylus. The visual interface itself becomes part of the manual interface. This feature allows for entirely new types of games and innovative game design.

Game Boy Advance (GBA)

Nintendo's *Game Boy Advance (GBA)* line —particularly the GBA SP and Game Boy Micro—still currently dominates the handheld market. For controls, it features a D-pad, action buttons ("A" and "B"), right and left shoulder buttons, and Start and Select buttons.

Nintendo   Nintendo

The newest handhelds in the Game Boy Advance family are the GBA SP (left) and the diminutive Game Boy Micro (right).

DS (Dual Screen)

The Nintendo DS, with its two screens, has the most interesting handheld design from an interface perspective. Games can utilize both screens simultaneously, and the bottom screen is a touch screen.

Nintendo

The Nintendo DS provides opportunities for innovative game interface design.

The controls of the DS are similar to the GBA—but they also include X and Y action buttons as well as the touch screen, which is operated via a stylus. The DS supports all GBA games (which don't utilize these additional interface elements or the second screen) and also DS-specific games.

In case these options weren't enough, the Nintendo DS also employs a microphone to allow for verbal commands. In *Nintendogs,* for example, the player teaches a virtual dog its name and various tricks—which it will perform when the player speaks the command words.

> One of my favorite manual interfaces is the touch screen for the Nintendo DS. Players have a stylus with which they can finally touch their games. We can perform complex surgeries, pet our adorable dogs, and race cars all within the hour.
>
> —*Trystan Coleman*
> *(Game Art & Design student)*

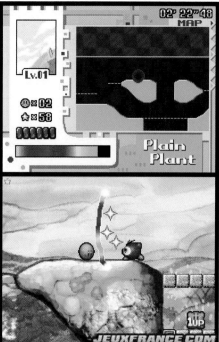

:::::: *Kirby: Canvas Curse*—An Innovative Interface

Kirby: Canvas Curse is an example of a game that utilizes the touch screen of the DS. The game is a 2D side-scroller in which the player helps a constantly moving ball, Kirby, navigate the game level. The top screen provides all the statistics—including Kirby's health, coins collected, and lives remaining.

The game is completely controlled with the stylus. Touching objects with the stylus can destroy, stun, or activate them. Drawing lines with the stylus creates rainbow paths that direct where Kirby moves and that can also protect him from enemies. Finally, when Kirby gains a special ability, touching him with the stylus activates it. *Kirby: Canvas Curse* is an excellent example of innovative interface design.

PlayStation Portable (PSP)

The *PlayStation Portable (PSP)* is Sony's first foray into the modern handheld market. It features a very large display screen, the same four action buttons as the PS ($\square$, $\triangle$, $\bigcirc$, and $\times$), left and right shoulder buttons, and both Start and Select buttons.

Sony Computer Entertainment America Inc.

The most striking feature of the PSP interface is its large screen.

The PSP, with its larger screen and better performance (and thus higher price tag) aims for an older market than the Nintendo handhelds. It is considered to be superior to the original PlayStation in terms of performance despite its handheld size.

Other Platforms and Interfaces

Several other platforms and interface types are prevalent enough to warrant discussion even though they are not currently dominant in the marketplace.

Mobile

The *mobile* platform is used to describe cell phones (except for the N-Gage, which is considered a handheld). Mobile phones provide substantial challenges to game developers.

First, games are only a secondary, or even tertiary, objective. General control options are non-ideal: a numeric keypad, a D-pad-like control located above the keypad, and a few additional buttons. The shape of the phone is somewhat awkward for holding with two hands, which is all but required for game-playing. Further, the buttons are generally not designed to be crisp and responsive as console controller buttons are.

Screen size for a mobile phone is exceptionally small and many are not in color. Games are saved on the phone itself (as opposed to using cartridges), meaning that storage space can be a significant limitation. Methods of getting games onto a cell phone are downloading them online or from a computer. The former method requires an additional service (web access) from the phone service provider, while the latter demands more technical savvy than the average cell phone user has; more to the point, it requires more effort than the average user is willing to invest.

The mobile platform, which is gaining in popularity, provides numerous interface design challenges.

The N-Gage: A Lesson in Hardware Interface Design

A multipurpose device, the N-Gage (launched in 2003 by Nokia) is a cell phone as well as a game platform.

Though its higher price point (when compared to the GBA) and a relative lack of high-quality games did not help consumer opinion of the platform, the biggest obstacles were interface-related. First, when used as a phone, it had to be held sideways—which some felt made the user look ridiculous. Second, to insert a new game cartridge, the battery had to be removed. While the practical effect of these two flaws might seem small, they had a huge impact on the appeal of the N-Gage as a gaming platform. A second model, the N-Gage QD, addressed these two interface design issues.

Nokia   Nokia

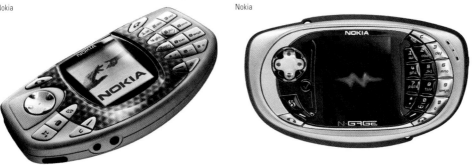

The Nokia N-Gage suffered from interface design issues.

Second, the mobile platform is lacking in standardization. Consistency, which is a fundamental goal of interface design, becomes exceedingly difficult to achieve because each cell phone manufacturer—and even various models within each manufacturer's selection—has its own design peculiarities.

The Dance Challenge

It's probably the most difficult to design manual interfaces for home console dance games. Imagine having to produce a 4 × 4 foot square that not only has to be packaged economically but has to work well. Most of the time, these are nonrigid mats with pressure sensors that get aggressively stomped on by hyperactive children. It can't fold or slide and it has to be able to stand up to the abuse required by the game. To do it right takes brilliant people. Joysticks, racing wheels, and handheld controllers consistently do the jobs they are designed for and the designers seem to have gotten a handle on them. Dance mats still need some work, I think, to really make them functional and entertaining.

—*Aaron Marks*
(President, On Your Mark Music Productions)

Don't Let the Controller Take Over!

Specialized controllers can really add to the game experience, and make many impossible game designs possible. *Guitar Hero* for the Sony PS2 would be impossible to play with a standard controller. However, unless you are able to bundle the specialized controller with the game, it is very hard to design a game, and very dangerous to design a game, to take advantage of a specialized controller. Utilizing a specialized controller exclusively will make your game become a much more specialized and hardcore game.

—*Troy Dunniway*
(Lead Game Designer, Midway Los Angeles)

Brave Firefighters is made available courtesy of Sega Corporation. © Sega Corporation, 2006

The arcade game *Brave Firefighters* uses a controller that mimics a fire hose.

Interfaces will eventually move from an analog input (buttons, joysticks, D-pads) to more intuitive controls (motion sensors, biorhythmic controls, thought interfaces).

—*Dung Chi Trinh*
(Game Development Student)

Input devices can create opportunities for more full body engagement with the game. *Dance Dance Revolution*'s dance platform provides additional benefits in what I call Serious Fun. In our research, people play *DDR* to improve their body coordination, they play instead of eating, and they play to lose weight.

—*Nicole Lazzaro*
(Founder & President, XEODesign, Inc.)

Beatmania and Singstar: Widening the Market through Manual Interfaces

Konami Digital Entertainment   Sony Computer Entertainment Europe

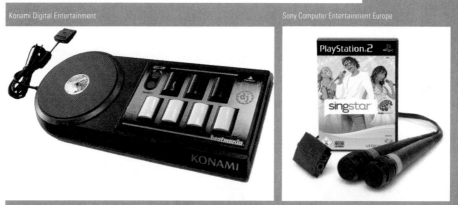

Beatmania features a set of five keys and a "turntable" with which you play out musical notes. It's really quite intuitive and a lot of fun. The whole tactile feedback revolution in Japan saw the development of some bizarre games, and ultimately saved arcades the world over. One of the best would have to be the addition of a microphone to the PlayStation and the advent of *Singstar.* That game has brought so many more gamers out of the woodwork. My mother would have never dreamed of buying a PlayStation before she saw *Singstar,* and now she's hooked.

—*Timothy Nixon (Founder & Creative Director, Straylight Studios)*

Enhancing the Experience through Manual Interfaces

Anything that can erase the artificiality of the human-computer interface is in my eyes a good thing. The dance pads are great because they involve the whole body as an input device. Force feedback steering wheels are great as they really get you "in" the experience. Most of these devices are expensive and limit the audience somewhat, but they do allow for a more sophisticated design for a more sophisticated user expecting an enhanced experience beyond point and click. All of them are great experiments and I think all can be fun. Something that makes the playing of games a more physical experience has the potential to resonate with people on a level that is a little deeper. For me, it is all about the experience that we can provide to the end user. If that experience can extend beyond just their ears and eyes and involve other senses, I think it is an enhanced experience.

—Joe Maruschak
(Creative Director, GarageGames)

Guitar Hero: Enhancing Immersion through Interface

RedOctane® is a registered trademark of RedOctane, Inc. Guitar Hero™ is a trademark of RedOctane, Inc.

Aside from the advantage that new manual interfaces allow you to design new types of games, they can also enhance the experience, most notably in terms of immersion. For example, *Guitar Hero* not only provides you with a guitar-shaped controller with a strap, but allows you to access the whammy bar—just the controller layout helps contribute to the illusion (delusion?) that you're actually playing a guitar and you're a rock star…that may be exaggerating a bit, but once you have that controller in your hand and you're playing the game, the number of "rock star" poses people get into just from holding the controller alone are priceless.

Chris Avellone (Chief Creative Officer & Lead Designer, Obsidian Entertainment)

Sony Computer Entertainment America Inc.

EyeToy: Full-Body Control

One exotic interface is the EyeToy, which was originally created for the PS2 by Logitech. The EyeToy is a digital camera and allows players to play games by moving their bodies. This movement is detected by the camera and used as a control mechanism in the game.

Unusual Manual Interfaces

Alternative manual interfaces include steering wheels, guns, fishing poles, dance pads—and even biofeedback machines! Since these can be expensive to produce, such unusual interfaces are most often used in arcade games, where they represent a relatively minor cost compared to the cost of the system itself.

For home consoles, exotic interfaces can cost more than the games themselves—making them less successful. You should not ignore the possible value of a custom interface, but in general you will find yourself confined to standard interface elements.

> The EyeToy opened up games to new markets by not requiring players to learn a video game controller. This is a big barrier to entry for non-traditional gamers.
>
> —Nicole Lazzaro
> (Founder & President, XEODesign, Inc.)

> *Guitar Hero* and *Dance Dance Revolution* would not be the same games without the controller. Pretty much the game revolves around the interface. Rarely does the user interface make the game.
>
> —Bob Mitchell
> (Senior Programmer, Sony Online Entertainment)

Harvey Smith is a game designer and creative director who has been making games professionally since 1993. Currently, he is studio creative director at Midway Studios-Austin. He worked at Ion Storm's Austin office from 1998 to 2004, acting as project director of *Deus Ex: Invisible War* and lead designer on the award-winning *Deus Ex*. (*Deus Ex* won the 2000 BAFTA and many other awards.) Prior to Ion Storm, he worked at Multitude, an Internet startup in San Mateo, CA. There he was lead designer of *FireTeam,* an innovative tactical squad game that was one of the earliest video games to feature voice-communications between players. Smith started his career at the legendary game company Origin Systems, working there for almost four years. Over the last decade, he has held roles in various design and leadership-related roles. From a professional standpoint, his passions are communications, team building, and game design. His creative interests are related to improvisational gameplay, player self-expression, and simulated game ecologies.

Harvey Smith
(Studio Creative
Director, Midway
Studios-Austin)

Everyone gets excited about the exotic input devices. On one hand, I think they're good opportunities for game designers to experiment with new forms of input. On the other hand, I think they're mostly gimmicks that don't equate to games being "better." The best interface devices are usually the ones you can forget completely. In the days of the Atari 2600, people tried to come up with a bunch of new input devices; most were not memorable. Some exceptional input devices are the paddle wheel for driving games and the guitar controller for *Guitar Hero.*

As you've learned in this chapter, you must consider the features and limitations of a game's platform before designing its interface. You have examined the manual and visual interfaces employed by all of the major game platforms. In the next chapter, we'll take a detailed look at game genres and discuss how they can influence the way interfaces are designed.

1. How do manual interfaces enhance the gameplaying experience? What is your favorite manual interface, and why? When applicable, discuss the controller's shape (if applicable) and both the layout and standard functions of the components.

2. How would you utilize a standard manual interface for an original game idea? Come up with a rough idea for a game. Which existing controller seems to be most appropriate for it? Label each component of the interface with its associated function.

3. "Exotic" manual interfaces such as guns and steering wheels have been utilized in electronic games since the arcade era. More recent exotic interfaces such as dance platforms, microphones and guitar-style controllers have enhanced the player's experience. Choose an electronic game that only has a standard controller and come up with a unique, exotic manual interface for it.

4. Choose an electronic game that is only available on one type of platform—whether it's arcade, console, computer or handheld. Let's say that there are plans to port the game to another platform. How will the new manual interface work with the game? In order to complete this exercise, you'll need to understand the functions of the existing manual interface. Whenever possible, avoid changing the way the game is played in order to make it work with the new manual interface.

CHAPTER

5

Genres:

game styles and visual interfaces

key chapter questions

- How do game genres affect interface needs?

- What are the established interface conventions for various game genres?

- What are the additional requirements of multiplayer game interfaces?

- What interface elements are common to multiple genres?

- How can existing interface conventions be applied to new game genres?

An interface's functionality depends upon what sort of feedback must be conveyed to the player and over what aspects of the game the player must have control. These elements are largely influenced by features such as depth of strategy, number of units or characters controlled by the player, presence or absence of dialogue, and many other factors. One common method of classifying games is by genre, and it is tempting to use genre to determine a game's interface needs.

In this chapter, we will investigate each of the major game genres and discuss their game interface requirements. We'll also examine some of the current popular conventions and what their strengths and weaknesses are. Finally, we'll look at how you might apply some of the interface conventions and needs from existing genres to new genres.

Classifying Games by Genre

One of the rules of thumb in interface design is to employ established conventions whenever possible. If a particular interface scheme is ubiquitous, it is generally better to stick with it as much as possible instead of asking the player to learn a new control scheme.

When designing a game, how do you determine what all of the current conventions are? Don't different games employ different configurations? Which ones set the standards that future games should follow?

Comparing game screenshots from different genres makes it very clear how the genre of a game can affect the way a game's interface is designed.

Stainless Steel

© Valve Corporation. Used with permission.

Real-time strategy games (*Empires: Dawn of the Modern World,* left) and first-person shooters (*Half-Life 2,* right) have very different interfaces.

Can we really generalize by genre to determine how a game's interface should be designed? Ultimately—and perhaps contrary to what you might initially assume—the answer is no. It's more important to understand how game *systems* are employed.

Sony Computer Entertainment America Inc.

Movement is a game system for an action game such as *Ratchet & Clank.*

::::: Game Systems

A game system includes one or more actions that the player can take. A game's systems, when combined, include all actions and options available to the player. If a player can do it, it's part of a game system. For example, in *Ratchet & Clank,* players can move Ratchet forward. This action is part of the movement system. They can also change Ratchet's direction and have him jump; these are also parts of the movement system.

A game's genre will sometimes (but not always) specify one or more game systems. For example, a first-person shooter—by virtue of the first-person perspective—requires a specific type of system for movement. However, as you will see, the combat system for a role-playing game (RPG) might be turn-based (e.g., *Final Fantasy X*), real-time (e.g., *Fable*), or a mixture of both (e.g., *Star Wars: Knights of the Old Republic*). Some interface elements (such as methods of accessing inventory, health indicators, and numbers indicating damage dealt) exist in the combat systems of all three of these games.

Bethesda Softworks

While both role-playing games, *Dungeon Siege II* and *The Elder Scrolls IV: Oblivion* have very different interface styles.

However, each game has its own requirements—since the details of combat vary considerably. For example, in *Knights of the Old Republic,* all of the player characters act simultaneously—and players can only control one at a time. In *Final Fantasy X,* players also control one character at a time—but each character acts in sequence, not simultaneously. Meanwhile, in *Fable,* players cannot control any of the companions their characters may have.

Still, it's useful to take a closer look at game genres for several reasons. First, many within the industry will discuss games by genre to communicate ideas. For example, by understanding the typical interface elements of a first-person shooter (FPS), you will better be able to communicate your ideas with others in the game industry. Second, examining the typical interface needs of each genre provides a good foundation in common game interface design issues. Third, for some genres, such as real-time strategy (RTS), the genre actually does dictate many aspects of interface design—even for games that initially seem quite different. These "interface-specific genres" will be discussed at greater length in this chapter—whereas "interface-diverse genres" will only be touched upon briefly. Later, you'll learn more about how to design interfaces for games that do not solidly fall into an interface-specific genre.

One of the first steps in designing an interface is to identify its functional requirements. What types of actions must the interface allow the player to do? Some genres are so well-defined that these requirements are quite similar from game to game. Since games of these genres typically have the same gameplay elements, they require the same functionality from their interfaces.

When a new genre emerges, its pioneer games tend to have some clumsy interface elements. When developers make new games for the genre, they attempt to improve upon its various elements—including the interface. They study other games in the genre, and the best ideas are often incorporated into new titles.

Genre: It's the Style—Not the Story

If your background is in literature or film, you've likely noticed that the game industry uses the word "genre" unconventionally. In game development, *genre* doesn't refer to setting or theme (science fiction, western, romance, mystery) as it does in film and literature. Instead, the word has come to refer to the style of gameplay. Even this definition is poorly defined in the game industry—with many inconsistent uses varying from company to company. For example, some publishers refer to games in the massively multiplayer online game (MMOG) genre as persistent state worlds (PSWs).

Action

The *action* game genre is vast—consisting of first- and third-person action games such as platformer (games involving many jumping and timing action-based puzzles), shooting, racing, and fighting games.

First-Person Shooter (FPS)

First-person shooter (FPS) games, made popular through the game *Doom,* are defined by two major factors: camera perspective and action-oriented gameplay. These two elements dictate much of the gameplay design—with different FPS games varying mostly by story, setting, and specific features such as available weapons and types of enemy behaviors (artificial intelligence, or AI) used by the opponents. As a general rule, similar gameplay elements result in similar interfaces. Therefore, because most FPS games play similarly, their interface needs vary fairly little when compared to some other genres.

With their emphasis on action and player skill, FPSs provide players with little information yet require considerable skill to master. As a result, their interfaces are among the most simplistic of all games.

Allowing players to customize their manual control schemes is especially important for skill-based games, such as FPSs. Character movement in an FPS is typically mapped to the WASD keys as well as the cursor keys.

Electronic Arts Inc.   Electronic Arts Inc.

In *Battlefield 2,* red indicators (circled in image on right) appear when the player character has been hit, providing clear feedback to the player.

Since FPS players cannot see their characters and are typically targeted by ranged weapons, it can be difficult to determine from which direction one is being attacked. Therefore, it is important for an FPS to provide this information to the player clearly. A flash of red to indicate that the player has taken damage—as well as an arrow showing the direction from which the attack was made—is a common method of providing this feedback.

Genre-Specific Controllers

As far as controllers for FPS games go, nothing beats a keyboard and mouse. Capcom's *Steel Battalion* comes with a very complex controller specifically made for that game. Nothing captures the feel of controlling a giant robotic tank than sitting in front of that massive control console. Driving games such as *Gran Turismo* and *Burnout* beg to be played with a steering wheel and pedals. It's almost a shame to play those types of games with anything other than their genre-specific controllers. There are also other games that without the controllers wouldn't be much fun—including *Guitar Hero, Donkey Konga, Dance Dance Revolution,* and *Samba De Amigo.*

—Ian Wall
(Senior Artist, Obsidian Entertainment)

Since players cannot see their own characters, it is difficult to incorporate dynamic interfaces into most aspects of FPS games. The fast-paced action makes it hard to show useful information through opponents' models as well.

Richard Taylor
(Lead Programmer,
Obsidian
Entertainment)

Richard Taylor began his career in the game industry at Black Isle, a specialized development team at Interplay—but he has spent the majority of his time at Obsidian Entertainment. His responsibilities often revolve around programming the back end of the user interface under the direction of a technical designer. As an interface programmer and an avid player, Richard has been exposed to a wide variety of game interfaces and has been able to use that experience in suggesting design and ease-of-use issues on the game interfaces he programs. He has led the programming teams on both *Star Wars: Kinghts of the Old Republic 2: The Sith Lords* and *Neverwinter Nights 2,* where he once again played a strong role in the implementation of the game interface.

For the most part, first-person shooter (FPS) interfaces are one-directional. They feed input to the player while the player controls the game by directly moving the character and the camera to different positions and firing weapons almost exclusively by the press of mouse buttons. Over time, a few basic expectations in feedback have become standards. Players sitting down to play an FPS expect their health, armor (if there is armor in the game), current ammo, and reserve ammo to all be available at a glance on the screen.

Once those basic pieces of information are available, games deviate with regard to what else they expose at a glance to the user. Some will include a display of weapons that the user has picked up and many will position a mini-map of the environment immediately surrounding the user. How much additional information is provided varies depending on what the FPS gameplay experience is intended to feel like from the designers.

Games such as *Half-Life 2* or *Doom 3* do everything they can to keep the player immersed in the game world. The minimalist interface reflects this with the lack of any more feedback besides the basic elements mentioned previously. Neither game has a mini-map. *Half-Life 2* doesn't have one as its levels are fairly narrow and restrict the user to following a easily perceived path through them. In *Doom 3,* exploring the levels was a large portion of the gameplay, so a mini-map was left out of that game too in order to let players figure out their own place with respect to various locations in the current level.

Other games, especially multiplayer games, intend for the user to be able to know a lot more about the state of the game at a glance. In *Planetside,* the player has a mini-map at all times, as well as a full-screen global map available with a button press. The mini-map shows a rough layout of the base that the player is in, or the outdoor terrain that the player was passing over. Also visible are indicators on the mini-map of the relative position to friendly players. If players have certain enhancements to their characters, they will also sometimes see red indicators of hostile players in the vicinity. Since the focus of *Planetside* is working with not just your immediate squad of up to 10 players, but also with your entire team of hundreds of players, it is necessary for the interface to give the player enough information to be able to enjoy the more tactical aspects of the game. If the designers had stuck with a minimal interface, players would easily get lost or spend more time looking around for players to interact with than actually engaging in combat.

One weakness common to most multiplayer FPS games is the means by which the player can communicate with other players. While the players can almost always type text in to speak to their team, squad, or all players, that text is very often put into the same general screen space as other automated text feedback, such as kill messages or chat macros being used by other players. This typically results in players' typed input flying off the screen within a fraction of the second that they type it—making it futile to try to communicate this way. *Planetside* avoids this problem by providing a full-featured chatbox similar to those found in today's MMORPGs. This allows player chat messages to be contained to their own reserved screen space, and players could resize that chatbox depending on personal preference. As a player that still prefers typed text over voice-chat systems such as Teamspeak, this is an interface design that I hope makes its way into future FPSs.

One important thing to keep in mind when designing multiplayer FPS interfaces is that the player needs to be able to perform actions very quickly. FPS games tend to move at a much faster pace than other game styles so it is best to try to figure out how to reduce controls and interface interaction down to single button presses or mouse clicks. Forcing the player to click through multiple screens or menus while actively playing the game will just get them killed for doing so and understandably frustrates them.

The Action Screen

Throughout this text, we'll refer to the main screen, the one on which all of the game's action takes place, as the *action screen*. Note that this is not an industry term; strangely enough, no word exists to describe this portion of the game. But for purposes of interface design, it is useful to define this most important screen.

Third-Person Action

Third-person action games include both platformers (such as *Jak and Daxter*) and shooters (such as *Max Payne*). These games are similar to FPSs in many ways, with the obvious exception of the perspective used. Melee (or hand-to-hand, such as with a sword or knife) combat is a little more common—though third-person action often uses ranged weapons as well.

Health

In most third-person action games, the player will have a certain amount of *health,* which is essentially a gauge of the amount and severity of mistakes the player has made. Health is generally the governing parameter affecting gameplay and as such is shown in the action window interface at all times—whether as a bar, a number, or some iconic representation of health (such as a heart).

Eidos Interactive Ltd.

Third-person action games, such *as Tomb Raider: Legend,* often clearly display ammunition on the action screen interface.

Ammunition

As with FPSs, third-person action games sometimes use *ammunition* as another limitation for the player. Information on how much ammunition is available for the currently equipped weapon is clearly shown in the action window—at least when the player is getting low.

A general guideline is that the quantity of any limited resource available to the player should be easy to determine. For example, *Max Payne* shows both ammunition and "bullet time" (a limited resource that allows the player to slow down the game enough to dodge an opponent's bullets) available. Don't hide this information within the interface; make it readily visible at all times.

Sony Computer Entertainment America Inc.

God of War uses a fixed camera.

Camera Control

While some third-person games, such as *God of War,* employ a fixed camera, free cameras are also fairly common. These are typically controlled on a console system by using the right analog stick. Some games have tried other methods, such as *Kingdom Hearts*—which uses the left and right triggers to rotate the camera.

Camera control is an essential feature because nothing is more important than what the player is looking at. With 3D games, it is difficult to ensure that what is being shown to players is what they want to see. For games with free cameras, it is important to include a command that will snap the camera back to the default view in case players get themselves "lost" by moving the camera too close or at a strange angle.

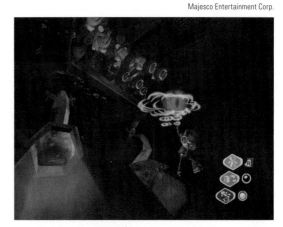
Majesco Entertainment Corp.

Platformers such as *Psychonauts* often use jumping as a gameplay element.

Jumping

Jumping is a gameplay element common to many third-person action games, such as all platformers. Jumping is somewhat controversial because the punishment for failing a jumping puzzle can be frustrating for many players. A failed jump can result in the player falling to his death, having to restart. Another problematic issue is when the player falls into the beginning of difficult region, thus having to complete the entire area again. These frustrations can be overcome through game design (by providing, for example, shortcuts to let players quickly bypass a section of the game they have already completed), though some would argue that they are an integral part of the gameplay.

My favorite interfaces are generally those that are unobtrusively integrated into the actual gameplay, while also being creative and fun to use. An example of this is the start menu for *Psychonauts*— which shows the main character, Raz, running around on a brain. To start the game, you have to run up to a door on the brain and jump in. Not only is this interface fun, it was seamlessly integrated into the quirky atmosphere of the game itself. While an interface doesn't have to be as complex as this, visual continuity, usability, and just plain fun always need to play active roles in a good game interface.

—Alan Dennis
(Game Art & Design Student)

Challenges and Frustrations

Remember that gameplay elements do not have to be frustrating to be challenging. When players fail, they should feel that it is because they made a mistake—not because the game didn't respond to them as they expected it to.

Note that these guidelines are relevant not just for jumping puzzles, but for any type of puzzle that requires precise timing by the player. If it looks to players like they should have succeeded, then let them succeed.

Sony Computer Entertainment
America Inc.

Gran Turismo 4 is a popular racing game for the PS2.

Racing

Racing games have straightforward interfaces due to the limited options required. During play, the player must be able to steer the vehicle, accelerate, and brake. Several camera views are typically provided. Passive interface elements include current speed, elapsed (or remaining) time, number of laps, and a mini-map showing nearby competitors.

These games will also have management screens on which players can modify their vehicles or choose the racetracks. These screens are designed similar to normal management screens. In arcades, racing games will employ steering wheel controls—which are also available for computers and some console systems for those who desire a more complete racing experience.

Vivendi Universal Games Inc.

Fighting games such as *Fight Club* involve "twitch" gameplay.

Fighting

Fighting games are characterized by their tactical, twitch (requiring quick reflexes) gameplay and fast pace of action. Typically, fighting games are one-on-one duels. The player controls one character, with the other being either controlled by another player or by the game's artificial intelligence (AI) system (non-player character or NPC). These games contain a large variety of characters, each with a distinct visual look and fighting style. The number of "combos," or possible moves, usually reaches into the dozens in modern fighting games. Some of these combos are easy to execute, while others require precision from the player.

Non-Player Characters

The term "non-player character" (NPC) refers to any entity with which the player can interact who is not also a player. The soldier who is your opponent, the merchant who buys your old equipment, and the bear wandering in the forest are all examples of NPCs. The term originates from the traditional pen-and-paper role-playing game *Dungeons & Dragons®*. By contrast, the player's character(s) is called a "player character" or PC (not to be confused with "personal computer").

Fighting games are at the extreme end of twitch action in combat. Since the player controls only a single character and fights only one opponent, the two combatants can be very large on the screen and the level of detail in their appearances and animations often exceeds that of other game types. As such, fighting games are better able than others to incorporate more of the interface into the game characters themselves. The characters can appear wounded when hit, and particle effects are large enough to indicate the success level of any attack.

Responsiveness

One of the key aspects to fighting game interface design is *responsiveness*. When players press a button or the analog stick, they want the game to act immediately. Even a delay of just a few frames can cause frustration.

Bottom-Load Animation

While a character winding up for a swing might be realistic, this can feel sluggish to the player. One way to overcome this problem is to "bottom-load" the animations. If the attack begins immediately and the extra animations occur at the end of the swing as part of the hit reaction, the player is still rewarded with exciting animations but will perceive that the character immediately responded to the player's order to attack.

Interrupted Moves

In some games, when players issue a new command, they must still wait for the character's current move to be executed before the new order is carried out. This practice might result in more realistic-looking animations, but it comes at the price of responsiveness. If the player reacts to the opponent's move—by trying to block an attack, for example—then it is frustrating to watch the character continue with a slow attack, leaving the player's character vulnerable to the coming blow.

The combat will feel better to players if their characters react very quickly to their commands—immediately switching to the block if that's what the player wants. While the instantaneous (or almost instantaneous) change in stance might look a little weird, very few will even notice given the intensity of the action. That's not to say that interruptible moves are always preferable—but minimizing the response time as much as the gameplay allows is generally a good idea.

Over-the-Top Ability

Many designers are tempted to make their games appear realistic. This direction can sometimes be a mistake, especially for combat in fighting games. Your first goal

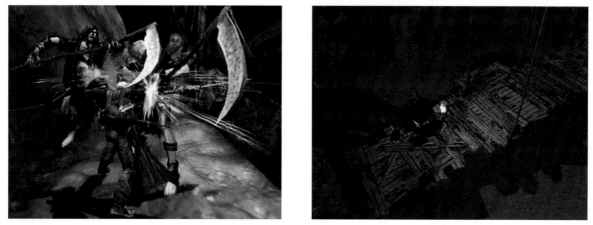

© Capcom Co., Ltd. Reprinted with Permission   ©Wizards of the Coast. Used with permission.

Notice how much more "exciting" the screenshot on the left (from *Devil May Cry 3*) appears. It's more cinematic than the screenshot on the right (from *Neverwinter Nights*) is—although it isn't as realistic.

is to entertain the player, not depict reality. Use your interface decisions to provide feedback to the player in ways that are exciting.

This aspect is one in which game developers can learn from the movie industry. People enjoy big explosions and dramatic effects. Use large and colorful particle effects for hits and blocks. Let characters jump higher in the air than normal humans can. Incorporate vibrant sound effects and colors whenever possible. If you push the limits of realism too far, you can always pull back a bit later.

These interface guidelines for fighting games can apply to many games that involve intense, twitchy action. Many other action games also fall into this category. These types of games are well-suited to the use of dynamic interfaces because the camera is focused on the player's character at all times.

Genres and Interface Complexity

Genres tend to have more of an effect on the in-game interface. First-person shooters (FPSs) work better with almost no interface since all the players really need to know is their health and such. In contrast, strategy games have a much more complicated interface, since there are a lot more components players need to access while playing.

—*Briar Lee Mitchell*
(Co-Founder, Star Mountain Studios)

Strategy Games

There are two main types of *strategy* games—distinguished by how time passes within the game. Real-time strategy (RTS) games are "action" games in which the player commands numerous characters (units) simultaneously. Additionally, in RTS games, all players are acting simultaneously. In turn-based strategy games (TBSs), on the other hand, only one player moves at a time—maintaining some of the gameplay feel of traditional board games, the roots of the strategy genre. All strategy games focus on *resource management* of characters and items (such as weapons, food, and materials).

Real-Time Strategy (RTS)

Real-time strategy (RTS) is one of the most standardized genres in terms of interface design. The reasons for this standardization stem largely from the complexity of the genre. RTSs are interesting from an interface design perspective due to how much their interfaces have evolved over the last decade. They also have heavy interface needs yet aim for an action-based play experience.

RTSs are almost exclusively developed for the computer platform. The RTS genre developed throughout the 1990s, when console games were less popular than they are today. The interfaces for these games became increasingly complex, adding new layers of features and controls for the player. These needs are well met through keyboard shortcuts, making them less suitable for consoles—which have "limited" manual interfaces that do not provide the options that RTS players have grown to expect.

Additionally, more complicated games tend to be less successful on console systems, which target a more casual audience. Finally, RTS games have often been on the demanding side in terms of system requirements due to the AI needs of maneuvering up to 100 or more units simultaneously—making the computer a more suitable platform. Since all computers employ the standard keyboard and mouse control scheme, the RTS genre could thus be standardized.

John Comes on Genre Interface Challenges

John was born in Reading, Pennsylvania, and grew up near Cleveland, Ohio. He received a Bachelor of Science in Mechanical Engineering from the University of Akron. After college, John and his older brother wrote a MUD (multi-user dungeon) from scratch: *Wolfshade MUD.* That is what got him into Westwood Studios where he quickly became a Senior Content Designer on *Earth & Beyond.* Prior to working at Gas Powered Games, John worked at Electronic Arts Los Angeles where he shipped *Command & Conquer Generals: Zero Hour* and *The Lord of the Rings: The Battle for Middle-Earth.*

John Comes (Lead Content Engineer, Gas Powered Games)

Each genre has different requirements for input. With a first-person shooter (FPS), you only need design around the motion of one character. With real-time strategy games (RTS) or most role-playing games (RPG), you're controlling a group of characters and it's easier to resort to an interface that supports selection and point or click to move. All genres have their own challenges but strategy games often have a high number of units and abilities. To design a fluid interface that makes it easy to view and issue orders on each unit and ability is a daunting challenge.

Dune 2, developed by Westwood Studios in 1992, is often acknowledged as the first true RTS.

RTS games, such as *Command & Conquer: Tiberion Sun,* often reserve a portion of the screen real-estate for the game interface.

The greyed-out buttons in the lower right show new options that will become available as the player advances through *Warcraft III*'s technology tree.

RTS Basics

RTS games contain some of the most complicated interfaces. An RTS is an action war game that allows a player to control dozens of units and buildings simultaneously, playing against between one and seven opponents (either other players or computer-controlled enemies) in games that last from 15 minutes to an hour or more.

The typical RTS includes several distinct phases of the game. First, players work to establish their initial infrastructure. In this phase, players will concentrate on collecting resources, scouting terrain, and building new structures. Through "rush" strategies, players can gamble to try to win the game during this early stage. The second phase involves advancing through the game's "technology tree," which is a path of advancement through new units and abilities. As one player gains a new technology, that player can try to exploit it against the other players—hoping to catch them unprepared to deal with the new threat.

The final stage of the game results when players have essentially gained access to all of the units and powers available to them. At this point, the game often becomes a battle of attrition as the players focus on resources and territory control to maintain more powerful armies than their opponents. At all phases of the game, an RTS requires the player to multi-task— managing resources, exploration, and combat at all times. The necessity to keep track of so many game elements in real-time places a great burden on the game interface to provide the player with an enjoyable experience.

RTSs are particularly interesting from the perspective of interface design. The complexity of these games makes the interface an increasingly important aspect of gameplay; some RTS players will claim that mastering the interface is a key difference between a skilled and novice RTS player. Due to this emphasis, many of the improvements in RTS games throughout the genre's development have involved advances in interface design.

Unlike most other genres, RTS games typically have a fixed interface on screen at all times. That is, while a large portion of the screen is dedicated to the detailed action, a section is reserved for interface elements. Efforts to minimize RTS game interface real-estate have typically been unsuccessful.

> I admire *Starcraft*'s simple but intricate interface. It's very clean—and most of the important components have hotkeys assigned to them. This makes the game flow much better and allows players to master the game without really worrying too much about the interface they are using.
>
> —*Welter Almeida*
> *(Game Art & Design Student)*

:::::: Skill-Based Games

The term "skill-based" is sometimes applied to games that require a certain degree of experience or hand-eye coordination to play well. These games are often not very forgiving of player mistakes—at least in certain situations. Typically, only action-oriented games such as fighting, FPS, and RTS games are described as skill-based.

World of Warcraft®, StarCraft®, Diablo®, and Warcraft® images provided courtesy of Blizzard Entertainment, Inc.

Activision Publishing, Inc.

StarCraft and *Quake 4* are both skill-based games.

Mastering a skill-based game requires a considerable amount of effort and even talent. Timing is a key element of any skill-based game; players must act precisely and quickly to maximize their success. Multiplayer games are often skill-based because the competition encourages players to invest the energy required to master them.

Mini-Maps

Though *mini-maps* have become common in many genres of games, they are most critical for RTS games. Unlike players of other game genres, the RTS player must be able to keep track of multiple locations simultaneously. The screen real-estate is too small to depict the entire battlefield at once, so only a close-up is shown. The mini-map, which displays the entire battlefield in an RTS, allows the player to see the big picture at all times. This feature allows the player to concentrate on a specific portion of the battle while still being aware of major occurrences elsewhere. In most RTSs, the mini-map can never be hidden because it's extremely important to gameplay.

Some RTS games "ping" the mini-map when an event occurs somewhere in the game world. A ping is a graphical (usually also accompanied by audio) cue that shows where in the game world an event took place. A keyboard shortcut will then immediately center the screen on the location of that event, allowing the player to quickly react to it.

World of Warcraft®, Starcraft®, Diablo®, and Warcraft® images provided courtesy of Blizzard Entertainment, Inc.

Like most RTS games, *Warcraft III: The Frozen Throne* provides a mini-map to help the player control the entire battlefield.

Unit Selection

Without exception, *unit selection* in a computer-based RTS occurs through the drag-select mouse functionality used in Windows. Players left-click on the screen, drag a box around the units and structures they wish to select, then release the mouse button to select them. To select a single unit, players instead left-click on that specific unit.

Double-Click Selection

As powerful as drag-selection is, its deficiencies became apparent as RTS games increased in complexity. Suppose players have two types of units in their armies—archers and pikemen. The archers are excellent at killing unarmored opponents, such as axemen—but they cannot harm the enemy's heavily armored knights. Meanwhile, the pikemen are great at felling the mounted knights—but they have difficulty against their axemen. When facing an enemy army with

Stainless Steel

Empires: Dawn of the Modern World includes a wide variety of units with unique advantages and disadvantages. Methods of quickly selecting classes of units are critical.

both knights and axemen, the optimum strategy is to target the knights with the pikemen and the axemen with the archers.

In reality, issuing these orders to the troops would be fairly simple. However, the cumbersome interface makes it difficult to quickly select all of the slingers and pikemen separately. A simple innovation, double-click selection, solves this problem. By double-clicking on a specific unit, all units of the same type on the screen are immediately selected.

Control Groups

Another interface challenge in RTS games comes from the fact that the player is simultaneously commanding troops spread far across the game map. Even with the mini-map, it is difficult for the player to quickly switch between locations on the battlefield. RTSs are also the origin of an interface concept known as *control groups*. While any group of units is selected, the player can press Ctrl-#, where # is any of the number keys. Thereafter, pressing that number key will select that same group of units.

In this way, the player can switch between armies across the map with a single key press. Pressing the number twice not only selects that control group, but also centers the screen on them. By not always centering the screen on the control group, the player can quickly order several armies to a specific location on the map.

Command Queues and Waypoints

RTSs are also the origin of the concepts of *command queues and waypoints.* Another tool designed to aid the player in multi-tasking, a command queue allows the player to issue multiple sequential orders to a unit or building. For example, a barracks can be instructed to continuously produce certain types of troops, or a platoon can be ordered to follow a patrol route.

Vivendi Universal Games Inc.

Players can use waypoints to order their troops to follow a specific path to a destination instead of the path chosen by the game's AI. Not only does the player have more control, but the routes become easier for the game to calculate—improving game performance. Waypoints are also used in RTSs to instruct newly built units to proceed to a specific destination or to order units to attack first one specific building and then another.

Waypoint paths, as shown in *Empire Earth II,* allow the player to dictate how units navigate through the map.

Enlight Software Ltd.

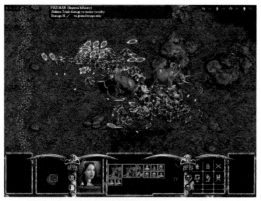

Warlords Battlecry 3 expanded the command queue interface option by also allowing interruptions.

Should the situation in the game change, the player may cancel any command queue and specify new, more appropriate orders. Some games, such as *Warlords Battlecry 3*, allow the player to interrupt command queues with new commands, with the units returning to their previous orders when the interruption is completed.

Command queues give the players great control over their units without requiring them to micromanage them. This feature makes the player feel like a "general" issuing orders.

Age of Empires III: The Complexity of an RTS

Microsoft

The more complicated the game is, the more difficult the interface is to design. A game like *Age of Empires III* probably has one of the most difficult interfaces to design. Trying to accurately control hundreds and thousands of units, build cities, change formations, manage your battles, and research technology is extremely difficult, which makes its interface not only extremely complicated to use but also to design and implement. Even by having "advanced" portions of the interface for advanced players, the interface is still extremely complicated. Having access to a keyboard and mouse makes having this kind of complicated interface possible, though it wouldn't be feasible on a console.

—*Troy Dunniway (Lead Game Designer, Midway Los Angeles)*

Battle for RTS Interface Standards

For many years, RTS games were dominated by three major franchises: Westwood Studio's *Command & Conquer (C&C)*, Blizzard Entertainment's *Warcraft* and *Starcraft*, and Ensemble's *Age of Empires* series. These RTSs became extremely popular in the mid-1990s—and many "clones" were created. Due to the complexity of the genre, most of these clones would adopt the conventions of the successful RTS games to make them more accessible to consumers. Two major areas in which these games differed were in mouse button controls and the location of interface elements.

C&C placed the interface on the right side of the screen, while *Starcraft, Age of Empires,* and most other RTSs used the bottom of the screen for the interface. The advantage of the latter convention is that the rectangular action window feels more comfortable to players than the approximately square action window that results from *C&C*. The interface choice in *C&C* has one major advantage, however: it allows the mini-map to be in the top-right corner of the screen, where it is most accessible.

The second major disagreement between *C&C* and its competitors was regarding how the mouse was used to select and order units. *C&C* employs a left-click control scheme—when one or more units are selected, left-clicking on a location orders the selected units to move to (or attack) that destination. Right-clicking, meanwhile, deselects the units. Blizzard and Microsoft games instead employ a right-click control scheme. Left-clicking is always used for selection and right-clicking to perform actions. This latter scheme appears superior because it is internally consistent.

Electronic Arts Inc .

World of Warcraft®, StarCraft®, Diablo®, and Warcraft® images provided courtesy of Blizzard Entertainment, Inc

Microsoft

The three major RTS franchises during the development of the genre were Westwood's *Command & Conquer* (top), Blizzard's *Starcraft* (middle), and Ensemble's *Age of Empires 2* (bottom).

::::: *Goblin Commander:* An RTS Designed as a Console Game

Jaleco Entertainment, Inc.

Some popular RTSs, such as installments in the *Command & Conquer* series and *StarCraft,* have been ported to consoles but have not met with great commercial success. One example of an RTS designed specifically for consoles is *Goblin Commander* (*Unleash the Horde* shown), which was developed by Jaleco Entertainment in 2003. Since drag-select is not an option for a console game, *Goblin Commander* had to find another solution. By holding down the square button, a selection box appears and gradually grows in size. Releasing the button selects all of the units that were contained in the selection box.

Exceptions

Note that while many RTSs follow the guidelines just described, some games classified as RTS appear quite different. For example, Relic's *Homeworld* looks and feels unlike any of the examples we've discussed. Even still, *Homeworld* makes use of many of the same RTS tools—such as waypoints, selection methods, and control groups.

Homeworld is a good example of the dangers involved in defining games by their genre. While sharing many elements with more traditional RTSs, *Homeworld* provides quite a different experience and appeals to a different type of gamer.

© THQ Inc.

Homeworld looks and feels unlike typical RTSs, but it employs many of the same interface elements.

You'll notice that many games are *cross-genre* or genre *hybrids* (include multiple genres), or they do not fit well in any genre. Consider a game such as *The Sims.* What genre does it fit into? It could be considered a role-playing game (RPG) because you are, in fact, playing the role of a specific person (or persons) in a fictional world. You advance your character and acquire possessions, much as you would in an RPG. It could also be a simulation game because it simulates social behavior in "real life." However, *The Sims* is "officially" a strategy game because of its resource management elements. Certainly, there are many differences between *The Sims* and either real-time or turn-based strategy games. Which interface elements does a game like *The Sims* need?

John Ahlquist on RTS Interface Design

While Lead Programmer at Electronic Arts, John Ahlquist developed the SAGE and SAGE 2 real-time strategy engine and tools for *Command & Conquer: Generals,* the *Zero Hour* expansion, and *Lord of the Rings: Battle for Middle Earth.* John previously worked for Altsys/Macromedia on Aldus FreeHand, and was one of the creators of Macromedia Fireworks. Prior to Macromedia, John spent seven years working for Texas Instruments developing Integrated Circuit CAD tools in the Design Automation Department. He is a second-degree black belt in Tae Kwon Do, and has been playing video games since *Pong.*

John Ahlquist
(Proprietor,
Ahlquist Software)

The real-time strategy (RTS) genre, including games such as *Command & Conquer: Generals,* is one of the more challenging categories for creating the interface. First, the interface must deliver a great deal of information to the player. At a glance, the player must be able to tell what several unit factories are producing, the degree of completion, the completion status of a base defense structure, and the recharge status of a superweapon. The interface must allow the player to select and specify a large number of actions—move, attack, deploy, garrison, mine, attach explosive. At the same time, the most common desired action is to either move or attack, so the player must be able to easily issue those commands without having to choose from all the possible actions. Finally, many commands are issued by the same gesture, a mouse click. The interface must make clear to the player the results of his action. Clicking on an enemy unit will result in an attack command, whereas clicking on the ground next to the enemy unit will result in a move command. It is very helpful if the interface provides feedback to the players before they click so that they can position the cursor to get the intended result (such as attack or move).

Turn-Based Strategy

Turn-based strategy (TBS) games are similar to RTSs in many ways. They tend to be very complicated and are most common on the PC platform. They require players to keep track of a large variety of parameters simultaneously. Since players essentially have unlimited time to consider their moves, however, interfaces for TBS games have more flexibility than those of RTS games. For example, in an RTS, the player must always be able to see the mini-map and the action screen—but in a TBS, the player can switch between full-screen interfaces, with each designed for a specific purpose. These purposes can include summaries of economics, military operations, trade, research, and espionage. Most TBS games will contain 5, 10, or even more unique full-screen interfaces—each customized to meet specific needs.

Due to this flexibility—even though they are typically even more complicated than RTS games—TBS game interfaces are less standardized. Furthermore, a sub-optimal TBS interface—while undesirable—is less detrimental to the gameplay than a poor interface for an action-oriented game would be. The precise interface needs for a TBS depend entirely on the specific game and on what strategic elements it contains. Applying general interface design principles is thus especially useful for developing a TBS interface.

Stardock Corporation

Each of the buttons at the bottom of the *Galactic Civilizations II: Dread Lords* screen opens a full-screen interface that focuses on one of the core gameplay elements.

Role-Playing Game (RPG)

Role-playing games (RPGs) allow the player to assume the role of one of more characters in the game. The definition of an RPG has changed over the years. Games

World of Warcraft®, StarCraft®, Diablo®, and Warcraft® images provided courtesy of Blizzard Entertainment, Inc.

World of Warcraft®, StarCraft®, Diablo®, and Warcraft® images provided courtesy of Blizzard Entertainment, Inc.

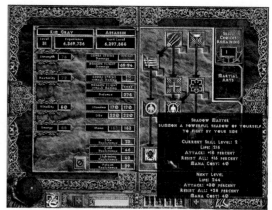

Role-playing games, such as the action RPG *Diablo II,* often have complex character advancement systems.

are considered RPGs if they contain features such as:

- characters that advance in power throughout the course of the game;
- an emphasis on story and dialogue; and
- an abundance of items for the player to find.

Any game with a type of "leveling" system, which refers to the player's character(s) advancing in power throughout the game, is said to have "RPG elements."

RPGs attempt to minimize the impact of the interface by allowing the advanced modes to share screen space with the action window.

Role-playing games often have separate interfaces for several elements, including character advancement, inventory, and maps. Let's take a look at many of the conventions used in RPG interface design.

Neverwinter Nights allows the player to access character inventory without concealing the action window.

What's an "RPG Element"?

In a literal sense, the core aspect of a role-playing game is that players are pretending to be someone else; they are playing a role. The term *RPG* would suggest, therefore, that character development and story are most important. However, you'll often come across games said to have "RPG elements." This term generally means that the character has statistics and can gain levels and abilities throughout the game. This type of gameplay first appeared in RPGs and has since been affiliated with that genre even though it's arguably not critical to role-playing.

Dialogue

Role-playing games often include a *dialogue* system through which the player communicates with non-player characters (NPCs) in the game world. In some games, such as *Fable*, the player acts as an observer of conversations that take place. In others, such as *Neverwinter Nights 2*, the player is an active participant and will select particular dialogue choices.

Genre Differences in Interface Design

Designing an interface for different genres can vary considerably. It all depends on how much information a player wants or how much information has to be communicated to the player to play the game. Also, whether it's a console game or not will affect the interface for each genre. As an example, an FPS needs a lot of immediate feedback—for ammo, loading, running, jumping, camera control—all available at a quick glance that never slows down the action. But in an RTS, you generally need to oversee the battle and a number of "fire and forget" interface mechanics in place in order to track and manage your resources effectively (set up building queues, assigning waypoints, grouping of troops—along with timer bars and resource outputs). The more information a player needs to play the game effectively, the more challenging the interface design becomes. Strategy games and role-playing games definitely fit into this category.

—*Chris Avellone*
(Chief Creative Officer & Lead Designer, Obsidian Entertainment)

In these dialogue-interactive RPGs, conversations with NPCs are an additional element of the gameplay—with the player's choices affecting various aspects of the game world. For example, if players offend a tavern owner, they might find they have to pay more for drinks. If another patron dislikes the owner, however, the patron might appreciate this action and reveal information that the players would not have otherwise received.

Bethesda Softworks

The Elder Scrolls IV: Oblivion utilizes dialogue as a gameplay element.

An RPG can have close to half of the gameplay occurring within conversations. Dialogue choices are used to both tell the game's story and to let players define what their character is like and what roles they will play. In *Star Wars: Knights of the Old Republic 2*, for example, players can decide through dialogue whether they follow the dark or light side of the Force; their decisions determine what quests become available to them as well as the reactions of their companions.

For the PC platform, RPGs, like FPSs, historically use the WASD keys for movement. In fact, this convention began with very early RPGs, such as *Wizardry*. It is common in recent computer RPGs to allow movement by left-clicking on the destination.

Tim Donley on Genre-Specific Information

Tim Donley
(Producer,
Bottlerocket
Entertainment)

Prior to entering the game industry 10 years ago, Tim Donley spent approximately 5 years designing toys. His educational background is in Industrial Design (he received a Bachelor of Science from California State University, Long Beach). In addition to Bottlerocket Entertainment, Tim has worked at Obsidian Entertainment, Black Isle/Interplay, Mattel Toys, and Sony Computer Entertainment. He also started a company (TriLunar) with a "super talented team of guys." Tim feels fortunate to look forward to his job everyday because he's doing what he truly loves.

Genres affect the information displayed on screen at any time. Real-time strategy (RTS) games tend to be concerned about unit production and management, so these are the things that take up space in their interfaces. In a first-person shooter (FPS), you are probably concerned about your bullet counts and your health—whereas in a role-playing game (RPG), you are looking at party member statistics, dialogue boxes, and combat information.

Genres are all challenging in their own ways. Personally, I think RPGs are the most challenging due to the amount of information being given to the player.

Having multiple party members, armor, statistic points, inventory, and quest information at the players' disposal throughout the game makes for some hard design decisions.

I also think more successful designs have been in the RPG category due to the inherent complexity of the genre. I'd like to point out two specific interface situations: In both cases, I was picking up a game I was not familiar with—the *Pokemon* ruby/sapphire games, and *Mario Golf* for the Game Boy Color. Within a few minutes into each game, I understood how the basic mechanics worked—and both games added layers of complexity so seamlessly as to be invisible. Each of these games had many complex interactions and statistics tracking, yet each one made it simple to understand what was going on. I never sensed that any information was out of place, unavailable, or obtrusive. For me, that's what all games are shooting for in interface design. These two stand out as great examples of games that were able to introduce the novice and still let the advanced players have all the control they needed.

Target Selection and Mouseover

For a computer RPG, *target selection* typically occurs through left-clicking. For a console game, some method of auto-acquiring a new target and cycling through available targets is common. An RPG can have many objects or creatures of interest on the screen at a single time. All of the relevant information would be overwhelming to the player if it were constantly visible. By showing this information only for a selected target, the player sees the details for one object or creature at a time.

Other methods of revealing extra information include *Fate*'s use of the ALT key to reveal any objects of interest on the screen.

Mouseover in a computer RPG also often provides this additional information. In many computer RPGs, mouseover also provides a context-sensitive cursor. For example, in *Neverwinter Nights,* the cursor becomes a door icon when over a portal that will move the player's character to another map.

Intracorp Entertainment

Intracorp Entertainment

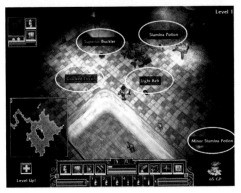

In *Fate,* the player can press ALT to reveal all interactive items. This setting can also be toggled.

Joe Maruschak on the Influence of Genres

Joe Maruschak
(Creative Director,
GarageGames)

Joe Maruschak began his career in gaming in 1996 as an artist working at Dynamix, creators of the Tribes franchise. At Dynamix, Joe contributed to the production of over 10 products in multiple genres, including first-person shooters, sports games, and casual games designed for the mass market. With the closure of Dynamix in 2001, Joe and a few other industry veterans formed the independent development studio BraveTree Productions in order to create and distribute online multiplayer games targeted at non-hardcore audiences. At BraveTree Joe served as lead designer and art director on BraveTree's first game, *ThinkTanks* and *ThinkTanks XBox* for the XBox Live Arcade. In 2005, BraveTree was acquired by GarageGames, where Joe is presently employed as Creative Director.

Genres definitely influence the ways certain game interfaces are designed. Real-time strategy (RTS), role-playing (RPG), and first-person shooter (FPS) games have clearly defined standards that developers cannot deviate much from without alienating the audience who buys such games.

My favorite game interfaces involve racing games. Giving feedback to the user about the behavior of the vehicle you are driving is key to getting the player to feel immersed. The feedback is very subtle—often small changes in the car's left or right lean, or the camera position in relation to the car that give the end user a sense of the car's interaction with the surface it is driving on (or flying through the air over). Since most people have ridden in cars and have a sense of what it looks like and feels like to drive a car, the small visual cues give them a ton of information about what is going on. If it is not just right, the illusion is broken and the player cannot suspend disbelief. If it is done well, it captures the essence of driving and is immediately and intuitively understood. It is my favorite because it is a really hard problem to solve. It is not just a purely visual effect—but it involves the confluence of the game physics, the track design, and the tweaking of the camera to present an illusion of a vehicle traveling over a surface.

However, most of my favorite interfaces are not [conventional] interfaces at all. They are types of gameplay where the player's interaction with the gamespace is so intuitive and natural that there is no need for an abstracted control and feedback interface. I would much prefer that if something is damaged, that it appear damaged and emit smoke. Most will intuitively understand the feedback given by something "looking" broken. I really don't like health and energy bars. In certain genres, they have become so commonplace that they have defined a standard that in some ways can become limiting, as I think it can inhibit the exploration of newer, more intuitive interfaces. With the strides being made in physics and graphics, we can show a lot more in ways that are less heavy handed and more natural.

Presently, I am more interested in ways to facilitate social interaction in game environments for players who are not hardcore gamers—so I try to stay away from established genres. I find it easier because I can just respond to what the games need. I feel boxed in by defined standards when something about the standard feels counterintuitive to me. Some of the standards are great, and some I am not so thrilled about.

Auto-Map

Similar to the mini-map in an RTS, the *auto-map* in an RPG helps the player navigate the game world. Its primary purpose is to indicate to players where they can go, where they have gone, and what is nearby. Unlike the RTS mini-map, the auto-map doesn't necessarily show the entire game world, though it does reveal more than the action window does.

"Old-school" RPGs such as *Wizardry, The Bard's Tale,* and *Might & Magic* had mapping as a primary aspect of gameplay. To solve the game, or at least to find all of the hidden places and items, players had to map out the game using graph paper—which was even included with some games. Obstacles such as tiles that would spin or teleport the player were included to make this process even more challenging. Now mapping is a task delegated to the game itself—freeing the player from this detailed work; hence the term "auto-map."

Some games, such as Gas Powered Games' *Dungeon Siege,* even allow the player to practically play the game using just the auto-map view. An RPG auto-map ideally includes information about all obstacles as well as anything with which the player might want to interact, such as enemies, NPC merchants, and items. How much detail is shown depends upon the particular game, however. For a game with many items often littering the floor, such as *Fate,* showing items on the auto-map is not practical, for example.

Mapping was necessary to find everything *Might & Magic II: Gates to Another World* had to offer.

Though intended to be played as from a third-person perspective, the auto-map for *Dungeon Siege* includes enough features to allow much of the game to be played from that view.

chapter 5 Genres: game styles and visual interfaces

Eidos Interactive Ltd.

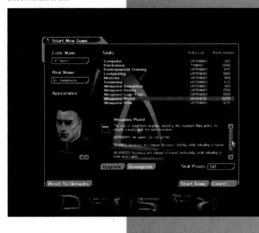

The complexity of the game will make a direct impact on the interface's layout and design. The more options and information to wade through, the harder it becomes to organize that information into a format where everything can be easily and intuitively found. In this sense, role-playing games are particularly hard to design interfaces for due to the sheer number of options available to the player. However, this doesn't necessarily need to be the case. *Deus Ex 2: Invisible War* attacked this problem by simplifying the way in which players customized their characters. While the original allowed the player to allocate talent points across a myriad of traits, the sequel simplified matters by constraining character development to the use of "biomods"—which would give the character a new tangible, useful skill. It was also a lot more intuitive than being given 50 points to distribute among traits such as swimming, side arm accuracy, and stealth.

—*Timothy Nixon (Founder & Creative Director, Straylight Studios)*

RPG Interface Challenges

Role-playing games typically make for difficult interface problems. First, those games carry with them massive expectations, based on the legacy of RPGs and the desires of the fans. Also, in order to represent a complex, evolving character in a richly detailed world, with a wide variety of inputs into that world, the game designer must juggle a lot of balls (and keep the text on the balls legible as they are flying through the air).

—*Harvey Smith*
(Studio Creative Director,
Midway Studios-Austin)

Quest Log or Journal

Another common interface element for RPGs is some method of tracking the player's progress through the game. RPGs can include more than 50 hours of gameplay and dozens of quests.

Journals, which are common in RPGs such as *Dungeon Siege,* keep track of a player's accomplishments and pending quests.

Without a means to keep track of everything they have done and need to do, it is easy for players to get lost—especially if they take a break from playing the game for several days or weeks.

The use of journals is an interesting aspect of game interface design because their purpose is similar to that of several work applications—namely organizing information. If a game has more than 10 or so entries, then it should be divided into subsections—such as area, time, or importance. Allowing players to sort their journals by these various categories is also helpful. Journal entries should include enough information to remind the players what it is they need to do and why. Whenever players make significant progress on a quest, the journal should be updated so that they know that they are going in the right direction.

In more recent games, it is common to indicate the direction of the next portion of the quest on a compass or mini-map. Then, even if players don't understand the details of what they have to do, they are still able to proceed. Though some developers might argue that this hand-holds the player, it is generally best to err on the side of helping the player too much rather than not enough.

Needs vs. Wants

The biggest hurdle in interface design is making sure you've got a comprehensive list of all the information the character *needs* to have—and then, if possible, all the information the player *wants* to have. For RPGs, we've found that catering to the hardcore players (the players who like to dig into the systems and gameplay mechanics) often means giving them a means to view the combat information in as much detail as possible so they can change their weapon combos and spells to maximize the damage they're doing—a symptom not unlike what you'll often see in *World of Warcraft* as people track their combat prowess through the combat box to see what they're doing wrong or right.

—*Chris Avellone*
(Chief Creative Officer & Lead Designer, Obsidian Entertainment)

Difficult Genres

Strategy and role-playing games (RPG) are probably the most complex genres for interface design because there is a ton of data to organize and display for a player. Often in strategy games, data is displayed in different ways depending on what the player is doing or manipulating at the time. This requires a lot of forethought in the ink and paper phase of the design. Sometimes you can make assumptions that make sense in a flowchart or on paper but then when you use it feel cumbersome or confusing. These types of interfaces often require a lot of back and forth and quite a bit of play testing before you're able to really hone in on what needs to be done to achieve a proper balance.

—*Ian Wall*
(Senior Artist, Obsidian Entertainment)

Stieg Hedlund
(Lead Designer,
Perpetual
Entertainment)

With a lifelong interest in games and visual storytelling, Stieg Hedlund became a professional designer of pen-and-paper role-playing games in his teens before beginning a career in electronic entertainment in 1987. Since then he has designed games of nearly every genre for a wide variety of computers, consoles, and arcade machines. He has successfully adapted to many diverse game development and production styles in environments ranging from small and entrepreneurial studios to some of the biggest publishers in the business, including working extensively in Japan. The list of companies he has worked for include Blizzard, Konami, SEGA, and Electronic Arts. In addition to being the lead designer of *Diablo II,* one of the best-selling PC RPGs of all time, and recipient of many of the industry's most prestigious awards, he also worked on some of Blizzard's other huge hits including *Diablo, StarCraft,* and the *Diablo II: Lord of Destruction* expansion pack. His credits with other companies include the acclaimed arcade beat-'em-up, *Die Hard Arcade,* best-selling Xbox title *Tom Clancy's Ghost Recon 2,* and *Tom Clancy's Rainbow Six Lockdown*— among many others. All told, he has shipped well over 30 titles.

My favorite game genre is role-playing. Unfortunately, role-playing games (RPGs) are very difficult to design due to the sheer amount of information that the player will want access to—which is usually overwhelming. I actually find that sports games are quite similar in how many stats players want and need access to. The challenge in both cases is to present all the complex data in a way that is simple to access and easy to understand.

Manual interfaces in arcade racing games such as those designed by SEGA really capture the feeling of driving remarkably well. Given that driving is something that many people have direct experience with, it would be easy to detect things that aren't right—but SEGA pulls it off beautifully. What you get out of these games is immersion. In fact, the experience is convincingly one of driving a stock car in a race.

Simulation Games

Simulation games all involve presenting a real-world system as a game. This diverse category ranges from economic simulations to sports games. Since these games focus on mimicking something from reality, they have some special interface needs.

Vehicle Simulations

Vehicle simulations typically strive for a control scheme realistic for the specific vehicle being simulated. For example, *Microsoft Flight Simulator*'s cockpit view provides controls designed to match those of the plane the player is flying.

Obviously, many shortcuts are included to make the simulation more user-friendly. However, unlike most games, part of the appeal in playing a simulation is mastering the realistic interface.

Steel Battalion is one of the most extreme examples of an exotic manual interface. This intense game is the epitome of a simulation in which the player mans a "vertical tank," a huge robot piloted by a human. The game's $200 price tag includes its custom control panel, which features two large joysticks, three foot pedals, over 30 buttons, and several other controls—even an ejection button protected by a cover so that it cannot be hit accidentally.

Simulation games, such as *Microsoft Flight Simulator 2004: A Century of Flight*—attempt to mirror reality and thus can have very involved interfaces.

Steel Battalion took simulation to the extreme, shipping with a $150 custom control panel for an interface.

> The joystick used in conjunction with flight-style video games is one of my favorite manual interfaces. It provides the smoothest control over an analog controller or mouse. Controlling the movement and direction of the aircraft in the game is easier and smoother from the wrist movement possible while using the joystick.
>
> —*Dan Cash*
> *(Game Development student)*

> My favorite manual interface would be the giant 40-button controller from *Steel Battalion*. Just the immersion gained through the controller alone is enough to make you feel like you are in one of the Mechs, battling it out!
>
> —*Brent LaDue*
> *(Game Art & Design Student)*

chapter 5 Genres: game styles and visual interfaces

Recognizing that only the most hardcore players would shell out so much money for a game, *Steel Battalion* is also difficult to play and master. Though it's excellent proof that an over-the-top interface and design is possible, its lack of success in the marketplace also underlines why custom manual interfaces are uncommon.

Flying Right!

I'm a big flight sim fan so a well-designed joystick is a must! It has to feel good in your hand, have a good range of movement, and have enough buttons in the right places to make easy use of the game's important features. A separate throttle controller is an excellent addition or having one available on the actual joystick is also a nice touch. Whether you're a licensed pilot or not, 'flying' with appropriate controls adds an entirely new dimension to the game experience—one that couldn't even come close to being duplicated with a standard keyboard/mouse configuration or a small handheld controller.

—Aaron Marks
(President, On Your Mark Music Productions)

PopTop Software Inc.

In *Railroad Tycoon 3,* players manage a financial empire centered around railroads and trade.

Process Simulations

Process simulations typically model economic systems, allowing the player to manage a process—such as a business or a city. These games are often similar in some respects to either real-time or turn-based strategy games, and arguments could be made to consider them strategy games instead of simulations. Unlike strategy games, which focus on the management of resources (real or fantasy-based), process sims always emphasize real-world procedures.

Like interfaces for turn-based strategy games, process simulation interfaces vary greatly from game to game. These games will typically include information such as time and current money in the active window and will have numerous other full-screen interfaces. Process simulations are most commonly PC games.

Sports & Participatory Simulations

Sports games are some of the best sellers because they appeal to casual players and have a built-in audience. Sports fans already know the rules, so they can jump right into playing the game. Moreso than many other types of games, the burden is on the interface to translate the controller into the game that the player already understands.

For any team-based sports game, such as football, the player generally controls one team member at a time but has a method of quickly switching to another teammate. Fortunately, most sports have a "key" player at any given time—the pitcher or batter in baseball, the quarterback or kicker in football, or whichever player has the ball in basketball or soccer.

One primary advantage of sports games is that they tend to change only slightly between versions. The rules generally change very little—so new editions will typically include the latest player stats, some new graphical capabilities, and other new features based upon what the development team learned from previous versions.

Interface needs for participatory sims—such as the sports (soccer) game *FIFA 06* and the music sim *Guitar Hero*—can vary greatly.

Adventure

The *adventure* game genre is loosely defined. Players navigate through adventure games by solving an assortment of puzzles. Combat is often a component of adventure games and they tend to be at least somewhat story-driven. Adventure games can differ significantly in how they play, but some interface guidelines apply to many games of this type.

As puzzle-oriented games, it is important for adventure games to provide the player with information about what to do. One of the biggest problems in developing adventure games involves creating puzzles that are challenging to all players without being too hard for some. In action games, difficulty settings can be used so that the player has more health,

The critically acclaimed *Indigo Prophecy* is one of the few recent additions to the adventure genre.

finds more items, or faces fewer enemies. With the exception of timing and jumping challenges, puzzles generally require players to figure something out. Given the items they have found or that are present in the area, how do they overcome obstacles so that they can continue? Since this type of challenge involves problem-solving and not reflexes, it is difficult to tune it for player ability. It is generally not practical to create multiple levels of puzzle difficulty, since doing so essentially requires creating multiple games.

One method of reducing frustration for players is to provide them with clear direction. As with RPGs, a quest log or journal can be used to indicate what the next step is. By hiding this help information in a journal, it is available to those who need it while not in the way of players who want to figure out the puzzle themselves. One option that hasn't seen much use in games is to also have such hints gradually become more clear as time passes. In Infocom's *Hitchhiker's Guide to the Galaxy*, a completely text-based adventure game released in 1984, new clues would sometimes be provided to the players until they managed to solve a particular puzzle.

Casual games, including most card games such as this version of solitaire *(Hardwood Solitaire)*, should have simple interfaces to appeal to their broad audience.

> I think we will see a rise in casual games that will bring game interfaces back to basics. More simplistic controllers will appear to capture other parts of the market.
>
> —Jesper Sorensen
> (Business Unit Manager & Game Director, ncom–web communities)

Casual

Casual games, such as classic card and arcade-style games, are typically designed to be very simple to play. Therefore, these games often have straightforward, easy-to-use interfaces. Casual games are more often found on computers than consoles and will normally be playable solely through the mouse so that players do not need to learn keyboard shortcuts.

Multiplayer Games

Although games from almost any genre can be multiplayer, the needs of multiplayer games are specific enough that it is useful to think of them as a group. The addition of multiplayer gameplay, whether cooperative or online, introduces several additional interface elements. These aspects are on top of traditional interface needs—making proper design even more critical. As you learned earlier, the more complicated an interface is, the more difficult it is to design. Note that these considerations are all with respect to providing feedback to the player.

Local and LAN-Based Multiplayer Interfaces

The term *cooperative* multiplayer (also known as *co-op*) typically refers to games that allow multiple players to play the game together using the same visual interface (such as a television). These games introduce interesting interface design challenges because players must be able to see what their characters are doing at all times. Several methods have been used to develop cooperative multiplayer interfaces; each has its own advantages and problems. Since most console systems only allow up to four controllers, support for more than four players is extremely uncommon.

Competitive multiplayer games have similar interface needs, though they involve players competing against each other instead of working toward the same goal. Cooperative and competitive multiplayer also apply to arcade games that utilize a single display for all players.

Local area network (LAN) games are typically PC games played on computers that are connected via a local network (typically in the same room or building). The interface needs of LAN games are more similar to those of online games (as discussed further below), though most of the online communication needs do not apply.

Shared Character

The *shared character* solution involves all players utilizing the same game character. This implementation was employed in some early console games, but it is very uncommon in recent titles. Basically, different functions of the character are controlled by different players, allowing each to play one role in controlling a complicated character.

For example, in *Microsurgeon,* a game released for the Intellivision system of the early 1980s, the player controls a surgical probe that traverses the patient's body attempting to rid it of blood clots, brain tumors, tapeworms, and other problems. The probe could move throughout the body and fire beneficial

Activision Publishing, Inc.

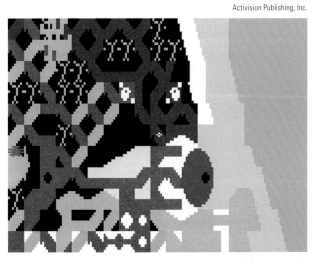

Microsurgeon allows two players to share control of the surgical probe.

antibiotics or electrostatic charges at the various "enemies." Since the Intellivision controller has only one "disc" (a variant of the current analog stick), the player holds down a button when pressing the disc to fire in that direction. When not holding down the button, pressing the disc moves the probe. In cooperative mode, the two players share control of the probe—with one player moving it and the other player firing. The game was designed to have two complementary challenges—both moving and firing—so that both players are entertained.

This last aspect is an important one to keep in mind. Any game with a cooperative mode should be designed so that all players are constantly entertained. A shared character interface is more of a gameplay than an interface decision; having both players control various aspects of the same character is a design feature that affects many aspects of the gameplay.

Restricted Camera

Gauntlet II employs a fixed, restricted, top-down camera.

For fighting games such as *Soul Calibur 2,* camera restrictions do not interfere with gameplay.

The most common method of supporting cooperative or competitive multiplayer is through *camera restrictions.* Restricted camera interfaces, which are used in many single-player games as well, allow each player to control their own character in a third-person (or top-down) view. As with the shared character interface, a single perspective is shown. All players' characters are forced to remain within the confines of the displayed area.

Sometimes, the camera shifts to provide a view that is essentially an "average" for all of the player characters. In these cases, the camera moves dynamically as the players change location in the game world—in some games zooming out as necessary to maintain all characters on screen. The desire to keep all characters of at least a certain size prevents how far out the camera can zoom. In other games, the camera is fixed to show a certain area of the game world (typically a single room), and players move around in that limited space.

In the arcade game *Gauntlet II,* for example, up to four players share the same screen. Characters are unable to move too far from other characters so that they are always onscreen. This interface can result in cases of characters becoming stuck and unable to reunite with their companions with the current camera view. In these cases, the other player(s) have to backtrack to allow their companion to rejoin them. This problem is one of the disadvantages of restricted-camera interfaces—though in the case of *Gauntlet,* it simply is part of the gameplay; it is one of the many challenges with which players have to contend. Perhaps for reasons due to technology limitations, *Gauntlet*'s camera remained at a fixed distance from the characters; in other words, it did not zoom in or out.

Fighting games are typically designed to utilize a small enough space so that a restricted camera has essentially no disadvantages. In these games, the same camera view suits both players equally—since seeing oneself and one's opponent are both useful.

Split Screen

The third solution for implementing cooperative or competitive gameplay is *split screen,* which sections off the display real-estate to allow each player to utilize one portion of it. For two players, the screen is typically split vertically—with one player's perspective shown at the top of the screen and the other at the bottom.

For three players, one will use either the upper or lower half, while the other two each have only a quadrant; for four players, the screen is split into equal quadrants.

The primary advantage of split screen is that it frees players to do their own thing in the game world. For any game that requires a first-person perspective (unless the 'shared character' implementation is used) or involves a large world, split screen is the only viable option; obviously, two people can't otherwise view the world through their own eyes using the same display.

Burnout 2 employs split screen for cooperative multiplayer.

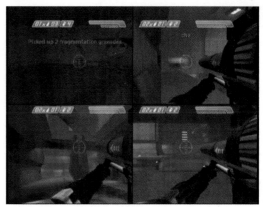

The multiplayer mode in *Halo* can be played simultaneously by as many as four players within a screen split into quadrants.

Interface design needs to go more in the direction of "blended" design. An example is *Halo's* bullet counter built into the gun—unobtrusive yet visible when needed.

—Irwin Robert Vasquez
(Game Development Student)

Sure, fun and playability come first. But I believe one of the reasons that *Halo* stands out above others that seem just like it is the background of "what-if" experimentation that lies behind those little snippets of story. Players feel they aren't patronized and that their play fits into a story that makes some sense.

—David Brin
(Author, Scientist & Public Speaker)

The principle disadvantage of split screen interfaces is that the available real-estate is greatly limited. In general, split screen is considered undesirable when a restricted-camera solution is possible. However, if players are to be able to operate in disconnected portions of the game world, few other options are available. Note that another disadvantage of split screen is that competing players can see what each other is viewing. In an FPS, for example, simply glancing at your opponent's portion of the screen can uncover the opponent's attempt to sneak up on you.

Nintendo

The Legend of Zelda: The Four Swords expands the visual interface to each player's Game Boy Advance.

Other Solutions

Other options for implementing cooperative or competitive multiplayer are also available. Some games for the Nintendo GameCube support play in conjunction with the Game Boy Advance.

In *Legend of Zelda: The Four Swords,* when players enter a dungeon, they play on their GBAs. This innovative implementation overcomes the typical interface problems by utilizing the GBA displays as additional visual interfaces. One disadvantage in this case is that the game uses the GBA's limited resolution for the GameCube elements, or otherwise the two game sections would look inconsistent.

:::::*Ratchet & Clank's* Multiplayer Mode

Sony Computer Entertainment America Inc.

Multiplayer games have a different set of needs because they need to be quickly accessible. On some of the *Ratchet & Clank* games (such as *Ratchet & Clank: Up Your Arsenal,* shown), Insomniac was able to pause the game when the player hit a button to change weapons. However, when they added multiplayer and co-op, this led to a lot of issues because you could no longer pause the game to switch weapons. The selection process had to become more streamlined and simple in order for players to access a wide variety of weapons in real time. When designing an interface, there is often a wide variety of things you must consider before committing to it. The more complicated the game, the more difficult the interface often has to become, but the faster the gameplay is, the more streamlined it must be. If you have a genre that is very fast-paced, multiplayer, and complicated, you may be in a lot of trouble trying to balance it all.

Troy Dunniway (Lead Game Designer, Midway Los Angeles)

Interfaces for Online Games

Online games are those played over the Internet. They may be played cooperatively, competitively, or even alone. For the purposes of interface design, only online multiplayer games require much in the way of additional considerations. Such games have several additional interface requirements. First, they need to provide players with information on their current Internet connections. Second, interfaces that ease communication with other players are extremely important.

MMORPGs: Evolving Interfaces

MMORPGs are challenging because they are played for months (and even years) and—supporting a wide number of play styles—often offer numerous controls. These games require interfaces that evolve over time so that the player has new things to do as their characters level up.

—*Nicole Lazzaro*
(Founder & President, XEODesign, Inc.)

I love customizable interfaces. MMORPGs are the best for this. Games like *EverQuest 2, World of Warcraft,* and *City of Heroes/Villains* are prime examples. Windows can be clicked and dragged to any location on-screen, opacity can be changed, hotbars can be customized for ease of use. Players should be able to completely customize their screens for play style and ease of use.

—*Trevor Kayser*
(Game Art & Design student)

"Traditional" multiplayer online games are usually very similar to LAN games with the exception of the distance between the players. Multiplayer games can support as many as 32 players, though maximums of 8 and 16 are more common. Massively multiplayer online games (MMOGs) support many more players in a single game world; numbers in the several thousand per server (computer) are common. Most MMOGs earn monthly revenue from players, who pay subscription fees. Keeping players happy is thus critical to an MMOG's success.

Connectivity and Lag

In online games, the player benefits from feedback on something single-player games are not concerned with: Internet connectivity. A player's connection to the Internet has a critical impact upon enjoyment of the game. The term "lag" refers to the delay experienced when suffering from a poor connection. Its symptoms are sluggish gameplay and poor response time.

Players might not recognize which problems are caused by lag and which are caused by their own computers. Online game providers receive many complaints from customers about poor Internet connections when the problem is often actually due to the players' computers being bogged down. By providing players with feedback on the quality of their Internet connections, player confusion and frustration are reduced because it helps them to identify the real problem—whether it is lag or something else.

Providing players with feedback as to the quality of their Internet connection also reduces player frustration by essentially preventing them from trying in vain to play. When players are directly told of the problem, they are more likely to simply give up and try again at a later time instead of struggling for many minutes with poor gameplay,

Online Communication

One of the primary appeals of online play is the ability to engage in *online communication* with other players. All of these communication systems involve interface design to at least some degree.

Forums

Forums contain postings by numerous players on a variety of topics. They allow players to communicate with dozens, hundreds, or thousands of others unobtrusively. Only those other players who are interested in the poster or the associated topic will read a particular message, reducing unwanted spam while also permitting mass communication. Forums are invaluable for the game developer to communicate with many of its players simultaneously. To allow better communication between players, some online games such as Kru Interactive's *Shattered Galaxy* provide forums that can be accessed within the game itself.

"Audio play" (chatting with fellow gamers during play) – which has been part of the PC gaming world for a while—is slowly catching on in the console gaming world. Xbox Live truly took this aspect of gaming experience to the next level and made the online console experience even better.

—*Daniel Kim*
(Concept Artist)

Chat

Communication with other players in real-time provides one of the primary appeals of online games. *Chatting* methods have thus been a focus of online games since their inception, and current communication systems have become fairly advanced. Primarily applicable to MMOGs, common features of chatting include a variety of message types:

- *Talk:* All players nearby will hear the message.
- *Shout:* All players on the current map will hear the message.

- ■ *Whisper:* A private message sent to a single player.
- ■ *Guild:* A message sent to all members of the player's guild. Guilds are semi-permanent, restricted groups of players and are typically formed by friends who meet within an MMOG.
- ■ *Team/Ally/Group:* A message sent to all members of the player's group, which is a sort of temporary guild.

Often, players will be able to turn each chat type on and off independently. For example, players can turn off shouts so that they aren't distracted during intense combat. It is also common for each type of message to be color-coded so that a player doesn't miss private messages from friends.

Some games also have various chat or shout "channels." Each channel serves a different purpose. One might provide tips for new players (and helpful veterans would also be found here), another might focus on assembling adventuring groups, and another would be a marketplace channel on which players would sell or auction items.

Who-Lists

Who-lists refer to any mechanism for determining which players are online and/or in a certain area. The purpose of a who-list is to enable players to find others with whom to communicate. Since online games often include cooperative play against other players or the environment, who-lists are typically designed to also help players find appropriate allies. In other words, they will indicate class, level, or whatever other parameters determine their role in combat. The who-list in Nexon's *Nexus: The Kingdom of the Winds* lists characters by class and relative power. It also uses icons and coloring to indicate special status and awards.

Who-lists serve a second purpose as well: they can be used to rank players and give powerful players recognition. Status is a very important element of online games, and allowing players to demonstrate their accomplishments to others provides a motivation for many.

World of Warcraft®, StarCraft®, Diablo®, and Warcraft® images provided courtesy of Blizzard Entertainment, Inc.

Friends-List

A *friends-list* is a variety of a who-list. It contains information regarding other players that have been specifically designated as friends. Generally, a friends-list will show when these players are online and where they are located. Friends-lists are also present in other online communication systems, such as any instant messaging program.

World of Warcraft's player list contains information on both friends and enemies.

It is common for a friends-list to require the "friend" to accept their addition to another player's list. This implementation prevents unwanted "stalking." However, some player lists in online games such as *World of Warcraft* allow players to get information about (and communicate with) both friends *and* enemies!

Ignore Lists

A robust communication system must also include methods of handling "griefers," or players who entertain themselves by disrupting the game for others. It is very expensive to handle these griefers through customer support. Automated methods of protecting players from others are most effective. A basic but effective method is an *ignore list.* When one player ignores another, they cannot receive private messages from that player and typically the game effectively removes them from the ignorer's game world—they cannot hear the ignored player's attempts to communicate and will not even see that player within the game world. This feature allows players to protect themselves without requiring additional work on the part of the publisher or developer.

Trading Systems

A major pastime in many MMOGs is item collection and creation. Therefore, *trading systems* (methods of trading items between players) are important because they support the item system and help enhance the community.

Online Marketplaces

Nexon's *Nexus: The Kingdom of the Winds* contains a rather unique transaction system. As with many MMOGs, the game includes a secure trading interface to prevent players from stealing from others. One area of the game includes a marketplace at which players can drop their items on the ground to display. These merchant players would hire guards to block access to the marketplace. Other players walk through the marketplace and can view the various wares, striking deals with the vendors whose items they desire. While primitive in some ways, the fact that the game's marketplace works more like a real-world flea market provides an interesting appeal—helping to establish the game's unique community feel. This marketplace serves as an example of how an interface can be used to develop a game's atmosphere.

One important component of any online transaction system is support for secure trades. Items represent players' time investment in the game and to have items stolen or swindled from them creates frustration that can cause players to quit a game.

Dofus, a massively multiplayer online turn-based strategy (MMOTBS) game, allows players to set up their items for sale and cost. When players log off, they can switch their characters to merchant mode. While players are offline, any player online can click on the offline players' merchants and buy their items if interested. This trading system is completely secure and also allows players to advance (by making money) passively and while offline.

Ankama Studio (www. dofus.com)

Dofus allows players to set up their shops while offline.

Timothy Nixon on Immersive Interfaces for Multiplayer Games

Timothy Nixon is the founder and Creative Director of Straylight Studios, a New Zeand–based interactive media company. He has helmed projects spanning communication design, web development, PC casual games, and portable games. In his current position as Creative Director he oversees the development of all projects from both an aesthetic and functional perspective, ensuring the quality and consistency of Straylight's products is maintained to the highest standard.

The main issue with multiplayer games is the player's ability to interact with teammates. Take a squad-based game, for example. In real life, it's quite easy to signal things to your teammates with hand signals—things like "there's someone behind that bush," or "run away." While you could simply type these in—or trigger messages to your team using hotkeys—the subtleties of the communication are lost.

Timothy Nixon
(Founder &
Creative Director,
Straylight Studios)

Voice communication takes care of the vocal aspect, and many games now have systems for pointing out things to other human characters in the world. Now developers are looking at integrating video chat into the game. The challenge there becomes preserving the player's sense of immersion in the game world when they see their friend's living room in the background of their video channel. A better way to move forward eventually will be sophisticated and dynamic character model animation that players can trigger intuitively to communicate the more subtle aspects of their message.

Bob Mitchell on Multiplayer Interface Design

Bob Mitchell
(Senior
Programmer,
Sony Online
Entertainment)

Bob Mitchell started in 1999 at Verant Interactive (working on *Trivial Pursuit Online*), where he learned the difference between the demands of a game interface and that of the engineering applications he had worked on previously. His game credits at Sony Online Entertainment include *PlanetSide* and *EverQuest II*. For both games, Bob was the primary user interface programmer.

Many MMOGs provide players with lots of different things to do. But in the end the user interface still has the same goal as it does in single-player game—staying out of the way while directing the player to the game objectives. One of our additional challenges is making the interface work for new players as well as those who play our game for hundreds of hours. I've really enjoyed working with the mod community that creates custom user interfaces for *EverQuest II*. They certainly make us think in terms of an open system instead of a locked-down interface that only does what we want it to do.

In this chapter, you learned about the various game genres and their standard interface conventions. You saw why it is important to use genre interface conventions as a guideline, but to always consider the specific needs of the game you are designing. In Chapter 6, you will begin to learn how to determine what these needs are and how to adapt interface conventions for games you develop.

1. What is your favorite game genre? What interface elements (visual and manual) specific to that genre contribute to that genre's playability? What interface elements would you change that would improve upon the genre?

2. Play three electronic games from different genres. Discuss at least five differences between their interfaces. Why do you feel these differences exist? Are they necessary in order for the game to be playable?

3. Discuss your original game idea from previous chapters in terms of genre. What is the game's dominant genre? What interface conventions are associated with that genre? Consider the goals players might have and the tasks they will need to accomplish in order to meet these goals. Create some original interface designs that can be used for your game.

4. After familiarizing yourself with the interfaces from any electronic game, change the game's genre. How would you modify one of the game's basic interfaces based on the goals and tasks associated with the new genre?

CHAPTER

6

Control Schemes:

empowering the player

key chapter questions

- How do you determine a game's interface control needs?

- What is the distinction between a mode and a system?

- What is a game system and what effect does it have on interface design?

- How can the usability of a control scheme be improved?

- What save-game options are commonly used and why?

As you've already learned, controls are at the core of any active interface. A solid control scheme will reduce player frustration and allow players to concentrate on gameplay instead of on manipulating the interface. In this chapter, we'll discuss how to identify a game's control needs and look at how to maximize control functionality and usability.

To illustrate the interface design process, let's consider the design of a hypothetical action role-playing game called *Fairy Tale* for the Xbox. *Fairy Tale* will include the typical lures of an action role-playing game (RPG): real-time combat, exploration, conversation with non-player characters (NPCs), character advancement, and finding and equipping items.

Throughout this chapter, we'll use the example of *Fairy Tale* to examine the steps involved in interface design. We will intentionally make some mistakes throughout this process to illustrate some nuances of the interface design process.

Visual Controls

In Chapter 4, you learned about control options associated with game hardware (manual interfaces). Control options on the software side (visual interfaces) are also important to consider. When the player clicks with the mouse or presses a controller button, what happens visually? The primary controls that the player manipulates include buttons, text input, and scroll bars—all of which appear on the display and are manipulated or activated by the player.

Buttons

Buttons in software interfaces are graphical representations of buttons used in manual interfaces. They are commonly used in computer games, in which they are operated by clicking on them with a mouse. Over the years, a number of button types have been established. As with most interface elements, it is generally wise to stick with the conventions unless you have a highly compelling reason to try something unusual. Most of these button types were developed for software applications other than games, but it is useful to maintain these conventions in games to lessen the learning curve for casual gamers.

Selection Buttons

Selection buttons are used to set options and other parameters for playing a game. Using a selection button keeps the player within the same interface, but it alters some aspect of the game. Typically, selection buttons are placed to the left of the text that identifies the purpose of the button.

Firaxis Games, Inc.

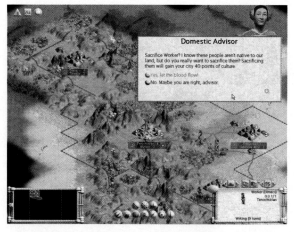

Radio buttons—such as those used in this Domestic Advisor interface from *Civilization III*—are used when only one of the options can be selected at a time.

Radio

Radio buttons are used for exclusive lists of items. Since only one of the items in the list can be selected at any given time, clicking on a list item "turns on" its button and "turns off" the button for the previously selected item. By convention, radio buttons are circles that display a "filled-in" center when activated.

Radio buttons are common in options screens, where exclusive choices are common.

Checkboxes

Checkboxes are used in lists of items that aren't mutually exclusive—meaning that several items can be chosen at once. They are squares that are empty when off and contain a checkmark when on. Clicking on the button toggles it from being on or off. Since the items activated by checkboxes are not mutually exclusive, toggling any one item has no effect on the others. In some interfaces, extra "check all" and "clear all" buttons are included to allow the player to easily change multiple settings at once.

Like radio buttons, checkboxes are commonly used in options screens and set-up screens.

Sliders

Sliders aren't buttons per se, but their use is similar. They are represented as vertical or horizontal lines with a marker that can be moved along the line. The line is a continuous measure of some parameter, such as volume. When the marker is at one end of the line, the parameter is at its maximum setting; at the other end is its minimum, which is often zero or "off." Sliders will include a number, either next to the slider or as a tooltip (mouseover help text) that appears over the marker, to indicate the exact setting.

Sliders are used in most game option screens for volume, but they are otherwise uncommon for game interfaces. Some games use sliders for discrete parameters. For example, *Warlords Battlecry 3* uti-lizes a slider for setting how much each player can spend on armies during the game.

Checkbox buttons—such as those used in this Custom Game interface from *Civilization IV* to select victory conditions—allow multiple options to be selected at the same time.

Interplay Entertainment Corp.

Star Trek: Starfleet Command uses a slider for game set-up.

Action Buttons

Action buttons cause an event to take place. The type of event varies from some effect happening within the game to switching to another interface. Action buttons are used in most games. Typically, the button will contain the text or an image that describes its function. In cases where an image is used, mouseover (for computers) or a help button (for consoles) will sometimes show a tooltip that describes the button's function.

Action buttons are often arranged in a list—such as any start menu, for example. They are also common in the Action Screen Interface, where they show what

World of Warcraft®, StarCraft®, Diablo®, and Warcraft® images provided courtesy of Blizzard Entertainment, Inc.

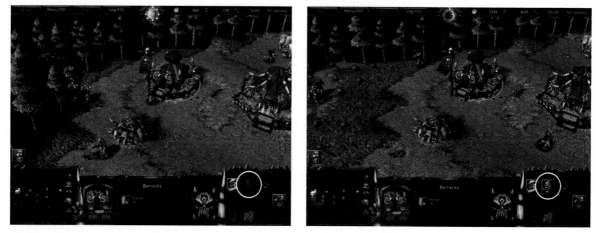

In *Warcraft III,* the button associated with a currently unavailable option is greyed-out (left, circled). When the option is unlocked, the button changes visually to indicate this and is no longer greyed-out (right, circled).

special abilities and other options might be available. For such abilities that have a time delay, a common implementation is for the button to go dark when it cannot be used. The dark button lights up gradually, allowing the control to double as a feedback mechanism for the player.

Greyed-Out Controls

One common convention for all visual controls is for them to be "greyed-out" when they cannot be used. In these cases, help information can explain to the player why the option is currently unavailable.

For console games, especially, it is best to put lists of action buttons together in a row or column. Doing so lets the player intuitively navigate the list using an analog stick or D-pad. For the same reason, you should limit the number of action buttons the player can scroll through, since the console player has no method of quickly jumping from one to the next and must cycle through each.

Text Input

Typically only used at the beginning of a game, text input is a control that is used by players to input their character name or similar information. Old arcade games used text input when players entered their initials after achieving high scores. For the computer platform, text boxes are used by first clicking on the box (if necessary) and then just typing the name using the keyboard.

For other platforms, the letters are displayed on the screen and the player uses some control—such as a joystick, D-pad, or analog stick—to move the cursor over a letter.

Pressing a button (on the controller) selects that letter. The player repeats this process until choosing an "enter" option (a "delete" or "backspace" option is also provided to undo mistakes). Text inputs for non-computer games are very clumsy—but since they are typically used only at the very beginning of a game, their poor usability is not a serious issue. Note that for these interfaces, it is best to list the letters in alphabetical order instead of presenting a keyboard layout—because this arrangement is more universally understandable.

Text input is also used in online games to allow players to communicate with each other. Online games are discussed in more detail in Chapter 5.

Due to the limited buttons on game controllers, text input (*Fable* shown) on console systems can be tedious.

Scroll Bars

Scroll bars represent a control-based solution to the problem of limited screen real estate. They are appropriate for any interface window that can contain more information than can be displayed in the space available. They are common in games, especially for computer games that tend to have longer lists of options.

In your designs, you should ideally provide enough space so that scroll bars are unnecessary. Scroll bars require the player to take an extra step to access the information or choices that they want. Still, for some types of information, the aesthetic burden of showing all of the information is too great (e.g., a list of saved games). Scroll bars are a very acceptable interface element in these cases. Note that scroll bars can be used in conjunction with some of the other controls. *Civilization IV*'s set-up screen, for example, has a checkbox list that is large enough that it also requires a scroll bar.

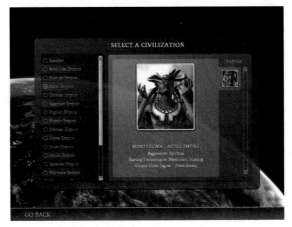

Scroll bars—such as those used in the "Select a Civilization" screen from *Civilization IV*—aren't desirable, but are an excellent method of increasing screen real estate.

Control Functionality

As you've already learned, the most important consideration in interface design is functionality. In order to create a fully functional interface, the designer must first identify every feature that the interface must accommodate and support. Many methods can be used to design an effective interface. We'll examine a top-down approach that considers the game's *systems* and *modes*. One of the advantages of this approach is that it allows the designer to simultaneously address both functionality and usability issues in an organized way.

> *T*he Lord of the Rings: The Battle for Middle Earth contained a very well designed interface. The interface stayed off the screen most of the time, allowing more of the action to be seen and popped up only when you needed it to be on the screen.
>
> —John Comes
> (Lead Content Engineer,
> Gas Powered Games)

Game Systems

Game systems include one or more actions that the player can perform while playing the game. For example, a combat system could include the abilities to attack and to block, while a movement system could include walking and running in eight directions. No player action can belong to multiple systems. So while it is possible to move during combat, the combat system does not by itself include the ability to move forward; that's part of the movement system. Note that this restriction is because of how a game system has been defined. The reason for this strict definition will become clear later in this chapter.

Game Modes

A game mode is simply a section of the game handled by a single interface. As an example, consider the game *Fable*—which could be described as having four modes: opening, action, cinematic, and management.

The *opening* mode includes the beginning menus of the game and allows the player to either start a new game or continue an old one. The player spends the majority of the time in the *action* mode, in which they run through the game world performing such activities as attacking, collecting, and talking. The *cinematic* mode is used for the game's cut scenes (non-interactive sequences). In cinematic mode, the player can't move around the game world and is instead passively watching specific events unfold. Finally, the *management* mode (entered by pressing the Start button) includes administrative functions such as inventory management and saving the game.

Note that even these four modes are insufficient to represent all of the game's interfaces. The management mode actually includes several sub-modes for handling options and game saving, inventory, personal stats, and experience-related stats. The action mode also includes the archery sub-mode in which the player can aim their bow from a first-person point-of-view (POV).

These four screenshots from *Fable* show the opening (top left) , action (top right), cinematic (bottom left), and management (bottom right) screens.

Determining an Interface's Control Requirements

To analyze the functional requirements for an interface, you should perform the following steps:

1. *Identify actions.* List all of the actions a player can take while playing the game.
2. *Identify systems and organize actions by system.* Every action should be included in one and only one game system.
3. *Identify modes.* List all of the modes in which the player will play the game.
4. *Organize modes by system.* For each mode, identify which game systems must be active.

Let's take a look at these steps for our hypothetical action-RPG, *Fairy Tale.*

Identify Actions

An *action* can be defined as anything players are able to do. It includes both actions that their character(s) can make as well as accessing system menus. If the player can do something, it is an action.

Diagram by Per Olin

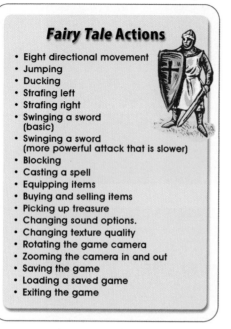

Fairy Tale Actions

- Eight directional movement
- Jumping
- Ducking
- Strafing left
- Strafing right
- Swinging a sword (basic)
- Swinging a sword (more powerful attack that is slower)
- Blocking
- Casting a spell
- Equipping items
- Buying and selling items
- Picking up treasure
- Changing sound options.
- Changing texture quality
- Rotating the game camera
- Zooming the camera in and out
- Saving the game
- Loading a saved game
- Exiting the game

Diagram by Per Olin

Fairy Tale Actions Divided by Game System

Movement
- Eight directional movement
- Jumping
- Ducking
- Strafing left
- Strafing right

Combat
- Swinging a sword (basic)
- Swinging a sword (more powerful attack that is slower)
- Blocking
- Casting a spell

Inventory Management
- Equipping items
- Buying and selling items
- Picking up treasure

Game Options
- Changing sound options.
- Changing texture quality

Camera Control
- Rotating the game camera
- Zooming the camera in and out

File Management
- Saving the game
- Loading a saved game
- Exiting the game

Suppose that after a brainstorming session, it is decided that the actions in *Fairy Tale* should include the items listed on the diagram to the left:

Note that this list includes some simplifications. For example, eight-directional movement is actually eight separate, discrete actions (or 16 if the game supports both run and walk modes). Yet even with the simplifications, this incomplete list is already fairly long. It may seem excessive to list all of the possible actions, but doing so will help ensure that every interface need is considered. Also, when an interface is implemented, the programmers will have to write code for each and every action that is possible. If the actions can't be listed, how can they be implemented?

Organize Actions by System

Due to the way a game system has been defined, we can use this list of actions to determine what the game's systems are. Remember that every action should belong to one and only one system.

For *Fairy Tale,* we might group the items in the action list into six distinct systems: movement, combat, inventory management, game options, camera control, and file management. In some cases, it is easier to first define systems and then think about all of the actions that must be included. For example, in any RPG, you will likely have a combat system. You can then think about the needs of that system.

Movement System

Let's consider the movement system for *Fairy Tale.* The character can move in eight directions and can also jump, duck, swim, and strafe (sidestep) right and left.

We might initially map these actions to the following controls:

- Left analog stick: character movement.
- Right analog stick: camera control.
- A button: duck.
- Y button: jump.
- B button: strafe left.
- X button: strafe right.

These button selections allow the position of the buttons to map to the type of movement. For example, pressing the topmost button (Y) causes the character to jump, while pressing the bottom button (A) makes the character duck.

Another option would be to map these controls to the D-pad, but this creates a usability problem. Both the left analog stick and the D-pad are on the left-hand side of the controller. In order for the character to execute a running jump, the player needs to be pressing these two controls at the same time; this is difficult to do unless the controls can easily be used by different hands.

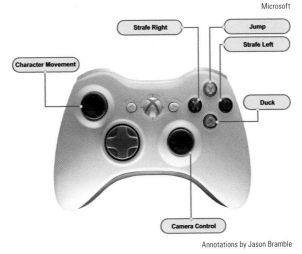

Annotations by Jason Bramble

The *Fairy Tale* movement control scheme for the Xbox 360.

We'll soon see the problem with this proposed implementation. However, in the context of a movement system, these controls appear to make sense.

Identify Modes

The next step is to determine the game's modes. Some modes, such as the opening mode mentioned earlier, are independent of the game design itself. Consideration of these modes can wait until later. What is most important is to consider the modes that the player will utilize during the course of gameplay.

For *Fairy Tale*, we'll plan to have the straightforward modes of Action and Management. The Action mode will show the character on screen and will be used whenever the character is doing anything. The Management mode will be used for actions that do not directly involve the character or his environment. Note that these are two of the modes we had identified as existing in *Fable*. We have omitted the opening mode and, for the sake of simplicity, *Fairy Tale* will not include any cinematics.

Organize Modes by System

For each mode, determine which systems must be active. In general, no game system will be active within more than one mode, but this is not always the case. The racing game *Burnout 3: Takedown*, for example, has one gameplay mode in which the player races other cars against the clock and another in which the player crashes their car into others to inflict as much damage as possible. The movement systems (including how the car is steered and accelerated) for these two modes are identical, yet other aspects of these modes differ greatly.

Electronic Arts Inc.

Electronic Arts Inc.

The standard racing and crash modes in *Burnout 3* both use the same movement (driving) system, though other gameplay aspects are quite different.

Let's see how we might break *Fairy Tale*'s systems down into action and management modes, as shown the diagram on this page.

For any mode, a control (such as an analog stick or a particular button) can be used more than once. Furthermore, all of the game's controls are at each mode's disposal. We can therefore use this arrangement of modes and systems to assign each action to a control. After this is done, an interface is functionally complete.

Diagram by Per Olin

Fairy Tale Game Systems by Mode

Action
- Movement
- Combat
- Camera Control

Management
- Inventory Management
- Game Options
- File Management

This procedure is just one method of creating a functionally complete interface. In practice, most interfaces are designed less rigidly and more by trial and error. Thinking about interfaces in terms of modes and systems can be helpful for some designers, but too restrictive for others. Develop your own method for determining an interface's functional requirements—just be certain to be thorough to minimize rework and frustration later.

Let's look at the Action mode. We've already assigned the movement controls. Following a standard convention of third-person games, let's assign the right analog stick to rotate the game camera and the right analog button to zooming in and out. Before considering how to incorporate the Combat interface into *Fairy Tale*'s Action mode, we should examine the issue of interface usability more closely.

Star Wars: Knights of the Old Republic 2 (KotOR 2) has an RPG combat system in which the player fights one or more opponents with their main character accompanied by up to two companions. The majority of fighting within the game occurs using this combat system. Yet *KotOR 2* has a second combat system. In one of the mini-games, the player controls the gun turret of their spaceship, the Ebon Hawk. Using this turret, the player shoots at enemy troops or ships. While this is also a combat system, the rules of the first combat system do not apply and the interfaces are functionally different. There is no character to move, no companions to switch to, and Force Powers and items cannot be used. The X button is used to attack in both modes to improve interface usability.

Control Usability

Usability is second only to functionality in importance and is just as critical for a game to be enjoyable. While functionality can be mapped out as shown in the previous section, usability is less quantifiable. If an interface allows all of the necessary actions, it is functionally sound. If it doesn't then it's not. Issues of usability are not as black and white.

Usability Guidelines

Maximizing a game's usability requires using common sense, judgment, and trial and error to determine the best control schemes. Before returning to the interface of *Fairy Tale,* let's look at numerous conventions and guidelines to maximize interface usability. Most of these stem from traditional user interface design. Note that at times these guidelines will be in conflict with one another. In these cases, it is important to consider the specifics of the game and which solution will yield the overall best result.

Convenience Should Match Importance

Perhaps the most critical guideline in designing control schemes is to make the most important functions the easiest to access. If attacking in an action game requires four button presses that navigate through several menus, the game would be frustrating to play and the pacing would be anything but exciting. For most games, the number of controls needed is substantial and not all can be given top billing. Some actions will require menus, sub-menus, or less convenient buttons or keys.

© Lionhead Studios Limited

In *Fable,* the white and black buttons on the Xbox controller are used to switch weapons.

When developing a control scheme for a game, the primary controls should be assigned to the actions that the player will execute most frequently. This is especially important for any actions needed during any real-time sequence—primarily because in these situations, the player will suffer more from control inefficiencies. For example, in *Fable,* the player needs to be able to switch weapons fairly easily—but this command isn't used very frequently in any given combat. Therefore, these actions are assigned (in the Xbox version) to the secondary controls of the white and black buttons. The player can still access these commands without entering any menu system—but they are of less importance than attacks, blocks, and other combat actions. Since in-game menu systems already create a break in a game's flow, these are conventionally assigned to the less accessible Start button. Note that games with very simple control schemes, such as *Tetris* or *Pac-Man,* do not need to consider this guideline.

Use Consistent Conventions

Consistency is a critical aspect of interface usability. Interface controls that look the same should behave in similar ways. This guideline applies to both visual and manual interfaces. For example, it's best to assign similar actions to similar controls. If a game has two attack types, assigning one to X and one to L1 would be confusing to the player. It would be better to assign the second attack to Y or one of the other primary buttons (or the first attack to R1).

The Tetris Company LLC/ Blue Planet

For a game with very few controls, such as *Tetris,* all actions can be assigned to primary controls.

For a game with different modes, the use of any given control should be similar between the modes, if possible. But be careful that this similarity does not lead to potential frustration. In *Dark Cloud 2,* which in general has a very well-designed interface, the player can use items in some specific locations. A saw can be used to cut down a certain tree to gain access to the next level. This action is accomplished by pressing the square button while at the tree, which opens a list of all of the player's items. The player then selects the saw.

However, anywhere else on the map, pressing the square button uses the hot-keyed item selected. While in both cases the square button uses an item, in this second case the item used is typically a limited-use item, such as a bomb. So if the player tries to use the saw, as in the first case, but isn't standing in quite the correct location, they accidentally detonate one of their few (and valuable) bombs. In this case, the square button is overused, resulting in an interface problem.

Sony Computer Entertainment America Inc.

In *Dark Cloud 2,* the function of the square key changes inconveniently.

In terms of visual controls, interface elements that perform similar functions should look the same. For example, buttons should look like buttons and nothing that isn't a button should look like one. Note that this guideline isn't absolute. Two buttons might look different, but they should contain enough similarities such that they appear to belong to the same category of interface element.

In the PC version of *Knights of the Old Republic 2: The Sith Lords,* action buttons include scroll bars that allow other actions to be assigned to the button in question. In the lower portion of the screen, the buttons are divided into several categories: defensive powers, healing items, and shields and other disposable items. Each of these buttons functions in the same way; clicking on the button itself activates that power or item, while clicking on the button's top (or bottom) scrolls to the previous (or next) power or item.

When in combat, buttons appear over the player's target that allow various offensive actions. These buttons look similar to the defensive buttons and, indeed, they work in the same manner. One primary difference is that the defensive buttons are blue while the offensive ones are red. Note that this color scheme is also used elsewhere in the game. For example, enemies appear as red and friendly characters as blue, further improving the interface's consistency. (This latter example is actually of consistency in feedback, not control.)

Accidental Mistakes Should Be Difficult to Make

Any action that might result in frustration for the player should be made difficult to accomplish by accident. This guideline especially applies to mistakes that can occur during an intense action segment of the game. For example, if the B and X buttons are used for various attack combos, but the A button opens up an inventory screen, the possibility for frustration is high because the player might accidentally hit the A button while switching between B and X.

Perhaps the most common interface design error that violates this principle is assigning certain commands to the left or right analog buttons. Through normal use of the analog stick, it is easy for the player to accidentally press in the stick,

Sony Computer Entertainment America Inc.

In *Dark Cloud 2*, switching between characters is accomplished using the analog buttons, which are easily pressed by accident while controlling a character in combat.

activating whatever action is assigned to the button. In *Dark Cloud 2*, for example, the analog buttons are used to switch characters—and there is no way to undo this character switch once it has been selected. This interface design decision is questionable, since pressing the analog button disrupts the flow of combat. One method of reducing this type of problem is to cause the analog button to only work if the analog stick is close to center. Then, if the player is pressing up on the analog stick and accidentally presses too hard, the button will not cause any effect.

Minimize Inconvenience

Any action the player must perform that does not directly lead toward their desired action is an inconvenience to them. This inconvenience is referred to as *excise* by Alan Cooper and Robert Reimann in their interface design book, *About Face 2.0: The Essentials of Interaction Design*—and we'll use this definition here. As a real-life example, suppose you want to watch television at home. One of the many steps involved in this process is paying your cable bill. To do so, you might write a check, put it in an envelope, buy stamps, put a stamp on the envelope, then mail the check. These steps are extra work you must perform in order to watch television. Online banking reduces the amount of excise required to watch TV because paying the cable bill online requires only logging in and clicking on a few buttons. Some online bill-pay services even allow you to automate the process, meaning that the excise is reduced to almost nothing.

Excise is undesirable and should be reduced as much as possible. One method of accomplishing this is by assigning any action that the player must perform frequently to one of the primary controls. This guideline is especially true for actions that must be accessed during intense gameplay. Any extra steps disrupt the fast pacing that the game is attempting to promote.

Easy Entry

You should make it as easy for a player to get into the game as possible. Repeated presses of the primary manual interface button ("Enter" for PCs, the main action button for a console) for the platform should take the player directly into the game. This means, for example, the "Play" option should be first and initially selected at the start menu.

An example of excise in some RPGs is the inventory system. In order to equip a new item, for example, players might enter a management mode, select item management, then scroll through several layers of menus to find the item they wish to equip. If players are trying to maximize a certain attribute, such as armor rating, then they must also compare all of their items manually to find the one with the highest armor value. Furthermore, armor is often broken down into many different locations such as headgear, torso, legs, feet, and hands. To switch from one's combat armor thus requires the player to go through this process five times. Item management systems like these are cumbersome and reduce the entertainment value of a game's items.

How could this excise be reduced? One possibility is to simply reduce the number of items in the game. Having fewer items reduces variety for the player, but it could be argued that the amount of excise involved in item management already makes the value of having so many items questionable. Another option would be to provide shortcuts that allow players to automatically maximize their armor for a given purpose. For example, players could choose to maximize their armor rating or their appearance and then equip the five armor pieces that will achieve that goal. For the player who enjoys further customization, the option to mix and match individual armor pieces could still be available—but other players would not be as burdened by the interface. It is possible, however, to take the concept of minimizing inconvenience too far . . . .

Don't Make the Player's Life Too Easy

In general, making the player's life easier is a good thing. Many of the interface design issues we've discussed involve doing just that. We don't want to frustrate players or punish them for minor mistakes. However, this philosophy could potentially be taken too far in game interface design. Taken to its extreme, it could lead to a game playing itself—with the player just watching.

In many RPGs (as discussed above), one element with which the players deal is item management. When an opponent is killed, the player can then loot the body—gaining gold or items. If players want to maximize his income in games such as the *Temple of Elemental Evil* or *Icewind Dale,* they must collect and sell all of the mundane equipment that the enemies were using. Since characters can carry a limited number of items, multiple trips between the town and dungeon are necessary. This type of gameplay is consistent with the pencil-and-paper roleplaying games, such as *Dungeons & Dragons*®, from which computer RPGs originated.

The Bard's Tale attempted to eliminate this tedious aspect of gameplay by instantly giving players gold when they kill their opponents. If players find a new weapon that is better than their current one, they automatically equip it—and the old one is converted into gold. This implementation makes

The *Temple of Elemental Evil* uses an item management system reminiscent of classic pencil-and-paper games.

inXile entertainment

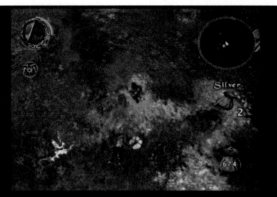

The Bard's Tale experimented with novel interface simplifications that often removed gameplay elements.

some sense; what players wouldn't instantly equip the new weapon they found? Several reviewers of *The Bard's Tale* noted that the game lost some of the traditional RPG appeal through this simplification. Part of the fun of an RPG is selling items to merchants and checking out new items to see if they are an improvement. By automating this process, some believe that the enjoyment of many players can actually be reduced.

The lesson to be learned here is that before simplifying a game's interface, make sure that you're eliminating tedium and not gameplay.

Design the Gameplay and Interface to Complement Each Other

This guideline basically encompasses all of the others, but is worth mentioning separately to stress the importance of how the gameplay and interface work together—or against each other. Whatever your game is, the interface should fully support it.

In *Star Wars: Knights of the Old Republic (KotOR),* the player has two primary types of weapons: melee (swords and lightsabers) and ranged (blasters and rifles). These weapons require different skills and are useful in different combat situations. Switching between a blaster and lightsaber requires the player to open up the management mode, access the equip screen, select the weapon slot, then choose the new weapon to use. This multi-step process interrupts the flow of combat. The game's combat is fairly easy and, while ranged and melee weapons had some different uses, it matters little overall which weapons players use. As a result, many players would forgo switching weapons. For these players, the excise involved in switching weapons exceeds the benefit of taking the time to do so. A smoother interface or a greater distinction between weapon types could make the different weapon types more entertaining for the player.

One of the improvements made in the sequel, *Knights of the Old Republic 2: The Sith Lords (KotOR 2),* involved a switch weapons action. Characters in *KotOR 2* had two weapon equip slots, though only one was used at a time. The player could thus switch weapons through a single key press and without leaving combat. By reducing the number of steps required to switch between ranged and melee weapons, the player was encouraged to make use of both styles of combat.

This improvement was not completely successful for a couple of reasons. First of all, while an effort was made to better balance the usefulness of ranged and melee weapons, the general tactics of combat did not change between the two games and it still mattered only slightly which was used. Furthermore, like in *KotOR,* the skill sets for ranged and melee weapons in *KotOR 2* were separate; most players would specialize in one type of combat or the other. They were thus encouraged to use only one of the types of weapons.

Another problem was that two weapon equip slots were inefficient because more than two types of weapons were available. Some weapons were good for fighting droids, others for combating enemy Jedi, and others for breaking down doors. To change which weapons were in each of the two equip slots required using an equip screen much like in the original *KotOR*.

The addition of the switch weapon button was an interface improvement over the first *Knights of the Old Republic,* but the fundamental design imperfections resulted in what was still not an ideal game system. The interface and gameplay were not fully in sync with one another.

Returning to the example of *Fairy Tale,* recall that the Action mode includes three systems: movement, combat, and camera control. We have already defined control schemes for the movement and camera control systems that appear solid. When we consider the combat mode, however, a usability problem becomes apparent. It is fair to say that during combat, the most important commands are swinging a sword and blocking. However, we have already assigned the most accessible controls (the X, Y, A, and B buttons) to the movement system! In our design of the movement system, we failed to leave open any of the primary controls.

Note that we could assign the four combat commands to other buttons, such as the D-pad or the left and right triggers and white and black buttons. Doing so would create a functionally sound interface. However, usability would be poor.

It is clear that the movement control scheme for *Fairy Tale* should be revisited. It's not clear that there's another good location for these commands, however. Strafing is only really useful during combat, and jump and duck also have obvious combat uses. Mapping any of these buttons to, for example, the white and black buttons would make them difficult to use during an intense combat.

The figure on this page—showing the following mappings—represents a possible solution to this problem:

- Left analog stick: character movement.
- Right analog stick: camera control.
- A button: magic attack.
- Y button: jump.
- B button: block.
- X button: sword swing.
- Left trigger (with X button): advanced sword swing.
- Right trigger: target lock.

Microsoft

Sword Swing

Advanced Sword Swing

Character Movement

Target Lock

Jump

Block

Magic Attack

Camera Control

Annotations by Jason Bramble

Another control scheme for the *Fairy Tale* action mode.

Now all of the combat commands are fairly accessible. The standard sword swing, magic attack, and block are all mapped to primary keys. The more advanced sword swing requires the player to pull the left trigger while also pressing the normal attack button. Jump is still mapped to the Y button, making it easily accessible in combat. The duck option still doesn't fit well into this interface, so it has been removed and any gameplay elements that were going to require ducking will also be removed.

What about the strafing options, however? These we have handled through a new feature, target locking, which is common in many third-person games. By pulling the right trigger, the active character locks onto the nearest enemy. Pulling the trigger again locks the character onto the next closest opponent, and so on. While locked onto a target, any movement left or right will automatically cause the character to strafe left and right. That is, the character will always face his target. Pulling back on the left analog stick, however, causes the character to lose their target and turn around and run, as normal movement would.

Think about what these interface choices say about the game and its gameplay. Given the priority that has been assigned to jumping, it should be a fundamental aspect of the game—even during combat. There should be obstacles that the player can avoid and targets that the player can hit through jumping and jump attacks.

Tecmo Inc.

The chaotic nature of combat in *Ninja Gaiden* would not work well with the movement control scheme devised for *Fairy Tale*.

Changing movement controls when a target is selected is another interesting decision. It is a good choice only if the nature of combat makes this type of movement desirable. For example, if the character is often attacked by opponents on all sides, such as in *Ninja Gaiden,* then the movement restrictions will be more frustrating than helpful.

Therefore, for *Fairy Tale,* we'd expect the player to normally face only a single opponent at a time, or at least to only be attacked from one direction. Still, even if this is the case, it would be critical to test out this control scheme at length. What can seem to be a good idea early in development might not work well in practice. If combat proves frustrating for the player, either the interface controls or the nature of combat will need to be changed.

A key guideline in interface design is that the character should always perform the action the player wants him to. So if combat is designed such that when the player moves left they want to keep facing their target, then this system might be successful. Note that the concept of changing movement controls while a target is locked is not a new one. This technique was employed in *Dark Cloud 2,* as well as other games.

Since the left trigger is used for a powerful sword attack, this aspect might be incorporated into the other primary controls as well. Perhaps the character has a power bar that fills up during combat and holding down the left trigger depletes it. The powerful sword attack can be revised to not be slower, but to instead use up this power bar. The left trigger can also be used for super magic attacks, blocks, and jumps.

Note that for a different type of game, such as an action platform that involves timing puzzles, the original movement controls might work well. It is due to the importance of combat in *Fairy Tale* that another control scheme was required.

Dark Cloud 2 changes movement controls when the player locks onto a target.

Save-Game Conventions

For any game that lasts a significant amount of time, some form of save-game feature is important. Being forced to redo something you've already accomplished is often frustrating; people want to make forward progress, not retread old ground. Saving the game typically involves storing the current state of the game world and allowing the player to pick up where they left off. All current game platforms support some sort of save-game option. A save-game feature improves a game's usability in several ways:

- The player can deal with long interruptions (sleeping, meals, phone calls) without undermining current progress in the game.
- The player can recover from a mistake (either perceived or actual) by loading a saved game.
- The player can freely experiment with new gameplay concepts without fear of reprisal.

Though few, if any, designers would advocate omitting save-game functionality, there are some compelling arguments to place restrictions on when or how often a game can be saved.

Saving the game reminds the players that they are involved in a game in which they are not fully accountable for their decisions. If they make a mistake, they can easily recover. Their choices don't really matter because nothing, except for the time elapsed from the previous saved game, is at stake. This mindset removes much of the tension and suspense that are part of the enjoyment of playing games.

One of the earliest massively multiplayer online role-playing games was Nexon's *Nexus: The Kingdom of the Winds,* released in Korea in 1996 and in the United States in 1998. *Nexus* is a fantasy RPG set in an ancient, mythic world loosely based on Korean mythology. When player characters die, they must return to a shaman to be resurrected. Unfortunately, all of the player characters' belongings remain in a pile where they died, forcing the players to then return to the location of their deaths to retrieve their items.

Though players could generally not directly fight each other, they could steal the possessions (the 'death pile') of a character who had died. This risk of loss created a sense of urgency for players who died; if they fail to return to their death piles quickly enough, someone else would steal their things. In response to player complaints over this form of theft, Nexon implemented "death pile protection"—in which a dead character's dropped belongings could only be picked up by that character. This solution is very similar to a save-game function; players are protected from their own mistakes.

Though this implementation eliminated the theft problem, it caused a new, less obvious one. The stress of having to hurry back to recover one's belongings had actually made the game more exciting. As a compromise, Nexon changed the death pile protection to only extend for the first 10 minutes after a character's death (and players were told that the protection only lasted 5 minutes)! In this way, players had a fair chance of fully recovering from their death, but they were also still driven by the sense of urgency. This example illustrates one of the potentially negative impacts of a save-game system: elimination of stress that contributes to a player's enjoyment of a game.

Saving the game can have other negative effects as well. It breaks immersion, by reminding players that they are playing a game. Saving the game requires memory storage and for some platforms can require the player to purchase additional hardware (PS2, Xbox360, and GameCube). Finally, saving the game takes time—potentially breaking the flow of the game experience.

Despite these disadvantages, it is widely believed that allowing players the control associated with being able to save the game is very beneficial for almost all types of games. Several options for saving games are described next, along with their benefits and drawbacks.

Save to Slot or File (Traditional Saving)

The standard save-game method *(save to slot or save to file)* involves the player opening the menu and manually saving the game to either a file (computer) or one of a limited or unlimited number of saved game slots (console). This method

DreamCatcher Interactive Inc.

Syberia allows a player to save games to slots and stores a thumbnail image of each save.

gives the player the greatest amount of control, but it also breaks immersion by transferring the player to a special screen that is essentially a file manager.

For some games, especially those on the computer platform, players can enter some text to describe their saved games so that they can later determine which previous saved game they wish to load. Some games also automatically include identifying information such as the elapsed time, the area or chapter of the game in which it is being saved, or a screenshot of what the player is seeing when the game is saved.

This standard saving is included in many games, even those that employ one of the following options as well. Some players desire this high degree of control, so it is seen as a good option to include.

Auto-Save

With *auto-save*, also called *checkpoint save,* the game saves the player's progress without any instruction from the player. Auto-saves keep immersion high by not interrupting the player. A message that the game has been auto-saved is often displayed, but without requiring the player to acknowledge it.

Auto-save is used to prevent frustration caused by the player's failure to save. It is typically performed in two types of cases. First, after a certain period of time, such as 15 minutes, an auto-save will be made. This implementation means that the player will never lose more than 15 minutes of time. Also, the saves are infrequent enough that they do not greatly disrupt the player's experience.

The second use of auto-saves is right before or after a particularly difficult part of the game. For example, in many action games, at the end of a level, the player will experience a "boss fight." Boss fights are combats against an especially powerful opponent (called a "boss") and succeeding in them is required for the player to progress in the game. These fights often involve pattern recognition or other tactics and are deadly until the player figures out how to defeat this particular opponent. These fights can last up to 15 minutes or more in some games. Auto-saving before a boss fight means that if the player dies when they first encounter the boss, they don't have to work their way to that point again. Auto-saving after the boss fight ensures that the player's accomplishment will not be undone by a future mistake.

::::: Auto-Save: Masking Poor Design?

Note that while auto-save is one way to reduce player frustration in difficult boss fights, there are other design methods of preventing frustration. One of the arguments used against auto-saving is that this feature is used as a crutch for lazy design. That is, the advantages of auto-saving wouldn't be necessary if the game were well-designed.

Giving the player hints that the boss fight is imminent allows the player to take suitable precautions and makes it more likely that they will either save the game on their own or prepare for the upcoming fight.

Boss fights—such as those in *God of War*—require special interface considerations.

Furthermore, many designers believe that boss fights should be designed so that the skilled player has a reasonable chance of surviving the initial encounter. A major source of frustration for players involving boss fights is when a game is overall very easy but then includes boss fights that are virtually impossible to succeed at the first time they are tried. The player, having breezed through the level with ease, is caught off-guard by an unexpectedly difficult fight.

By better balancing difficulty of the game throughout, this frustration can be reduced. If a player knows to keep on their toes, they will not be surprised by a suddenly difficult encounter. Auto-saving is therefore not as necessary because the game doesn't take "cheap shots" at the player and does not lure him into thinking the game is too easy. Not using attacks or obstacles that instantly kill the player also reduces the necessity for auto-saving.

One of the limitations of auto-saving is that there is generally only one auto-save slot available. In games in which the player might want to take a different path (such as many RPGs), auto-saving becomes insufficient. For example, in *Neverwinter Nights 2,* the player can influence the course of the game through his dialogue choices. In some cases, the choices made by the player significantly affect the direction of the game. If players learn later on that they wished they had made a different choice earlier, they might find that the most recent auto-save occurred after that fateful decision.

This problem can also occur in difficult action games in which players might work

Homeworld's persistent gameplay results in potential save-game dilemmas.

their way into a very difficult situation and find that their last auto-save is at a point where the game will be close to impossible to win. For example, in the RTS *Homeworld,* the players' resources at the beginning of each mission depend upon what resources survived the last mission. If players performed too poorly early on in the game, they might find some of the later levels extremely difficult. This design decision could force players to load a saved game from a mission or two earlier in order to "correct" their mistakes. If these saved games have been overwritten, players might even have to start from the very beginning. Note that another method of addressing this problem would be to scale the game's difficulty based upon what the player's resources are, thus lessening the importance of loading saved games.

Quick-Save

Microsoft/Bungie

Quick-save allows the player to save the game at the touch of a single button. It has many of the advantages and disadvantages of auto-save, but gives the player more control and hurts immersion slightly more. Its advantage over normal saving is that it does not interrupt the player with a load/save game menu. Quick-save almost always involves a single save slot, which can be loaded via a single quick-load button.

Since the player controls when a quick-save takes place, the problem of overwriting a needed saved game is worse than it is for auto-save. In other words, since the game decides when to auto-save,

Most FPS games, such as *Halo: Combat Evolved,* allow quick-saving.

the designers can prevent the game from choosing this option when the player's demise is imminent. However, with a quick-save, the unfortunate player might choose to save the game when they have unwittingly ensured his death—thereby forcing them to load older saved games. One way to address this issue would be to keep track of the last few quick saves and allow them to be loaded from the traditional load game menu.

Limited-Save

A hybrid system of the traditional and quick-save methods, *limited-save* allows the player to choose to save the game only at certain locations or under certain conditions. This method—used in *God of War,* for example—is implemented when

Sony Computer Entertainment America Inc.

the designers do not wish players to be able to save anywhere and at any time. This method can increase the tension in the game (as discussed at the beginning of this section). Immersion is still disrupted, but the problem of the players saving while doomed is eliminated. Its advantage over the auto-save option is that players can choose if they wish to use it. Thus players are more conscious of when the game is saved and they can avoid overwriting a previous saved game.

God of War allows the game to be saved at specified locations.

Another advantage of limited-save occurs in games such as RPGs in which the player might return to the same location on multiple occasions. For example, in *Dark Cloud 2,* players will tend to save their games at the same locations, but after having advanced their characters. Auto-save doesn't work particularly well in this case because the game doesn't know when the player wants to save. For a purely linear game without backtracking, this option is generally inferior to the auto-save method.

Unusual "Save-Game" Implementations

A side effect of saving games is a player mentality referred to as "save-load." Save-load game playing involves players saving the game before any major decision, then reloading the saved game if they don't like the result of their choice. It results in a different gaming experience and is generally seen as undesirable. For any fairly difficult game, it encourages players to spend a fair amount of their gaming time watching save and load screens. It undermines a game's difficulty and provides a strong argument for simply making games easy enough to not require it.

Designers have experimented with many methods to reduce the prevalence of save-load gameplay. These novelties are efforts to affect how the game is played and thus what the game experience is like.

Firaxis Games, Inc.

Alpha Centauri's Iron Man mode rewards infrequent saving.

One variant is the Iron Man mode for the turn-based strategy game *Alpha Centauri.* In Iron Man mode, the game still allows players to save the game whenever they like. However, when the game is saved, the program automatically exits. Though still possible to play the game using the save-load strategy, the penalty for doing so is more significant—since it's necessary to restart the entire game, which takes some time. As a result, players are more likely to endure their mistakes and play the game normally. The reward for playing in Iron Man mode is a 100% bonus to your final score. By discouraging saving the game and rewarding players for this play style, the game provides a good incentive to play it as originally intended and to accept any mistakes.

Fire Emblem for the GBA also uses an innovative save-game methodology. The game involves a few dozen levels or chapters. Three save-game slots allow saving at the beginning of any chapter. However, whenever any unit is moved within a chapter, the game is auto-saved into a special saved game slot. Therefore, if a move was a mistake, players are stuck with the results unless they wish to replay the chapter from the beginning. A single chapter might take an hour or more to complete, so players must weigh their desires to undo the mistake against the amount of time required to do so.

In *Fire Emblem,* the player has many units—each a character with their own personalities and abilities. The death of a character in battle can be a major loss, but the game wisely provides players with far more units than they can deploy at any given time. Thus, losing units doesn't have a great impact on the player's ability to win the game. If a favorite character is lost, the players might choose to restart the level—but the game design helps encourage

Fire Emblem employs an innovative save-game methodology.

players to press on, resulting in their own unique experiences with the game. Player reaction to this unusual design decision is mixed—but it definitely affects the style and appeal of the game.

Another unconventional method to address the save-load style of gameplay is used in *Metal Gear Solid.* In this game, the players' total number of saved games is tracked as they play—providing an incentive for players to stick it out. The game even mocks players if they've saved the game frequently. Sometimes special content is unlocked if players completes the game without ever saving. These implementations are perhaps too "hard-core" to affect how most players approach the game, but they are still interesting experiments.

In this chapter, you learned how to identify the control needs of an electronic game. You should now understand the distinction between game modes and game systems and the importance of thinking in these terms when designing a complicated interface. You have also examined control usability issues, including saved game conventions. In the next chapter, this discussion will be expanded from how the player communicates with the game to how the game communicates with the player: feedback schemes.

1. Unlike other forms of entertainment, games allow the "audience" (players) to have control over their entertainment experience. The interface directly enables this player control to exist. Play an electronic game for at least 1 hour. How does the game allow for player control through interface design? Does the game ever take away player control? How?

2. Describe the 4 main game modes discussed in this chapter. How are interfaces used within these modes in games you played?

3. What 4 steps do you need to follow in order to analyze the functional requirements for an active interface? Perform these steps for both an existing game and an original game idea.

4. What are the 6 main interface usability guidelines for designing control schemes? Analyze an existing game and discuss whether or not each of these guidelines are followed.

5. There are several methods possible for saving the game. Discuss the "save-game" methods introduced in this chapter. Come up with an original game idea. Which method would you implement for your game?

Feedback Schemes:

informing the player

key chapter questions

- What is the purpose of *feedback* in interface design?

- What types of feedback should always be available to the player?

- How can the *usability* of a feedback scheme be improved?

- What *aesthetic* guidelines should you consider when developing a feedback scheme?

- How can an interface aid in *immersion?*

Now that the design of interface control schemes has been explained, the second major purpose of the interface can be addressed: feedback. Keeping the player informed via feedback is as necessary as allowing the player to provide input to the game (control).

All passive interfaces exist to provide the player with the information he or she needs to play, understand, and enjoy the game. Additionally, feedback also plays a part in the design of active interfaces. A thorough understanding of the role of feedback is necessary to entertain the player, and this aspect of design is especially important for games intended to appeal to more casual gamers.

Feedback Functionality

Strictly speaking, feedback elements of interface design are inherently issues of usability, not functionality. Still, it is useful to broaden the definition of functionality when considering feedback. A game's feedback is functional if it provides the player with all of the information necessary to make the player's choices meaningful. This statement doesn't mean that the player must be given all of the relevant information. In fact, withholding information from the player is often an intentional gameplay element. For example, strategy games will often conceal the map with a feature known as "fog of war." Some early real-time strategy (RTS) games, such as *Command & Conquer,* did not employ fog of war, but it is now a common feature that enhances a game's strategic elements.

> The most common game interface design mistake involves insufficient user feedback on what players should be doing.
>
> —*Gordon Walton*
> *(Studio Director, Bioware Austin)*

::::: Hiding Information within the "Fog of War"

Activision Publishing, Inc.

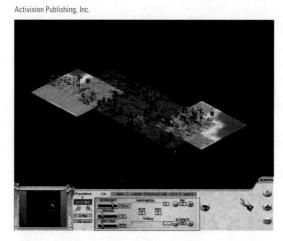

In *Civilization: Call to Power,* "fog of war" is used to create tension and allow for more strategy.

Strategy games often limit the mapping information available to the player. There are three levels of knowledge the player might have regarding an area of the map. Areas to which the player has never been are masked with a "shroud." The player is given no information about what is concealed under the shroud. Areas that are within the view range of one of his units or buildings are completely visible. The current status of all terrain features, buildings, and troops are clearly shown in both the action window and the mini-map.

Areas that the player has visited during the game but that are not currently within view of one of his units or buildings are masked by the "fog of war." In these regions, the player can see the terrain and buildings that were in the area when he was there last, but no troops are visible. Furthermore, if new buildings have been built or existing buildings have been destroyed, the player does not have this knowledge. The fog of war is typically depicted by those sections of the map being greyed out.

By hiding mapping information from the player, the game incorporates another layer of strategy. Typically, RTSs provide many tactics that are powerful under certain circumstances, but that can easily be countered by a properly prepared opponent. Instead of just firepower and defensive might, espionage becomes important. If a player can see what their opponent is building and where they are moving their troops, they will better be able to counter their strategy. Some units have invisibility, high view ranges, or special abilities that uncover fog of war at a distance, making them excellent scouts. Players must balance their development of offense, defense, and espionage to win.

Exactly how much information the player needs depends upon the specifics of the gameplay. When designing an interface's feedback scheme, the designer should carefully determine the effect of each piece of information on gameplay.

Mandatory Feedback

Some types of feedback are required for almost all games. Only under unusual circumstances should this information be kept from the player.

Player Status

The most basic information a player needs is the status of his own position. Unlike some other types of information, player status feedback should almost always be visible onscreen.

Player Location

One of the primary goals of feedback is to ensure that the players always understand what options are available to them at all times. The most critical of these options are those involving *player location*—including the players' surroundings, and where they can and cannot go.

At its simplest form, the player's location is shown through the contents of the active screen. In most games, players are looking either through their characters' eyes or at their characters in the world. This is often insufficient, however, since many locations in the game environment might look the same. Landmarks—such as trees, buildings, and rivers— greatly aid players in identifying their locations within the game world and help prevent them from becoming lost or confused. For games with larger environments, mini-maps (see p. 118) are another common method of helping to convey both where the player is and where the player has been.

> As players get more involved, they want feedback that involves personal consequence—not just physical sensations, but a sense of almost-real win and loss.
>
> —David Brin
> (Author, Scientist & Speaker)

Player Health

The term *player health* refers to how long the player has until the game is over. This could be time/lives remaining or the actual health of the player's character. The greater the penalty for the player's death, the more important it is to constantly inform the player of his health. For this reason, many games employ warning signs such as a flashing health gauge to warn the player of imminent death.

Atari Interactive, Inc.

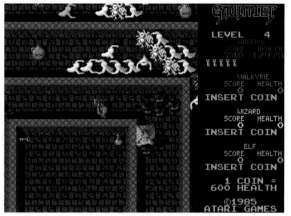

In the classic arcade game *Gauntlet,* an ominous voice warned the players when one of their members was low on health.

Combined with a heartbeat that increases in pace as the player gets closer to death, the interface provided both feedback and entertainment value through increased tension. Fortunately for the player (and unfortunately for the player's parents), all they had to do to increase their health was to insert a quarter into the machine.

Gauntlet uses audio cues to warn the player that it's time to insert another quarter.

Similarly, a change in the player's health must be clearly indicated. In many first-person shooters (FPSs), the screen flashes briefly when players are hit—clearly informing them that they have lost health.

Feedback Is Essential

Interfaces don't have to be big to be good—but they must provide the information the player really needs at any given moment. The best interface is completely seamless and invisible—but, of course, this isn't necessarily practical. The interface is part of the feedback mechanism for the players; it's important to make sure the players cannot only access the information they need, but also that the information they're receiving is useful.

—*Tim Donley*
(Producer, Bottlerocket Entertainment)

Voiceover

The term *voiceover (VO)* refers to having voice actors read any dialogue or text in the game. Including VO in a game can greatly increase immersion. Hearing characters' voices adds to their personalities, making them feel more alive and real. It's one more tool designers can use to flesh out their characters.

Some games avoid using VO for player characters so that the players can imagine what their avatars sound like instead of having a voice forced upon them. Also, in any game in which the players can choose what their characters say, having VO for the player character can greatly increase the amount of lines that must be recorded.

Voiceover is a major undertaking and expense for any game with a significant amount of dialogue, such as a role-playing game (RPG). Localization of a game for foreign languages further expands the expense of VO. Still in any modern game, VO is all but required for the game to feel of high quality.

While a complete discussion of VO is beyond the scope of this text, it is useful to understand some of the resulting complexities. In particular, the project timeline is greatly impacted. Normally, the bulk of game design content is implemented fairly late in development. When voice must be recorded, however, it is important for all dialogue to be written early enough for this process to take place. After the VO is recorded, it has to be incorporated into the game. Any changes or bug fixes that affect dialog require that additional lines (called "pick-ups") be recorded. These can be expensive and difficult to coordinate well.

Alien Voiceover

One trick to reduce the burden of VO is to utilize "alien" voiceover. Any game with non-human species can have these non-player characters (NPCs) speak in fabricated languages. In these cases, the "voiceover" is simply several dozen lines of gibberish that sounds like what that species' language might be like. Lines are recorded for different emotional states (e.g., angry, happy, scared) so that the lines will sound appropriate for what the NPC is saying. Besides reducing the number of lines that need to be recorded, alien VO provides another huge benefit. Since it does not need to be recorded specifically for each line of dialogue, it is much easier to change later.

Another potential problem with voiceover is that it increases the quality of the dialogue required. While many game designers are competent writers, writing dialogue for voice actors benefits from specific training and experience. A line that reads fairly well might sound terrible when spoken. Few game designers have sufficient scriptwriting experience to truly capitalize on the potential of voiceover, yielding games that feel less polished.

Player Abilities

When trying any new game, players quickly learn what options are available to them. If at any time these options change, players will be confused unless the change is clearly communicated to them.

For example, in *Fire Emblem,* a unit can be put to sleep, in which case it cannot be given any actions. To depict this state, the unit has a series of "Z"s appear above its head. This simple feedback explains to the player why he is unable to select and move that particular unit. Without this visual cue, the player might feel the game was broken.

Similarly, the addition of new options should also be conveyed. Grabbing a certain flower in *Super Mario Bros. 3* allows Mario to launch fireballs at his opponents. When he

Nintendo

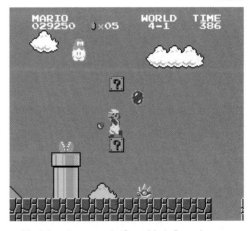

Mario's appearance in *Super Mario Bros.* changes when he can throw fireballs.

Nintendo

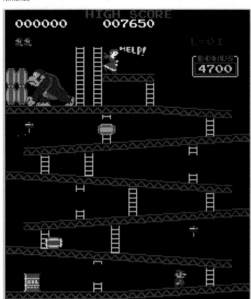

In *Donkey Kong,* Mario's hammer flashes for a few seconds before vanishing.

has this ability, Mario's outfit changes, making it clear to even the first-time player that he has new powers. Note that besides informing the player that he has a new option available, this implementation also rewards the player with the graphical effect of a new appearance.

Often, changes in abilities last for a limited amount of time. In these cases, it is common to give the player some warning before the effect ends. For example, in *Donkey Kong,* Mario can acquire a hammer. While Mario is holding the hammer, the rules change; he can no longer climb ladders or jump, but is able to smash the barrels rolling toward him.

A few seconds before the hammer goes away, returning Mario to his former vulnerable status, it begins flashing—alerting the player. The effect is similar to the yellow light in a stoplight. Preparing the player for what is to come prevents frustrating mishaps.

Goals

Another critical type of feedback is the player's current goal and the player's status toward achieving it. This goal could be either short-term (such as reaching the next level in an RPG), or long-term (such as progress toward completing the game). Providing information on goals is important because it informs the players about their progress through the game.

Firaxis Games, Inc.

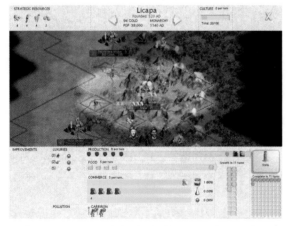

The action screen of *Civilization III* provides feedback on multiple important goals.

For a game with many goals, not all of this information needs to be prominently displayed, but it should all be made available to the player—and the most interesting or important goals should often be shown. Sid Meier's *Civilization* series is well-known for its ability to provide the player with a constant stream of both short- and long-term goals. In *Civilization III*'s action screen, current wealth and progress toward the next technological advance are always visible. Additionally, each city's progress toward both production and population growth is shown below the city name. Note that this last piece of information is an option that players can toggle off if they prefer a cleaner interface appearance.

Other goals—such as victory points, total culture, and progress toward the space race—are available through other interface screens. The designers decided that this information was of less immediate importance to the player.

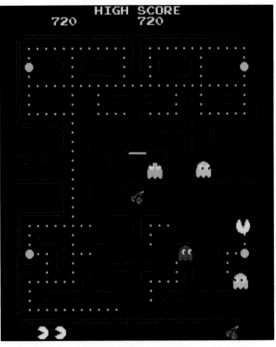

Pac-Man is a simple example of providing player status feedback.

The above guidelines apply to most types of games. For example, even in a simple game such as *Pac-Man,* players are always aware of where they are, in which direction they're moving, and how close they are to death (i.e., how many lives are remaining). The player's abilities do not change throughout the course of the game—with the inability to move through walls or ghosts (except when powered-up) immediately made clear to the player.

Exceptions to these guidelines are typically limited to specific situations or occur with particularly unusual gameplay elements. For example, players might not realize that they are in an anti-magic area until attempting to cast spells. Not informing players of this limitation can create tension and excitement. Still, it is generally best to at least provide players with clues about the situation. As always, the game world should be consistent. For example, when entering the anti-magic area, the players' enchanted swords might stop glowing—suggesting that the region they are in is special in some way.

Feedback Usability

Issues that improve a feedback scheme's usability primarily involve common sense. As with usability for control schemes, several guidelines provide a solid basis for feedback scheme design. As mentioned earlier, feedback is generally rooted in usability rather than functionality—with most feedback-related interface features designed not to make a game playable, but more enjoyable and less frustrating.

Don't Require Confirmation

Confirmation dialogues are common in game interface design to prevent players from performing actions that they might regret, such as accidentally selling valuable items or overwriting a saved game. Indeed, these types of mistakes could be extremely frustrating to the player. Confirmation dialogues, however, are inconvenient—requiring players to complete an extra step when they do know what they're doing. If players perform the action often, they'll become accustomed to quickly accepting the confirmation dialogue—eliminating its usefulness. The better practice is to make it both difficult for the player to make the mistake and to provide an *undo* option in case the player does make a mistake.

How does one prevent the player from making mistakes? Consider accidentally overwriting a saved game. One common way this type of error might occur is when players think they are loading a game instead of saving; instead of loading the desired saved same, they overwrite it. This error is much less likely if the screen that handles loading a saved game looks very different from the screen associated with saving a game. Players then receive a visual cue that reduces the chance they will make the mistake in the first place.

Undo functionality is rarely included in games. It can be cumbersome to code and difficult to implement in an intuitive way, such as in the case of a saved game. In order to allow the player to undo a saved game mistake, extra memory is required to store both the new saved game and the old one that might have to be restored. When does the act of overwriting a saved game become final? It could be much later before the player realizes a mistake, and even a robust undo option might not provide the remedy.

One powerful method of dealing with this problem is to minimize the size of saved game files, making overwriting them unnecessary. When an essentially limitless number of saved game slots are provided, overwriting saved games simply isn't desirable—so the player is less likely to accidentally do so. Frequent auto-saving, and backing up more recent auto-saves, also provides players with what is essentially an undo option. If they accidentally obliterate the most recent saved game, they at least have an auto-save that does not greatly set them back. Note that because of the control players have over their hard disk space, these saved game issues are generally not relevant for computer games.

BioWare Corp.

In RPGs such as *Knights of the Old Republic,* a sell confirmation dialogue is an easily implemented solution to the problem of accidentally losing valuable items.

Other types of mistakes suggest their own solutions. In many RPGs, accidentally selling an item can be a costly mistake. The item might be either gone forever or marked up by the merchant who bought it—making it costly to undo the error. (It is common for merchants to sell items at much higher prices than those at which they will buy them.) One solution to this problem is to allow players to buy back any items just given to a merchant at the same price at which they sold them. Doing so requires little extra effort and doesn't disrupt the game balance in any way. This solution could potentially confuse players, since the next time they return to the store the item will be at a higher price. Perhaps the temporarily discounted item could appear in a special font color with help text that explains its price—or maybe the shopkeeper explains the policy to players when they first sell items to the merchant.

World of Warcraft takes this concept one step further by allowing players to buy back, at no loss, recently sold items from any merchant within the game. Some may argue that this unrealistic solution undermines immersion; clearly, Blizzard decided that usability is more important.

Provide Progress Bars

Whenever any action requires more than a few seconds to complete, a progress bar should be used to show how quickly the action is being completed. Progress bars perform two major functions. First, they indicate to the player that the game has not crashed and that the desired action is being performed. Second, they provide the player with an estimate of how much time remains before the game will be ready.

BioWare Corp.

Following this cinematic in *Star Wars: Knights of the Old Republic,* the player is immediately involved in an action sequence.

In some games, cinematics require up to 10 or more minutes to load (depending on the platform). If the game doesn't provide players with information on this loading time, they might think the game has crashed. In some cases, the player is immediately involved in an action sequence following the cut scene. Therefore, players who are tired of waiting for the cinematic to load might leave their computers or TV monitors—only to return and learn that they have lost a battle (or even the game itself).

In this case, the best solution would be to optimize cinematics to ensure that none of them take too long to load on systems that meet the game's recommended system requirements. Failing that, a progress bar that includes "time remaining" information would certainly reduce the frustration experienced by the player. Another method to address this particular problem would be to require player input before beginning the action sequence.

Remove Unnecessary Tutorial Information

Tutorials are key tools in teaching players how to master a game. To the player who already knows the rules, however, a tutorial and similar help information is an unnecessary obstacle to enjoying the game. Always provide the player with the means to skip or disable extra information such as tutorials. For example,

Nintendo

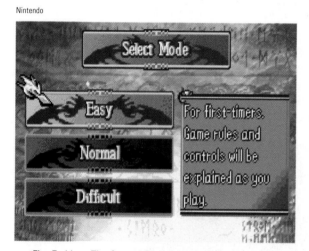

Fire Emblem: The Sacred Stones wisely makes its tutorial optional, especially since gameplay has changed little from the original version of the game.

Fire Emblem: The Sacred Stones includes three difficulty settings. The second option (Normal) is the same as the first (Easy)—except that tutorial help is not provided. If the player has already played through the game, or if they know how the game plays from playing the original *Fire Emblem* (the gameplay is identical), then they are able to avoid the tedium of a tutorial.

Furthermore, while it is critical to take into account the needs of the novice player, it is unwise to design an interface for the novice. At the very least, provide players with settings that they can modify—allowing them to use a more advanced interface that better suits the more experienced player.

::::: ToolTips

Microsoft

ToolTips are a specific form of pop-up help used in traditional interface design.

Within the game industry, pop-up help is often referred to as ToolTips, though this term is technically inaccurate. ToolTips are a specific type of pop-up help used in traditional interface design. ToolTips are used exclusively for toolbars and iconic controls and, unlike pop-up help in game interfaces, are not intended to help the beginner learn the interface. Rather, they serve to remind a more advanced user who may not have used the application in a while.

Accommodating Both the Novice and Expert

For me the biggest challenge is finding the balance between tailoring the interface to the first-time user and accommodating the seasoned veteran. While it is definitely true that the game must engage people within the first 30 seconds, the interface that allows this ease of accessibility may not also be the most efficient for the proficient player. This can lead to an interface that frustrates the long-term player, and ultimately dulls their overall experience of the game.

I'm personally a huge advocate of having as little "interface" visible as an overlay of the game world. It detracts from the experience, and reminds you that you're playing a game as opposed to interacting with an organic world. If you do have to overlay anything, it's always important for it to feel part of the world, so aesthetics matter in this respect.

—Timothy Nixon
(Founder & Creative Director, Straylight Studios)

Pop-up help is context-sensitive help information that follows this principle. For PC products, moving the mouse cursor over a button or interface element causes—after a half-second delay—a small pop-up window to appear that provides information on what the button or element does. For console games, a help control is sometimes provided. When pressed, it causes the selected item's information to appear.

Nintendo

In *Fire Emblem,* the right shoulder button causes help to appear for the currently selected item, character, or interface element.

Neverwinter Nights displays status conditions through icons that appear near the character's profile.

Like many games, *World of Warcraft* color codes its health and mana bars to allow the player to easily distinguish between them.

Pop-up help aids the player in learning the game's controls—but it can later be ignored after the player has figured out what various icons mean. It can also help players quickly remember how to play a game they haven't used in a while. Pop-up help does not inconvenience experienced players because it is unobtrusive and also requires action (either leaving the mouse stationary or pressing a button).

Use Consistent Conventions

Consistency is as important in feedback mechanisms as it is in controls. Elements that provide similar information should be displayed in the same way. For example, if a fighting or RPG has status conditions (e.g., poisoned, enraged, stunned), these should be represented through a consistent method.

It is equally important for elements that are different to be visually distinguishable. For example, if you have both a health bar and a mana bar, these should be different colors.

In Chapter 6, you learned about the importance of using color conventions for control schemes. It is likewise important to maintain color consistency between both feedback and controls

The Effectiveness of Colors

Colors can be more effective in communicating what's going on than straight numbers. (In RPGs, we try to provide for both options, since some of the hardcore players prefer to see numbers to calculate damage, to hit, and see results of their damage.) Also, a concept artist for an interface to help balance out the design is not a bad thing. It helps maintain overall consistency, and the more the feel and colors of the interface matches the game world, the more unobtrusive the menus and options will be.

—Chris Avellone
(Chief Creative Officer & Lead Designer, Obsidian Entertainment)

when possible. In some games, for example, red buttons are used both for attack buttons and for feedback concerning enemies.

Note that this concept of consistency applies to all types of feedback supplied by the game and not just those elements that are traditionally considered to be part of the

interface. For example, in *God of War,* the player finds cracks in a wall at one point in the game. A ballista at that location can be fired at the wall, destroying it and opening up a secret area. Throughout the game, when players see similarly cracked walls, they know to search for ways to break through them.

In such cases, the designers have used the interface to teach the player a gameplay element. By reinforcing this learning through consistent use of the established conventions, the designers are able to reward the player and provide a more immersive experience.

Sony Computer Entertainment America Inc.

In *God of War,* cracked walls can be destroyed, allowing access to new regions.

Adapt the Interface Based on the Game's Stage

Some games change greatly in terms of scope and complexity as the game progresses. For these games, the ideal interface for the end of the game can be very

different from the interface used for the game's early stages. Turn-based strategy games are an obvious example of this phenomenon.

In *Civilization III,* for example, the player's turn begins with separate notifications about the various events that occurred between the end of the player's last turn and the beginning of the current one. At the start of the game, the player might own a single city—and everything that occurs at the city will be relevant and useful in achieving success. A small mistake at this stage could severely cripple the player's position.

Firaxis Games

Civilization III: Conquests lets player set which event messages will appear at the beginning of their turn.

Later in the game, however, the player might control dozens of cities; wading through these events can be tedious. Furthermore, because the player's position is so large, the status of any specific city becomes much less important. Therefore,

Civilization III lets the player toggle these event messages on or off. This option allows the interface to adapt throughout the course of the game to suit the player's specific needs based upon both their play style and the stage of the game.

Master of Orion 2, another turn-based strategy game, uses a similar implementation but also adds another mechanism to address this issue. A report screen lists all of the major events that happened in-between turns. This interface design allows the player to quickly scan through events without forcing them to confirm event dialogues.

Atari Interactive, Inc.

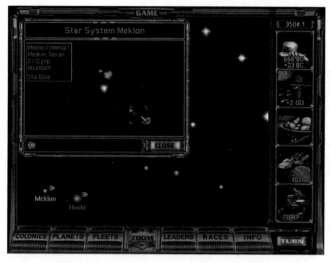

Master of Orion 2 includes a report screen that unobtrusively summarizes important events instead of interrupting the player with them.

Less Is Better

An interface should be as unobtrusive as possible without undermining its functionality. The more information provided to the player, the more likely he is to become confused or frustrated. Before revealing some specific information to the player, consider whether or not it is truly necessary to the gameplay.

Hide Unneeded Information

Hiding unnecessary information is the primary purpose of in-game menus. The player doesn't need all the information all the time, so we can hide much of this feedback in menus that the player can access when desired.

As an extreme example, consider the many game options often provided, such as sound volume or screen resolution. When at the options screen, this information is important because it is why players are there: to set these options the way they desire.

Out of the Park Developments

Title Bout hides infrequently needed information in menus.

However, it would be a useless distraction to have a sound volume bar always visible onscreen.

Use Heads-Up Displays When Appropriate

Another method of reducing the impact of an interface is through a *heads-up display (HUD).* A HUD is a transparent portion of the interface that conveys information without severely obstructing the player's view of the action. HUDs are very common in FPSs and in any game that emphasizes fast-paced action.

A possible disadvantage of HUDs is that the transparent interface can result in some information being unreadable when shown on top of a busy background. When using a HUD, consider slightly larger fonts and interface elements to make them more readable under all conditions.

Allow Customization

One method of reducing the interface is to allow the player to change exactly which portions of it are visible. Different players desire different levels of feedback from the game. Experts at an FPS, for example, might be skilled enough to not need a constant reminder about how many bullets they have left before they need to reload. By allowing players to turn interface elements off when desired, you give them the power to decide what is more important to them: feedback, or the size of the action screen.

Some games, such as *Command & Conquer: Generals,* allow the player to disable most of the interface to increase the size of the action window. A better design, however, is to let the player have separate control over each aspect of the interface, resizing or minimizing each component separately.

Valve Corporation

HUDs, such as in *Half-Life 2,* reduce how much an interface obstructs the player's view of the action.

Electronic Arts Inc.

Electronic Arts Inc.

In *Command & Conquer: Generals,* players can view all of their options (top) or collapse the interface (bottom).

::::: MMOGs and Customization

Interestingly enough, the fairly new genre of massively multiplayer online games (MMOGs) leads the way in terms of interface customizability. Games such as *World of Warcraft* and *Everquest II* have extremely flexible interfaces. Why are MMOGs so advanced in this regard?

World of Warcraft®, StarCraft®, Diablo®, and Warcraft® images provided Blizzard Entertainment, Inc.

World of Warcraft currently has one of the most advanced user interfaces.

The primary reason MMOGs have highly customizable interfaces is due to the amount of time players spend within the game. A typical console game will provide 10–20 hours of gameplay. Some longer or highly replayable games (such as those with unlockable content) might provide closer to 50 hours of gameplay. By contrast, a hardcore MMOG player will play up to 50 or more hours every week and the average subscriber plays an MMOG for three to four months.

The more time a player spends within a game, the more advanced the interface should be because novice users and expert users require very different things from software. Due to the vast amounts of time MMOG players will invest into those games, the interfaces must accommodate a level of user expertise that isn't required by most games. Additionally, these players are typically paying subscribers. If their needs aren't met, they will stop paying for the game. By the time players become experts in non-MMOGs (and thus by the time they want more from the interface), they have already paid for the game. Therefore, the incentive for great interface design is much greater for subscription-based games such as MMOGs.

Finally, MMOGs often provide a variety and depth of gameplay beyond that of other types of games. To entertain players for hundreds of hours, MMOGs need to continuously provide new challenges and options. This results in a very complicated interface, making the ability to customize it even more important.

Incorporate Feedback into the Game

The best method of reducing the negative visual impact of an interface is incorporating the feedback into the game itself. Virtually all games accomplish this to at least a limited degree. For example, in any third-person 3D game, an interface element isn't needed to show a character's facing. This information is implicitly included within the character model itself; just by looking at it, the player can tell which direction they are facing. Similarly, signposts in a game can be used to inform the player in which direction to go or what is in a nearby building.

This guideline returns to the concept of dynamic interfaces that was discussed in Chapter 2. Remember that interface design extends beyond static elements and menus; anything that provides feedback or control should be viewed as a part of the interface.

The advantages of working the interface into the game itself are very compelling. In the real world, extra interfaces aren't often needed; the components of reality provide people (the players) with sufficient information to live their lives. Games are at a major disadvantage when compared to the real world, however. Games can only convey visual and audio information. Other important forms of feedback such as the weight of a shield and the pain of an injury cannot be as easily conveyed.

This signpost in *The Elder Scrolls III: Morrowind* gives the player information and is also a natural part of the game world.

Audio as Feedback

Audio is vital in interface design. Much like tactile and visual feedback, audio is another important means of communicating information to the player—such as when: a new game hint pops up; the journal is updated; your attack isn't working against an enemy; your spell has misfired; and you have successfully clicked a button on the interface. All this positive and negative feedback is essential to letting the players know if any of their actions have succeeded or if new information is available. Audio is one of the best ways to give this to the player.

—*Chris Avellone*
(Chief Creative Officer & Lead Designer, Obsidian Entertainment)

Audio is one of two elements that link directly into the consciousness of the player. If the audio is coordinated perfectly with the actions and decisions of the players, they will be immersed that much more quickly. A gun shot that is coordinated with the right sound and controller vibration is impossible to ignore. Until I started to study vision I didn't really think that we 'rank' our senses in terms of believability. If you touch an optical illusion, you always doubt your eyes. Touch is believed more by the consciousness than the brain. Audio is more believed than the eyes and is truly 3D, whereas our vision is just a little portal into the world.

—*Mark Terrano*
(Design Director, Hidden Path Entertainment)

Additionally, players want a level of detail that real life does not provide. In the real world, a boxer doesn't know that his opponent has exactly 15% of his stamina remaining. He only knows that he's landed many good blows, and that his opponent's breathing is labored and his movements are becoming sluggish. While the experienced boxer might even be able to predict how close his opponent is to collapsing, the player is less experienced. Furthermore, game technology is not at the point where such fine details can be conveyed accurately.

Player Perception

One important aspect of game design to keep in mind is that what matters is player perception, not reality. For example, if a magic potion increases players' damage by 20%—but the game doesn't explicitly provide this information—players might not feel like they have gained an advantage. Dynamic interface elements—like new special effects to represent attack bonuses or new armor the player can wear—are a great method of providing feedback and entertainment simultaneously.

Still, experimenting with methods of providing feedback through in-game elements is an excellent way to reduce the amount of interface needed. For example, suppose a sword-fighting action game allows a player to build up energy to perform a special maneuver. This type of gameplay is found in many fighting games in which a power meter shows the character's progress. Instead of showing a power meter onscreen at all times, the character's magic sword might serve as the power meter itself—with the sword becoming increasingly red with heat until it bursts into flame when the character has accumulated enough power.

Minimize the Interface through Gameplay

Another method of reducing interface clutter is through gameplay decisions. Often in game design, the interface is of secondary consideration. In Chapter 6, you learned the importance of designing the gameplay and control scheme to complement each other. This design methodology can be applied to feedback schemes as well.

Think carefully about the goals of your game and adapt its feedback scheme to fit those goals. One of the best ways to minimize an interface is to simplify gameplay. A very common feedback element, as discussed above, is the health bar. But are health bars necessary for all games?

Super Mario Bros. 3 is simple enough that it doesn't require a health bar. Most enemies are killed with a single hit, and so is Mario. When Mario eats a mushroom, he grows to a larger size, which essentially doubles his health by allowing him to absorb a hit before being killed. By increasing his size, the gameplay changes (because he can now reach higher places and has trouble squeezing into tight areas) and the health bar information is incorporated directly into the appearance of the character. Note that this is an example of a dynamic interface element; the player's health is displayed not through a static interface element but within the game components themselves.

What are the repercussions of this design decision? With such a limited health system (in the best case, Mario is killed after taking only two hits), the player doesn't get many chances. The gameplay must take this into account by providing frequent checkpoints and multiple lives. For some players, *Super Mario Bros. 3* could be discouraging. A particularly difficult section of the game

The gameplay of *Super Mario Bros. 3* doesn't require a health bar.

might require dozens of failed efforts before the player can proceed. However, this challenge is also part of what makes the game fun. *Super Mario Bros. 3* is also internally consistent: the gameplay and interface support one another.

One could easily imagine a game similar to *Super Mario Bros. 3* that has more difficult situations, requiring more precision from the player to not be hit by enemies. To achieve the same overall difficulty level, this game might include a health bar, allowing the player to make more mistakes before having to restart. This game would have a more obtrusive interface and would appeal to a different kind of player.

Minimize the Interface through Technology

New technological solutions can also reduce how much interface is required. Graphics technology has progressed to the point where many types of feedback can be built into the game's action without requiring additional interfaces. For example, damaged opponents appear hurt within many action games—preventing the need for health bars. For an older RPG like *Phantasie III*, this option was not available and numbers had to be used to indicate health. The technological limitations resulted in the interface dominating the screen, with only a small section of the screen revealing the game world.

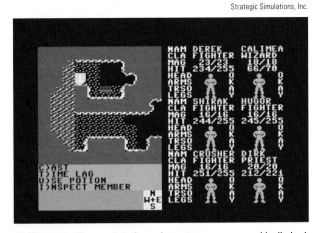
In *Phantasie III,* many interface elements were governed by limited technology.

::::: Wizardry: Ahead of Its Time

Sir-Tech

Even in the 1980s, Sir Tech—the developer of the *Wizardry* series of RPGs— understood the importance of minimizing a game's interface. The developer allowed the player to toggle some interface elements on and off as desired. The party's health and status information and compass were separate "windows" (long before the concept of windows had been truly established) that could be disabled to reveal more of the active window. Given *Wizardry's* limited graphics, the impact on immersion was overall minor, but the concept was a very advanced one in terms of interface design.

An interface issue faced by many games involves loading times. Most games contain too much content to be loaded into the system's memory at any given time. Therefore, as the player moves from one area to another, the game needs to load new data into memory. Though generally not a critical problem, it would obviously be better to not break up the action of game by eliminating, or at least minimizing, loading times.

In some older games, such as *Ultima V: Warriors of Destiny* (which spanned four double-sided 5.25" floppy disks), players have to switch disks during some area transitions. Improved data storage media, through the now popular CDs, solved this aspect of the problem—but the larger issue of loading times continues to plague most modern games.

Electronic Arts Inc

Ultima V requires players to switch between eight disk sides during play.

chapter 7 Feedback Schemes: informing the player

One improvement to mitigate the negative impact of loading screens was to make them at least partially dynamic. Some games, such as *Warlords Battlecry III*, include hints on loading screens. Graphical changes to the loading screen also add to the player's entertainment while waiting.

Technology offers better solutions, however. As memory becomes cheaper and thus more plentiful, more data can be loaded by the game at any given time—reducing the frequency of load times. Improved processor speed

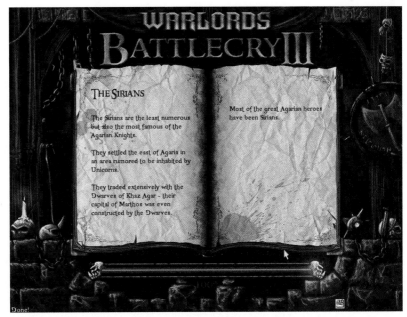

Warlords Battlecry III uses hints and minor graphical changes to make load times a little more interesting.

decreases the duration of loads. Better graphics require more data, however—so at the same time, the amount of data that must be loaded is generally increasing.

Gas Powered Games' *Dungeon Siege* provides another technological solution to the loading screen issue. Using what is referred to as "streaming" technology, the game loads new data behind the scenes without disrupting the game's action. As the player

moves from one area to another, the data needed for the new region is gradually loaded into memory—while data from previously visited regions is discarded. From the player's perspective, except on slower machines, the loading process is invisible.

This implementation does have a few trade-offs, though. Besides its technological challenges (a streaming system is more difficult to program), this system requires careful resource management. Each area of the game has more stringent restrictions with regard to how many models, textures, and other resources are allowed than a game that employs loading screens would.

Dungeon Siege employs streaming technology to eliminate load times.

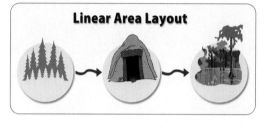

A streaming loading system benefits from linear area design (left), but a non-linear layout (right) makes it more difficult to eliminate loading delays.

Additionally, the area design must be fairly linear or at least have long passageways connecting various regions. For example, suppose a game contains three areas: a forest, a cave, and a swamp. If a player could rapidly get from the forest to both the cave and the swamp, all three areas would need to be in memory in order to prevent loading delays. To prevent this burden, the entrances from the forest to the cave and from the cave to the swap would be far apart, so that only two (the forest and the closer of the other two areas) would need to be loaded.

::::: Memory Limitations

Any game requires a certain amount of information to be loaded into memory in order to operate. To view a single character on the screen, its model, animations, and textures must all be in memory. Therefore, displaying twin human warriors requires roughly half of the memory as showing one warrior and one spider. To reduce memory, various characters can share information. If the spider were instead a goblin, for example, it could possibly use the same animations as the human. Better yet would be a bandit character—which might use the same model and animations as the warrior, but different textures (e.g., armor, face).

World of Warcraft uses low-poly models that share animations, in part to conserve how much memory is consumed.

Whenever a new area is loaded, the graphical information for the creatures and objects is stored in memory. The greater the variety of graphics in any area, the longer this process takes and the more powerful the video card required. Through careful game design, similar creatures can be placed in an area to allow the memory requirements to be reduced. Allowing players to change their graphical settings to use lower-quality models or textures also helps, especially for players with weaker video cards.

For an MMOG such as *World of Warcraft,* this limitation can be especially important. The game must be able to have one of every possible player model and texture available at the same time. For a single-player game, even one that allows the player to choose their appearance, high-poly models can be used because only one of those appearances must be in memory at any time. *World of Warcraft* thus uses relatively low-poly models and few texture variants, but compensates with a distinct artistic style that generally results in a favorable impression of the game's graphical quality.

Note that this aspect of memory limitations is only one of many considerations. Another graphical limitation, for example, is supporting many characters onscreen simultaneously. Displaying information onscreen requires processing power, while having that information ready to show requires memory. Both of these limitations, along with many others, must be considered.

The Nintendo DS is a good example of using technology to improve feedback schemes. The dual screens allow one to serve as an action window while the other provides feedback information. This layout cleans up the action screen while still making the desired information readily available. When compared to the GameBoy Advance version, the DS interface requires fewer control presses to provide the same feedback.

All guidelines should be used judiciously. It's important to always keep usability issues in mind when designing game interfaces. Remember that the goal of the interface, from a feedback perspective, is to clearly present to the players the information that they need.

Nintendo

Advance Wars for the DS utilizes two screens to improve its feedback scheme.

Aesthetics

Since feedback involves presenting information to the player, aesthetics are an important consideration. While it is important for feedback to be provided clearly and completely, it is also desirable for it to be visually appealing and to match the artistic style of the game.

General Guidelines

User interface design is a fairly new area of research, but numerous aesthetic guidelines have already been established. Many of these are commonsense guidelines and are similar to those in other design-related fields such as advertising and interactive media.

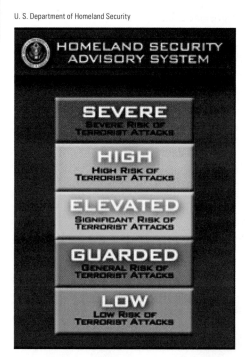

The Homeland Security Advisory System uses colors to emphasize the likelihood of terrorist threats.

Color

Color is a valuable tool in interface design because it can differentiate interface elements while adding minimum complexity. However, indiscriminate use of color can lead to a confusing or unpleasing interface. As a general rule, the number of colors to use in an interface is the minimum number required to achieve the design goals. Using more colors lessens the visual impact of each and thus reduces the overall effect of colors.

Creating a Mood

"Cool" colors—such as blue, purple, and green—tend to have a calming effect on people, implying safety and harmony. "Warm" colors—such as red, orange, and yellow—create anxiety and excitement and can imply danger. The effects of warm and cool colors are readily apparent in everyday life—as shown by their use in traffic signs and lights or the Homeland Security Advisory System currently used in the United States.

World of Warcraft®, StarCraft®, Diablo®, and Warcraft® images provided Blizzard Entertainment, Inc.

Red is often used in game interfaces (*StarCraft* shown) to alert the player to dangerous situations. Note the red and yellow representations of the selected, and damaged, units in the bottom section of the screen.

Keep this distinction in mind when selecting a color scheme for an interface. For example, red is often used to indicate unit health when the unit is close to death, while green is used when it is fully healed. Besides having been established as a standard convention, the use of red in this case is believed to affect the player at a physiological level—increasing their anxiety—which is appropriate for the situation within the game.

Use warm colors when you want to elevate the player's alertness and stress and cool colors when you wish to provide the player with a "break" or to convey that a situation is under control. Keep in mind that color contrast is important when colors are used in this way because the player will adapt to whatever standard the game sets. For example, if your entire interface is red throughout the whole game, the color's ability to impact the player will be diluted. Players will become used to the color scheme, and it will cease to have the desired emotional impact. It would be more effective to use both warm and cool colors so that the contrast will have the desired effect.

Improving Visibility

Colors can also be improved upon to accentuate important interface elements (color differentiation) or otherwise improve visibility. Brighter colors (and warmer ones) are easier to read on the dark backgrounds common for games. Blue is harder to read and is less desirable for elements such as text.

Color differentiation is the process of using different colors to provide feedback to the player. One common use is to clearly and concisely show that two seemingly similar elements possess different properties. Colors used in this way should contrast with each other so that the player can easily tell them apart. As a general rule, it is best to use no more than four or five colors for this purpose if the colors designate discrete differences.

Diablo II, for example, uses color for item text to indicate the item's relative value. Mundane items are grey, magic items are blue, very rare items are white, special "set" items are green, and unique items are orange. At a glance, players can thus tell which items they care about and which items they can ignore. The use of color prevents players from having to read the entire name of

World of Warcraft®, StarCraft®, Diablo®, and Warcraft® images provided Blizzard Entertainment, Inc.

Diablo II employs color differentiation to tell the player which items are important.

the item. Players can concentrate on the game's action without worrying about accidentally passing up a valuable item.

However, if *Diablo II* had another five item 'types,' the benefit of this color coding could be lost. It would become difficult to determine whether an item were pink or red, for example, preventing the player from acquiring the desired information. Additionally, if so many colors appeared in item names simultaneously, the player could become confused by the excess of information. In interface design, if this type of situation arises, consider consolidating the types into a smaller number of options. For example, armor, weapon, and ring status could also be integrated into the game's color coding scheme (with armor having one set of colors, weapons another, and rings a third)—but the developers wisely decided to use the item graphics and name to convey this less critical information. That is, the player cares more about getting the most valuable item than getting the weapon, so the item's value is the more important information to convey. For another game, color differentiation by item type instead of item rarity might be more appropriate.

When displaying a spectrum of possibilities, using more than four or five colors can be appropriate. For example, a health bar might use a dozen or more colors ranging from red to green. In this case, having so many colors does not cause confusion because the exact shade of color used is not especially important.

:::::Guild Wars: Color Differentiation

In *Guild Wars,* characters are largely defined by their 'skills,' which include spells, abilities, and passive effects. For skills that affect other characters, some damage the target over time, others damage them when a specific action is performed (such as every time they attack), and others reduce their speed. With dozens of possibilities, mapping a color to each of these effects would at best be useless and at worst confuse the player.

NCsoft Corporation

Instead, *Guild Wars* uses skill icons to show these status effects. Although these are still difficult to read easily, the players learn the symbols of the important skills with time—and they can then tell at a glance what is affecting them. Were colors used instead, no amount of experience with the game would allow the player to easily distinguish between the fine color differences.

Guild Wars' status effects are an example of when color differentiation would have been a poor design decision.

So how, then, does *Guild Wars* choose to employ color differentiation? Colors are used to designate which class uses the skills. Purple skills are used by Mesmers and green ones by Necromancers, for example.

This use of color is visually appealing, but it is not especially useful from a feedback perspective. Knowing whether a player's character is affected by a Necromancer's or Mesmer's "hex" (a negative effect that lasts for a certain period of time) isn't very important. What is important is the knowledge that the player's character is being affected by a hex. Any character has skills from only two classes, so this use of color differentiation isn't very necessary when sorting one's own skills.

A more useful implementation might have been to color-code positive and negative effects of certain types. For example, red might indicate a skill that inflicts damage immediately—while purple is used for hexes that inflict damage under certain conditions or over time. It then is trivial to determine which effects on a character are good and which are bad. It would also be easier for the new player to figure out which of his own skills he wants to use in a heated combat.

Color differentiation is often used to provide duplicate feedback information. For example, the selection circle around units in *Command & Conquer Generals: Zero Hour* changes in both size and color to provide information regarding the unit's health.

It is not always advantageous to use color in this manner. Color differentiation should only be used when the extra layer of feedback is necessary. In *Fire Emblem,* for example, a character's currently equipped weapon is always at the top of their inventory list. As soon as the player learns this very simple rule, it is obvious which weapon is equipped—since the ordering of the inventory list has no other effect. Color-coding the inventory list to show which item is equipped is unnecessary—adding to interface color while adding nothing.

Electronic Arts Inc.

Color differentiation is employed in *Command & Conquer Generals: Zero Hour* to emphasize critical information: unit health.

Nintendo

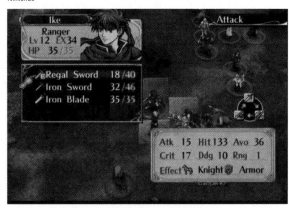

Fire Emblem wisely does not use color differentiation to identify which weapon is equipped.

While the font used in *Diablo II* helps establish a fantasy atmosphere, it's somewhat difficult to read and a cleaner font might have been a better choice.

Text

Typography is a fundamental and straightforward aspect of interface design. Since interfaces are used to convey information to the player, text typically plays some role. Some general guidelines for font selection can help keep an interface clean and legible.

Guidelines for font selection and use include:

- Use as few different font types within a game as possible.
- In general, use left-justified text.
- For PC games, use at least a 14-point font. For console games, a larger font size, such as 18 point, is preferable. The more intense the action on any given screen, the larger the font size should be.
- Font readability is far more important than font aesthetics. While ideally the font used will convey the feel of the game, err on the side of legibility if necessary.
- For any given purpose, always use the same font. For example, if a game has a number of system menus, they should all be using the same font.
- Use no more than three different font sizes or styles on the same screen.
- San serif fonts are generally more readable than serif fonts.
- If your game is going to be localized into other languages, allow at least twice as much space as is required for the English version. Many other languages, such as German, tend to use more characters than English to convey the same meaning.
- When possible, use iconic symbols (see below) instead of in-game text, primarily because they are easier for localization. For example, if you have a sign that says "Blacksmith," you'll have to create new art for that sign for every language to which the game is localized. By contrast, a sign with a picture of an anvil on it would require no translation.

Icons

Icons are an excellent tool for interface design in games and in software in general. The purpose of icons is to provide considerable information while creating minimal screen clutter. The key to using icons is to make them accurately represent whatever is being shown. For example, *Sims 2* uses icons that all players can understand because they are from real-life. Buttons to speed up and slow down the flow of time use symbols that were established for VCRs, for example.

> One of my favorite active visual game interfaces would definitely be the one used for *The Sims 2.* This interface allows players to view their progress in the level and to seamlessly point and click—controlling their Sims' lives while still being fully immersed in the game. This interface is a help rather than a hindrance. We are sometimes bombarded with too much interface, which decreases the player's suspension of disbelief. However, *The Sims* got it right.
>
> —*Trystan Coleman*
> *(Game Art & Design Student)*

Electronic Arts Inc.

The Sims 2 makes good use of icons to create an interface that is clean yet easy to read.

Even for games in which everyday icons would not be useful, icons are still valuable tools because they are a compact method of conveying information. For example, icons are used to great effect in some strategy games, such as *Civilization 3* and *Master of Orion 2.* Though these games use a lot of numbers, they are masked by icons. Once the player learns the meaning of the icons, the interface becomes very easy to use. Perhaps even more important, though it might take some time for a player to learn the icons, they are less intimidating to the new player than numbers would be.

Icon Symbology

Symbology for icons can be very difficult — usually because you have to deal with two separate problems:

1. You sometimes have to convey foreign game concepts to the user with a symbolic icon.

2. You have to do this in a very small space (64 x 64 pixels or less), and it has to be easily recognized.

Icon symbology usually requires a lot of trial and error, since sometimes the best symbol for a particular icon might not read well at a required size. A console game has to have enough pixel density to read well on a television. Issues like these can make symbology and iconic representation very challenging.

—Ian Wall
(Senior Artist, Obsidian Entertainment)

Firaxis Games, Inc.   Firaxis Games, Inc.

Icons (in *Civilization IV,* left) and numbers (in *Civilization: Call to Power,* right) are both used to display information.

Some guidelines for icons include:

- All icons for a particular aspect of the game should be the same size and use the same style.
- Icons should be small. Large icons defeat the purpose of saving screen real-estate.
- Icons should contain minimal detail. Highly detailed icons can be difficult to read and less distinguishable from similar icons.
- For PC games, use pop-up help (mouseover text) to explain what an icon represents.

Immersion

Immersion involves creating a game environment in which the player can get lost (in a positive sense). Immersion is a general goal of all games to some extent, though the method in which it is achieved varies by game type. For example, a player of a puzzle game such as *Tetris* or *Meteos* certainly doesn't feel like he is part of that game world. However, these games can be immersive in that the player can become so engrossed in the game that they lose track of their real-world surroundings.

Immersion is typically accomplished through the game design. The role of interface design in the process is simply to not break that sense of immersion. A poorly designed interface frustrates the players, forcing them to remember that they are playing a game and thus disrupting their enjoyment.

One method through which interfaces can help achieve immersion is with "seamlessness." A seamless game system is one that does not create a break within the game world. Seamlessness is good because it does not distract players, and instead lets them enjoy the game.

A *mini-game* is a sub-game that uses gameplay different from that of the basic game. Typically, mini-games are short and simple. For example, *Star Wars: Knights of the Old Republic* includes a mini-game called Pazaak—a card game similar to blackjack that can be played to gain money and some items within the game. When playing Pazaak, a new interface appears that shows the cards the player is holding as well as the cards that have been played on the table. This implementation is not seamless because it does not keep the player within the game world.

A seamless version of this interface might have involved the player's character sitting at a table with an opponent. The camera could have shifted to be behind the player, showing the cards. In front of the player would be the table, showing the cards that have been played as well as the current deck. Note that seamlessness isn't necessarily the most desirable option, however. For example, if Pazaak were complicated enough of a game, it would not be feasible to implement it in this seamless way described while still conveying all of the necessary information. Also, implenting a mini-game in a seamless way can require

BioWare Corp.

The interface for the Pazaak mini-game in *Star Wars: Knights of the Old Republic* is not seamless.

much more effort—which could be spent elsewhere to improve the overall quality of the game. Remember that the "perfect" solution is often not the best one for achieving your goals.

Earlier in this chapter, we discussed how *Dungeon Siege* uses technology to reduce the amount of interface needed. Its streaming technology allows the game world itself to be seamless. By eliminating loading screens, which break up the game's flow, the immersion of the game is improved.

In this chapter, you learned about the importance of feedback in interface design and how to achieve both functionality and usability. You also examined some aesthetic guidelines and how to use interface appearance and design to improve immersion. In the next chapter, you'll learn about the interface design process.

1. Feedback is an essential component of game interfaces. Play an electronic game for at least 1 hour. How does this game provide feedback to the player through interface design? Is there any missing information that you feel should have been conveyed? What would need to be modified in order to convey this information?.

2. How do aesthetics play a part in providing feedback to the player? Analyze the aesthetics of a game's interface. Do the aesthetic components enhance or detract from a player's ability to access game information?

3. What are the 6 main interface usability guidelines that allow for feedback? Analyze an existing game and discuss whether or not each of these guidelines are followed.

4. What are 6 methods for reducing clutter in passive interfaces? Critique a game interface that you feel is too cluttered. What methods would you use to reduce clutter? Create a sketch of the modified interface.

5. Create a feedback scheme for your original game idea in the form of a heads-up display (HUD)—conveying at least 5 information elements (such as health and location) to the player.

Part III:
Practice

CHAPTER

8

Process of Interface Design:

how interfaces are created

key chapter questions

- What are the roles of each development team member in interface design?

- How should the production pipeline and methodologies for interface design be structured?

- What are some common interface design mistakes?

- What are the elements of an interface design document?

- How can the effectiveness of an interface be assessed?

We've already discussed various interface features, effects of platforms and genres, and control and feedback mechanisms. Now let's examine the *process* of developing an interface. On larger projects, interface development is a multidisciplinary task. We'll discuss the various roles involved in interface development and how they interact with each other. We'll also examine communication and documentation standards used to assist in the development process. Note that details might vary from company to company; the roles outlined in this chapter represent one common and effective division of responsibilities. Common interface design mistakes and tips from game industry professionals also appear throughout this chapter.

Roles in Interface Development

The four primary roles in interface development are the same as those involved in game development in general: designers, artists, programmers, and quality assurance (QA).

Illustration by Ben Bourbon

Teamwork is important in most aspects of game development, including interface design.

As you've already learned, consistency is extremely important in interface design because it improves usability. For example, if the right analog stick controls character movement during combat in a game, it should also control character movement while not in combat. Otherwise, players must learn multiple control schemes depending upon what they are doing within the game.

In general, there are few industry standards for interface design; many aspects of the process are still subjective and based upon individual opinions. Thus, often only one designer, artist, and programmer will be directly involved in this process for a game. Limiting the number of people involved greatly improves consistency. Additionally, though the quality of a game's interface can have a large impact on a game, it is a fairly contained task that does not require a large number of people to complete.

Designers

Interface design begins with functionality, which is determined by the game design. It is the game *designer*'s responsibility to determine what the requirements of the interface are. What aspects of the game can the player control? What feedback must be related back to the player? How much of the screen can be devoted to the

Illustration by Ben Bourbon

Designers are responsible for an interface's control and feedback

interface elements? The answers to these questions are the responsibility of the designer, who analyzes a game's control and feedback needs (as discussed in Chapters 6 and 7).

The designer is ultimately accountable for the quality of the interface and creates an *interface design document (IDD)* that is used both by programmers to code the interface and by artists to create its aesthetics. Depending upon the specifics of the team, the designer might be more or less involved with the technical or artistic elements. For example, the aesthetics of an interface might be governed by the general tone of the game, but otherwise determined by the art team instead of the design team.

In practice, the task of interface design will sometimes fall on a programmer or artist involved in its implementation. Depending upon their experience, this situation is not ideal. Designing good interfaces can be a very complicated process and is best handled by a specialist (although a programmer or artist could certainly be an interface design expert).

Designers Are Not Artists ... or Programmers!

Keep in mind that *designers* are unique to the game industry and are a completely separate group from artists and programmers. Many people from other industries—such as software development (where programmers are sometimes considered "designers") and interactive media (where artists are also seen as "designers")—don't have a firm grasp on the role of a designer in the game industry. For a more detailed discussion differentiating roles and responsibilities of game industry professionals, see the first book in this series—*Game Development Essentials: An Introduction* by Jeannie Novak.

Illustration by Ben Bourbon

Programmers

Programmers incorporate the interface into the game. They convert the IDD into a working implementation. Since the interface must work intimately with the remainder of the game engine, a programmer often works in conjunction with the designer in the early stages of interface development. Sometimes the elements of an interface are not very compatible with the details of the game engine and have to be dropped or modified to be implemented in a timely fashion.

Programmers implement the designed interface.

Programmers thus also guard against poor design. They are involved in the finest details of the implementation and thus are likely to find any major oversights. For example, when hooking up a combat interface, a programmer might discover that no method of retreating was included in the design. Programmers are most involved with the functionality of an interface.

Illustration by Ben Bourbon

Artists

Artists are responsible for the aesthetics of the interface and thus directly impact the secondary goals of immersion and atmosphere. Generally, less-senior artists will be involved in interface design because the concepts are fairly straightforward; also, interfaces are typically 2D and thus do not require expertise with 3D development packages.

This does not mean that aesthetic interface design is easy or unimportant. The interface is a very prominent portion of a game's graphics and can influence the player's opinion of the game's aesthetics.

Artists ensure that an interface provides immersion and atmosphere.

chapter 8 Process of Interface Design: how interfaces are created

Common Art-Related Mistakes

Common mistakes I see in user interface design usually revolve around art, as they tend to be the most obvious. Often artists try to make the art of the interface the focal point. This is usually a mistake because, if anything, you want the user to focus past the user interface, and focus on the game content itself. A good user interface is one that you don't notice. When a user interface works with you, it's intuitive to the point where you're not really thinking about each action and hunting for buttons; those are the interfaces that are doing their job the best.

Ian Wall
(Senior Artist, Obsidian Entertainment)

Mark Terrano on Interface Design Process Techniques

Mark Terrano (Design
Director, Hidden Path
Entertainment)

Prior to co-founding Hidden Path Entertainment, Mark worked in the Xbox Advanced Technology Group as a Technical Game Manager. In this role, he was able to work with game developers worldwide to help them make the best possible Xbox games. Previously, he worked with Ensemble Studios on the *Age of Empires* series as a designer and programmer. He was also a network specialist involved in every area of computing, from stock markets to oil pipelines. When not working, he enjoys Seattle, playing music, and—of course—all kinds of games.

Game interfaces are far too complex to learn and use. True immersion starts after the interface has disappeared from the player's conscious decision-making process. The more buttons, colors, and modes, the longer this process will take.

If you are designing for a PC, try designing the experience for a console controller—or if you are using a mouse, think about a mouse with no buttons. What would you do if you had to cut the number of controls in half? Pare down the interface to the essentials, and the game will always benefit.

Make interfaces easy to change, and don't be afraid to change them regularly. Build time for interface tuning into the schedule, and spend a lot of time with people that have never played your genre, never played your game, or never played games at all. Use an interface specialist or usability engineer if you can to do more formal studies. If not, read up on low-cost usability studies and run your own.

Interfaces in games-in-progress tend to be like that old beater car that you "just get used to." Some pieces don't work, some are unsafe, and some work sporadically. Nobody fixes them because early on the interface isn't priority and everyone adjusts around the broken bits. The problem is when developers end up at E3 or a publisher evaluation with the jalopy. We see it all the time.

Iterate as much as you can. Get a working interface going first and keep refining it. Change up the basic assumptions and conventions when the gameplay changes (even though everyone howls). Many games with significant interface problems just failed to evolve the interface when the experience changed during development.

Quality Assurance

Typically, *quality assurance* (QA) does not dedicate a specific person to interface testing. Instead, QA tests aspects of the game by system or functionality. For example, a tester might be assigned to the game's combat system or character customization system. Since interfaces are tied to functionality, testing every system of the game results in QA being exposed to all aspects of the interface.

Furthermore, the interface is a very exposed aspect of the design; any serious flaws are generally obvious to even the untrained player. However, some aspects of interface design are more subtle—and a test plan that specifically includes interface issues will result in a more consistent and polished interface. Finally, besides just finding bugs, a good QA team will also identify problems with the interface's design.

Illustration by Ben Bourbon

Quality assurance is the last line of defense against a poor interface design.

Troy Dunniway on the Interface Design Process

Troy Dunniway is an award-winning, seasoned game designer, director, and artist with over 15 years of industry experience. Prior to joining Midway, he was Lead Designer at Insomniac Games—where he worked on *Ratchet Deadlock* for the Sony PS2. Troy has also worked at Ubisoft, Electronic Arts, Westwood Studios, and Microsoft. He has shipped dozens of action, platformer, fighting, flying, RTS, FPS, and RPG games for almost every console platform and the PC. Troy has also written dozens of articles on game design.

Without the right tools, any kind of game interface can be difficult to implement. Being able to quickly prototype, implement, change, and refine the interface is difficult with most tools. So, the needs for each project and each company will vary widely from project to project. The more complicated the interface, the tougher it is to implement.

Troy Dunniway (Lead Game Designer, Midway Los Angeles)

chapter 8 Process of Interface Design: how interfaces are created

When designing an interface, you must constantly ask yourself if each aspect of the interface is needed. If it's not really needed, then get rid of it, minimize it, or make it disappear when it's not important. You have to worry about functionality first.

It is often important to think about how the interface is balanced on the screen, arranged, or grouped. Some games have gotten away with throwing the entire interface into one small corner of the screen or have random interface components spread all over. This often isn't the best route to take because the interface will never feel integrated.

Every game has different needs. For some games, such as *The Legend of Zelda: The Wind Waker,* the game interface is truly just that: an interface set over a virtual world, and one that reminds you constantly that you are playing a game. Other games such as *Star Wars: Republic Commando* try to explain the interface and justify it as some kind of HUD, VISOR, or other interface that you are really using as part of your adventure. Regardless of the game, you need to come up with a good theme and use it to the fullest.

Common Mistakes in Game Interface Design

The most common mistake I have seen is a tendency of developers to present the end user with too many choices too early in the game. Many developers want to expose everything to the end user as they feel that most want more choice in how the game is configured. For hardcore gamers and for the development team, this might be a great thing, but for someone new to the game, it is overwhelming. Players initially have no idea what the difference is between, say, 20 different weapons in a game. If they are introduced to everything all at once, with no explanation, it makes them feel powerless and stupid.

Another mistake I have seen is when the developers either intentionally or unintentionally ignore existing interface standards and make it confusing for the player to navigate. If an interface exists for a particular type of functionality, the developers should understand it and use it in a way that should be intuitive to the end user. In some genres, certain interface standards have become so commonplace that not adhering to them would be marketplace suicide.

Both of these mistakes have a root cause. The root cause is often that the designer of the game has an idea of how he/she wants players to interact with the game and has not put enough thought into how they actually interact with the game (or has not done enough testing to understand the issues involved).

Joe Maruschak
(Creative Director, GarageGames)

Interface Design Pipeline and Methodology

A *pipeline* is a process by which some task is completed. One logical pipeline for interface design is described below—although others are certainly possible depending upon the nature of the company, the game being created, and the project's overall timetable.

The nature of game development requires that interface design be approached in an *iterative* fashion. That is, the interface will be revised numerous times throughout the duration of the project. Game development tends to be very "organic"—with various elements of the design or project changing as it progresses. A new feature might be desired or a planned feature might not be working out. If the game uses a licensed engine, some features promised by the company making the game engine might not be implemented in time—forcing aspects of the game to be changed. The project might be progressing too slowly, causing content or features to be cut so that the game will be ready on time.

Interface design is especially vulnerable to the often chaotic process of game development because an interface is one of the first components needed and one of the last ones that can be evaluated. Some sort of interface is required very early on in a project in order to test and experiment with any aspect of the game—but until all of a game's features have been finalized and implemented, it's not practical to assess how good the interface is. Like many aspects of game development, it is generally best to attempt to fully design the interface, with the knowledge that it will change and evolve as the project continues.

Game interface design typically begins with the establishment of the functional needs of the interface. What can the player do? From these functional needs, a designer creates an IDD, which also contains specs related to the design's usability and accessibility.

> **I**f it's not needed, get it off the screen!
>
> *Tim Donley*
> *(Producer, Bottlerocket Entertainment)*

> **I**nterface design for truly 3D games is the hardest. How do you provide players with ready control over motion in three dimensions?
>
> *Frank Gilson*
> *(Senior Developer for Online Games, Wizards of the Coast)*

> **T**he real balancing act in game interface design is between information that is always needed and information that is only intermittently required.
>
> *Stieg Hedlund*
> *(Lead Designer, Perpetual Entertainment)*

Prototyping

A *prototype* is a minimal implementation designed to demonstrate that a certain technology, gameplay structure, or other feature works and will be an asset to the game. The term "prototype" is often used interchangeably with "demo"— though the latter is usually for public consumption, while prototypes are primarily a tool for the developer. Whenever an aspect of a game involves significant risk, it is beneficial to develop a prototype. Since prototypes are a minimal implementation, they allow you to see how an idea will work before investing a tremendous amount of effort in it. Prototyping is also applicable to interface design. In particular, when you are creating an interface for an innovative game feature, developing a prototype allows you to test your design with minimal expense. Remember that the interface plays a critical role in how enjoyable a game is to play. Without a functional interface, it will be impossible to accurately ascertain how well the system you are prototyping works.

Paper Prototyping

As a first step in the development of an interface, "paper prototyping" can be a great process as it is very low cost and quite dynamic. Your subject has to use imagination a little, and it can get a little messy with scissors and glue, but it can be quite beneficial.

Timothy Nixon
(Founder & Creative Director, Straylight Studios)

After the designer has created the IDD, it is reviewed by the programmer—who considers how each aspect of the interface might be implemented. The programmer's job is two-fold. First, the programmer must determine how the interface will be incorporated into the game. If any element of the interface appears too time-consuming or technologically demanding to implement, the programmer will work with the designer to find alternatives. Second, the programmers evaluate the design's usability, serving as a second opinion on whether or not the interface is well-designed.

After the programmer and designer have reached an agreement, an artist reviews the design. Is the layout aesthetically appealing? Would any elements of the interface break the player's immersion or damage the overall feel of the game? While the designer should have taken these matters into consideration in the original design, it can be beneficial to have an artist's feedback as well.

The programmer then creates a mock-up interface that is functionally correct and usable, but without any accompanying artwork. At this point, the interface is tested thoroughly by designers and then quality assurance. The goal

Diagram by Per Olin

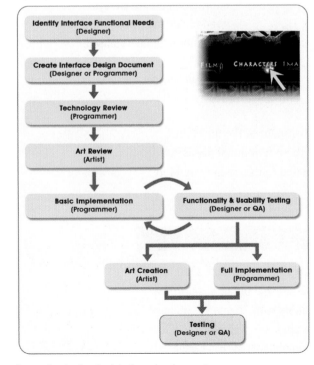

A sample pipeline for interface development.

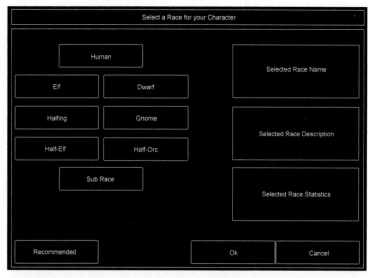

A mock-up interface (top), and a completed interface (bottom) from *Neverwinter Nights*.

is to analyze the interface's usability. Is it easy to use? In what ways can it frustrate the player? The interface is modified until it appears to be optimally usable and functional.

At this stage, the aesthetics of the interface are fully developed. Any changes to the interface will require art changes, so waiting until the interface has been well-tested to create the artwork saves resources. After the artist has created the artwork needed for the interface, the programmer incorporates it into the game and the interface is complete. The final interface is tested in QA along with other game features.

I prefer games with zero visual interface elements, or something as close to this as possible. I love games that present themselves as seamless portals into some interesting, richly detailed world.

Harvey Smith
(Studio Creative Director, Midway Studios-Austin)

Less Is Best

I believe that the most common interface design mistake is to keep all the information on the screen that the player may ever need. The interface should only be there when the player needs it to be there and be off the screen when they don't. Any interface that pulls the player out of the game experience needs to be reevaluated.

John Comes
(Lead Content Engineer, Gas Powered Games)

Don't Wait Too Long

The most common interface mistake that developers make is waiting too long to design the interface. By the end of the project it's often too late to make many changes. Doing simple interface wireframes and concept art during pre-production is key.

Nicole Lazzaro
(Founder & President, XEODesign, Inc.)

Interface Design Document

An *interface design document (IDD)* is intended to communicate an interface's details to the programmer and artist who will implement and create it. Typically written by a designer, a well-organized IDD will ensure that the interface meets the desired specifications. The IDD also aids in finding any flaws in the interface design by forcing the designer to fully consider the implications of their decisions.

Purpose of Interface Design Documents

As with all aspects of the game development process, documentation is very important to interface design. While it takes additional time to write and maintain good design documentation, the general belief is that ultimately time is saved by taking this additional step.

Good documentation serves two primary purposes. First, it helps designers organize their thoughts and thus fully design whatever aspect of the game they are describing. By describing all aspects of an interface, the designers must consider how its various components interact.

Second, it communicates the design to the other team members. With a strong design document, it is much more likely that the interface will be implemented as the designer intended. When ideas are only verbally communicated, it is easier for people to forget details or to misinterpret what was said. Furthermore, documentation is useful for new team members or those who were not present during any initial discussions of a particular design.

Integrate Interface into Gameplay

Ask yourself constantly, "Can the player be shown this information in any other way? In any simpler way?" The more you can make the interface part of gameplay, the better. For example, many FPSs use the simple convention of showing your character reloading his gun when he runs out of ammo. That is about as simple as it gets when it comes to interface feedback.

Tim Donley
(Producer, Bottlerocket Entertainment)

Document Format

An IDD should use the same format as other technical design documents for the project. One possible format would be to include the following components:

- Summary: A brief description of the contents of the document.
- Revision History: A log of significant changes made to the document. Whenever the document is edited, a comment is added to the revision history that indicates the date, the person making the edits, and the basic nature of the changes made.
- Table of Contents
- Body: The description of the system, interface, level, and other game features being designed.

The remainder of this section discusses the components that should be included in the body of an IDD.

Avoid Information Overload

Presenting too much information and features to players all at once causes many players to give up on a game. Instead designers should either simplify features to a core set or gradually introduce advanced features as players master the beginner ones. For many players, especially new ones, that first hour of play makes all the difference between loving a game and leaving it.

Nicole Lazzaro
(Founder & President, XEODesign, Inc.)

Information overload is the number one big mistake, especially with long text on tutorial screens. Tutorials screens should contain very little text, and simple, well-designed tutorial illustrations. Some players don't read in-game text, so the only hope that you have in getting through to them is through clear and immediate tutorial illustrations. Try and make them as exciting as possible as well. A still, flat graphic isn't nearly as exciting and engaging as an animated, highly stylised introduction piece with matching voice-over.

Timothy Nixon
(Founder & Creative Director, Straylight Studios)

Diagram by Per Olin

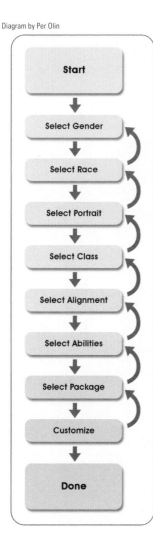

A sample interface flowchart for character creation in *Neverwinter Nights*.

Interface Flowchart

The purpose of an interface can often be described in a mere sentence or two. For example, the description of the Race Selection screen in an RPG such as *Neverwinter Nights* might be: The Race Selection screen allows the player to choose the race (dwarf, human, elf, etc.) of their character. Yet the detailed explanation of how this interface should work spans several pages!

While this level of detail is necessary to successfully implement an interface, it is cumbersome for the reader to comprehend and evaluate. The interface flowchart is a graphical depiction of an interface's functionality that bridges the gap between the one-sentence purpose of an interface and its lengthy, detailed description. Each screen of the interface is represented by a box, with arrows indicating how different interface screens and elements relate to one another.

The "Too Many Steps" Problem

One common game interface mistake involves the "too many steps" problem. User interfaces often contain unnecessary screens or button presses. Interfaces need proper design, layout, and testing just like any other software feature. Make sure to include usability testing when designing a game interface.

Frank Gilson
(Senior Developer for Online Games, Wizards of the Coast)

Interface Mock-up

An interface mock-up is a quick sample that illustrates the interface's layout and proportions. The mock-up aids the designer in communicating to the artist what the interface should look like from a usability perspective.

Typically, a mock-up does not attempt to illustrate any aesthetics, since this is the domain of art, not design. A mock-up is important because it demonstrates how all of the controls and feedback will be presented to the player. If an interface is attempting to convey too much information, the mock-up will often make this problem clear.

A sample interface mock-up.

Using Style Guides

From a visual perspective, the most important activity in ensuring a slick design and interface is the development of "style guides." These are essentially rules that dictate how the interface should look and feel. They usually contain color and font directions, logo/icon guides and examples, element spacing and balance rules, and other guides concerning the number of objects on screen seen at once.

Timothy Nixon
(Founder & Creative Director, Straylight Studios)

Interface Technical Specifications

While the flowchart and mock-up provide the graphical representation of an interface, the technical specifications explain all of the details required to implement it. These include what happens when any button is pressed or moused over and when information is updated.

Unfortunately, creativity, time, and money aren't the only constraints on game developers. Technical limitations can render some of the otherwise best ideas worthless. For consoles, the technical limitations are well-known, since all players will have the same processing power, video RAM, and more. For computers, the technical limitations are less clear because each computer has different capabilities. Regardless of the assumed technical limitations for a computer game, some players will find it running slowly on their systems—while others will have excess computer power that you aren't utilizing. For console systems, some interface aspects—such as how controller buttons are referred to by the game—must meet detailed specifications set by the manufacturer. Terms such as TCR or TRC refer to this type of requirement.

A detailed discussion of technical constraints is outside of the scope of this text, but keep in mind that they could play a role in the interface design process. For example, each texture you use in an interface requires some memory, and complicated animated sequences may also cause problems—especially if they can occur when the game is already requiring many resources, such as during combat. Always look for ways to keep anything you create as manageable as possible. An object that the player never sees close-up can, for example, be created with many fewer polygons than one that the player can examine in detail.

Avoid Clutter & Complexity

A common interface design mistake is clutter: when the interface demands your attention more than the gameplay itself. I am a big fan of clean interfaces that are visually unobtrusive and fairly intuitive to use during gameplay. To that end, I really appreciate the lack of interface with *Ico* as well as the new *King Kong* game.

Drew Davidson
(Faculty, Entertainment Technology Center, Carnegie Mellon University)

Players don't have time to scan an interface that is very complicated while trying to play an action game of any kind. If you keep up tons of interface, mini-maps, objectives, and other information on the screen while the player is trying to play, it becomes information overload for most players—causing lack of understanding and frustration. If the information on the interface isn't immediately needed, it is best to make it disappear somehow.

Troy Dunniway
(Lead Game Designer, Midway Los Angeles)

The Race Selection screen for *Neverwinter Nights* is part of the character creation process.

For this book, we have created a sample Race Selection Screen based on our *Neverwinter Nights* example. Note that this is just one screen within the character creation interface diagram shown in the previous section. The Race Selection Screen:

- allows players to select the race of their characters during the character creation process.
- consists of an immobile window, shown over the MainMenuBackground.
- is accessed by clicking the Race button on the Character Creation Screen.
- accesses the Character Creation Screen when Buttons 4 or 5 are activated.
- accesses the Sub Race Dialogue when Button 2 is activated.

When this screen is accessed from the Character Creation Screen, the following code is activated:

$raceSelected = if **!$player.Race** then **$recommendedRace**
　　　　　　　else
　　　　　　　$player.Race

Text Areas

Text areas are shown in the figure as lettered blue circles.

A. Title Bar

Contents: **windowTitle**
Initial Value: "Select a Race for your Character"

B. Selected Race Name

Contents: Plural form of Selected Race
Initial Value: if **!$player.race** then "Races"
else
textPlural($player.race.name)

C. Race Help Text

Contents: Help text for Selected Race
Initial Value: if **!$player.race** then **helpText("Races")** else
helpText($player.race.name)

Buttons

Buttons are shown in the figures as numbered orange circles. When the mouse pointer is within any button on the interface:

- While the left mouse button is depressed, the text within the activated button is shifted downward by **activatedButtonTextOffset** pixels.
- When the left-mouse button is released, if it had been depressed while the mouse pointer was within the button, the button is activated and **whenActivated** is triggered.

1. Race Selection Buttons

Purpose: These buttons allow the player to select character race. They also show the currently selected race.

At all times, **length(race[])** Race Selection Buttons are shown. The contents of Button 1 is **$race[i].name.** If **length(race[])** is even, then buttons are paired horizontally. If **length(race[])** is odd, then the first button is centered, with the remaining buttons paired horizontally (shown).

Exactly one Race Selection Button is selected at any given time. The selected button uses a different background.

Initially, the button corresponding to **$player.race** is selected. If **$player.race** is undefined, then the button corresponding to **$recommendedRace** is selected.

The race corresponding to the selected button is the **$raceSelected.**

Contents of button 1: **$race[i].name**

whenActivated:

- This button is selected.
- **$raceSelected** = race corresponding to the selected Race Selection Button.
- The previously selected Race Selection Button is deselected unless it is the same as the selected button.
- **textPlural($raceSelected.name)** is displayed in Text Area 2.
- **helpText($raceSelected.name)** is displayed in Text Area 3.
- Sound **menuButtonActivated** is played.

2. Sub Race Button

Purpose: Allows players to name the races of their characters. The statistics for this custom race are the same as those of the Selected Race. The Sub Race Button is located below the last Race Selection Button and is centered horizontally.

Contents: "Sub Race"

whenMouseover: Button border is replaced with the mouseover button border.

whenActivated:

- **$player.Race = $raceSelected**
- The Sub Race Dialog appears and becomes the active window. (See corresponding documentation {not included in this example}.)

3. Recommended Button

Purpose: Selects the recommended (easiest) race for the player.
Contents: "Recommended"

whenMouseover: Button border is replaced with the mouseover button border.

whenActivated:

- **$raceSelected = $recommendedRace**
- The corresponding Race Selection Button is selected.
- **textPlural($raceSelected.name)** is displayed in Text Area 2.
- **helpText($raceSelected.name)** is displayed in Text Area 3.
- Sound **menuButtonActivated** is played.
- The Recommended Button's background is changed to the **selectedButtonBackground** for **showButtonActivatedFrames** frames.

4. OK Button

Purpose: Sets character's race and returns to Character Creation Screen.
whenMouseover: Button border is replaced with the mouseover button border.

whenActivated:

- ■ **$player.race** = **$raceSelected**
- ■ Sound **menuButtonActivated** is played.
- ■ Race Selection Screen is closed and player returns to Character Creation Screen.

5. Cancel Button

Purpose: Returns to Character Creation Screen without changing the player's race.

whenMouseover: Button border is replaced with the mouseover button border.

whenActivated:

- ■ Sound **menuButtonActivated** is played.
- ■ Race Selection Screen in closed and player returns to Character Creation Screen.

Assumptions include:

- ■ **textPlural($string):** returns the plural form of **$string** or **concatenate($string,"s")** if no plural form is specified. Capitalization is retained (e.g., plural of "Elf" is "Elves," plural of "elf" is "elves").
- ■ **helpText($string):** returns the help text associated with **$string.**
- ■ **$player** is an object containing all player information.
- ■ **race[]** = array of the available races. A race is an object that contains the statistics related to a race.
- ■ **$player.race, $selectedRace** and **$recommendedRace** are also race objects.
- ■ **selectedButtonBackground** refers to the graphic used for a selected button.
- ■ **showButtonActivatedFrames** is the number of frames a button appears selected for when it is activated.
- ■ After a button is activated, **whenMouseover** is false unless the mouse is moved off of and back onto the button.
- ■ Contents for a button is the text displayed within the button on the screen.
- ■ Button dimensions and acceptable distances apart are standardized.

Don't Fill the Vacuum

Game designers make one major interface mistake repeatedly: People fill up the control surface just because it's there. Their features expand to fill the vacuum. If the control has 24 buttons, they use them all. In reality, maybe the game is only really centered around four or so inputs from the player to the world.

Harvey Smith
(Studio Creative Director, Midway Studios-Austin)

Streamlining the Process

You'd expect game interfaces to be well designed and perfect for the job they're created for, but unfortunately, some fall short of the mark. The ability to navigate through both game features and the gameplay environment are the most important elements of an interface and I don't know how many times I haven't been able to access certain features or would have to dig too deep in a menu system to accomplish something—it can be very frustrating! I think something as simple as allowing a player to access the most often used features of a game easily can streamline the process and let the player actually enjoy the game more. This includes everything from the onscreen interface and menu system, hot keys assigned to a keyboard/mouse interface for PC games, to specifically designed handheld controllers with appropriate buttons, triggers, or joysticks. Get it right and the player will love you for it!

Aaron Marks
(President, On Your Mark Music Productions)

Chris Avellone on Common Interface Design Mistakes

Chris Avellone wanted to make computer role-playing games (RPGs) ever since he saw one of his friends playing *Bard's Tale 2* on a Commodore. He went to the College of William and Mary where he got a piece of paper that claims he has a Bachelor's degree in English. He started writing a bunch of short stories and RPG material after graduation—some of which got published. (Most of it didn't.) The submissions that were accepted were enough to get him hired at Interplay, and he worked there for 8 years before co-founding Obsidian Entertainment with a bunch of other ex-Interplayers and ex-Black Islanders who'd also worked there a long time. Chris has worked on *Starfleet Academy, Die by the Sword, Conquest of the New World, Red Asphalt, Planescape: Torment, Fallout 2, Icewind Dale 1, Icewind Dale: Heart of Winter, Icewind Dale: Trials of the Luremaster, Icewind Dale 2, Baldur's Gate: Dark Alliance, Lionheart, Champions of Norrath,* and *Star Wars Knights of the Old Republic II: The Sith Lords.* He is currently a designer on *Neverwinter Nights 2.* Chris's mom still isn't exactly clear on what he does on a day-to-day basis, and neither is he.

Chris Avellone
(Chief Creative Officer & Lead Designer, Obsidian Entertainment)

One major interface design mistake is not identifying frequently used options and making them easily accessible on the console controller or with a single mouse-click in a PC game. Another is not recognizing the localization issues in a game interface that may pop up later on when you're trying to translate the game into other languages. What may fit nicely on the screen in English may not fit when the game is translated into German and you're suddenly presented with a word that's five times longer than what the interface can handle.

Along the same lines, embedding any actual text into a game interface screen as part of the *art* instead of part of the *code* usually causes the same localization problems. It's hard enough to do foreign language versions of a game. However, if you have to redo the art for a game interface, too—in 10–12 different version for 5–6 screens—you're asking for headaches, especially if you're going for a simultaneous worldwide release. That's generally why Obsidian's a big fan of icon-driven game interfaces with pop-up tool tip text. This is very easy to localize and for anyone in any language to understand.

Sometimes designers have the urge to reinvent the wheel with the interface for a new game, and I think this can work against them. Part of an interface's success comes from people recognizing the layout from previous games and other similar games within the same genre and being comfortable with it. If you make them learn a brand new set of rules for the sequel or the same genre with much of the same conventions just for the hell of it, you're throwing up another obstacle to them playing. In general, I say reinvent the interface only when you feel it's necessary to enhance the gameplay experience—never do it just for the sake of change.

For PC games, a poorly designed (and coded) installation screen is also a killer. If it isn't as user-friendly as possible (for example, auto-detects for hardware and video cards), then you've just thrown up an obstacle to the user right there. Don't make it hard for people to play your game.

Usability Testing

Due to the complexity of interface design, it is necessary to thoroughly test an interface's effectiveness. The two main methods used to test interfaces are internal testing by designers and quality assurance, and focus group testing by players outside of the development process.

Internal Testing

terative testing is the true path to a great interface.

Bob Mitchell
(Senior Programmer, Sony
Online Entertainment)

Internal testing involves using quality assurance to determine that the interface accomplishes everything it needs to. As with any organized, trained testing, interface testing requires a detailed test plan. Designers are also well-suited to test the interface for usability. Also, because the interface is a very "exposed" aspect of the game, all members of the team will be able to evaluate and comment on it.

Focus Groups

A focus group test involves getting a group of people who have not been involved in developing a game to playtest it. These testers could be family and friends of employees or even team members who are less involved in the gameplay and design, such as producers or artists. Ideally, a focus group would be done with those outside of the company, but organizing such a test can require a good deal of energy and is only practical for large projects. While companies can be contracted to conduct focus group testing, be careful when selecting one. Some are not familiar with the actual factors that affect game entertainment value and sales and their findings may not be accurate.

Illustration by Ben Bourbon

Testing is an important aspect of interface design.

Observing new people try a game can point out problems that otherwise can be very difficult for developers to find. Even a poorly designed interface can become easy to use if one spends enough time with it. This fact can cause problems as developers become accustomed to their own interface mistakes, which renders them unable to see the problems. Focus group testing can overcome this type of blindness by exposing an interface or gameplay system to players who are completely unfamiliar with it.

Timing

One dilemma of focus group testing involves when it should be performed. Focus groups are only useful if they are conducted early enough in development to allow changes to be made. But early in development, a game's systems and graphics might be too rudimentary to provide the tester with an accurate representation of what the game will really be like. For example, if a focus group tests a game with many bugs, they

Testing from the Outside

Focus groups and field testing outside of the company is paramount! Anyone who designs an interface is too close to the project to really stay objective about it. A fresh set of eyes and hands will focus more on the functionality and ergonomics of a unit like the player will, independently and without office politics. You can do it without these steps but to really make the consumer happy, I'm a firm believer in bringing in the outside help.

Aaron Marks
(President, On Your Mark Music Productions)

will not enjoy the experience. It may be difficult to determine which problems they find are due to any design errors and which are simply because the game is unpolished.

One general guideline is to only use a stable version of the game for focus group testing. Everything that the testers are exposed to should work as intended, even if not as fleshed out as it eventually will be. If possible, conduct focus group tests at multiple points in development. After a working prototype is developed is a good time for the first focus group tests. Be careful to weigh this feedback carefully, however, as the early state of your game might be part of the reason for any problems that the testers encounter.

For the purpose of evaluating an interface, late focus group testing can still be valuable. Many aspects of an interface are easy to change, even late in development. For example, if testers are getting confused because of how some commands are attached to certain buttons, it is a trivial programming task to change those bindings.

Tester Supervision

Always have team members, probably producers or game designers, observe the testers. If you rely only on written or verbal summaries from the testers, you will often not get a good picture of what the true problems are. However, by watching them and observing their frustration and excitement firsthand, you will gain a much better insight as to how to solve any problems.

Criticism

One rule of thumb to keep in mind is that "the focus group tester is always right." If testers are confused or frustrated, then something is wrong with the design—and it should be fixed. It is easy to blame the tester for not understanding something that seems simple, but the bottom line is that if a tester doesn't understand, then many of your players won't either. Confusion and frustration are not a matter of opinion. They are valid reactions that you do not wish your players to experience. Be especially open to any criticism offered by more than one person.

While the primary purpose of focus groups is to identify problems, focus groups can reveal positive aspects as well. If testers are especially entertained by a specific aspect of the game, consider expanding upon it. For example, if your game includes graphical customization of the main character (such as hair color and style) and you find your testers spending considerable time on choosing their appearance, you might want to add more of that element to the game.

Nicole Lazzaro on the Interface Testing Process

Nicole Lazzaro is an award-winning interface designer and an authority on emotion and the player experience. A frequent speaker at industry events, she writes extensively on games and why people play them. She has spent more than 15 years designing successful experiences for all levels of players and users, from novice to expert, in many game genres. Her work on the emotional and cultural content of play has improved the player experience for more than 40 million people and helped expand the game industry's emotional palette beyond the stereotypical range of anger, frustration, and fear. Nicole founded XEODesign in 1992 to bring her expertise in player-experience research and design to the mass-market entertainment and consumer-creativity industries. Her clients have included Sony, LeapFrog, Mattel, Sega, PlayFirst, Monolith, The Learning Company, Xfire, Broderbund, Roxio, Ubisoft, and Maxis. Her ground-breaking research on "Why We Play Games: 4 Keys to More Emotion Without Story" has generated phenomenal interest. Prior to her fascination with player experiences and games she worked in film and earned a degree in Psychology from Stanford University.

Nicole Lazzaro
(Founder & President,
XEODesign, Inc.)

Player feedback is essential to delivering a play experience with a wide range of appeal. Game interface features should be tested for usability. If the art interferes with operating the interface, the art will need to be toned down to make the interface more usable. Some aspects are part of the challenge and should be frustrating, other aspects such as saving a game should be easy. Hiring an interface designer and working out the interface early on in the project saves time and money. If the interface is not clear in a black and white wire frame, it will not become easier to use by adding art.

Too many people confuse user testing with market testing. To improve the functionality of the interface it is very important to watch people who haven't seen your game play for the first time unassisted. Talking with players seated around a table (as in a marketing focus group), if done well, can answer questions about packaging, price, and positioning. However, this style of testing will yield very little data on *player experiences:* what it feels like to play your game.

My advice to others is to bring in people from your target market and watch them play. While they play don't provide help. Instead give them a card with a basic description of the game and watch to see how much they can discover on their own. Pay attention to how they do so. In looking at your results don't let players design your game. (That's the game designer's job.) Do listen to what they have to say, and note what they try to do and how they try to do it. These are clues to increasing usability. Pay attention to what they find fun or not fun. Look for patterns in their needs and interests. If I'm not completely surprised by at least one thing in a study, I run the study again.

Also, never run your own observation sessions. Watch them; but don't be there in the same room. You'd be surprised at how easy it is to influence the player. I have someone else run observations on my own designs. The insights of a neutral third party are highly valuable. Plus they will come up with angles on your design that you hadn't thought of, and others you've forgotten about. Be sure to watch the observations, preferably in person. Don't just rely on the report. Player experiences are qualitative and happen over time. You'll get a deeper visceral understanding of a player's pains and joys by being there.

In this chapter, you learned the process through which interfaces are designed, documented, and tested. In the next and final chapter, you will put together all of the knowledge you've learned by developing an interface for a hypothetical game.

:::CHAPTER REVIEW:::

1. Take a single screen from any game and write an IDD for it. Follow the example in this chapter to create your document.

2. Create a production plan for the interfaces associated with your original game idea. Discuss the roles and responsibilities of team members, the production pipeline, and methodologies. Pay special attention to the prototyping process.

3. Create a test plan for the interfaces associated with your original game idea to ensure the effectiveness of your interfaces. What method would you use to test your interfaces? What guidelines would you have your testers follow?

4. What are 5 common interface design mistakes? How will you avoid making these mistakes when you develop your original interfaces?

5. Choose 2 interfaces from your original game idea (such as HUD, character creation, inventory, main menu) and create an IDD incorporating both interfaces. Make sure you include all the necessary components—including flowcharts, mockups, and technical specifications.

CHAPTER

9

Prototype Interface Design:
putting it all together

key chapter questions

- Is it possible to create any style of interface for any given platform?

- How are control and feedback schemes guidelines put to use?

- How might the interface for an unconventional genre and platform combination be designed?

- What are the most important tools to use when designing a game interface?

- What types of game interfaces might be used in the next 5, 10, or 20 years?

Throughout this text, you've learned a great deal about interface design. In this final chapter, you will bring together all of your knowledge to develop a game interface. Most of the examples throughout this book have concentrated on mainstream games and interface conventions. While it is critical to understand what is currently being used, the next step in expanding your interface design abilities is to apply this general knowledge to an unusual design. In this chapter, we'll be exploring the interface for a unique game: a real-time strategy (RTS) game for the Nintendo DS.

Various quotations and tips from industry professionals also appear throughout this chapter that express thoughts on the future of interface design. Through these quotations, you'll see how many industry experts see this dynamic field progressing. Do you agree with their thoughts on the future? How do you feel interface design will grow and evolve?

Illustration by Ben Bourbon

Interface Design for Caesar's Quest

Caesar's Quest (CQ), a hypothetical game discussed in *Game Story & Character Development* (part of the *Game Development Essentials* series) by Marianne Krawczyk and Jeannie Novak, is an RTS that takes place during Caesar's rise to power within the Roman Empire. The basic game concept and backstory are discussed below. In this chapter, we'll be designing the interface for *CQ*. Developing this interface will require that we flesh out many aspects of the game's design as well. Keep in mind that our development of *CQ* focuses on how unusual interface design challenges can be met.

While customizable interfaces have existed for a long time, truly adaptive interfaces still have a long way to go. Artificial intelligence will assist the player as well as guide enemy character behavior. Ultimately we are heading toward experiences which truly "wrap" themselves around our personality—first simply by interpreting the way we play the game, and eventually truly sensing our intention far quicker than we could possibly hope to manipulate using a game pad.

—Timothy Nixon
(Founder & Creative Director, Straylight Studios)

Game Design Documentation Elements

The following is a list of relevant game design documentation elements associated with the hypothetical game, *Caesar's Quest (CQ)*, discussed in *Game Story & Character Development*:

Genre

The genre for this game will be *real-time strategy (RTS)*.

Theme

The game's theme will focus on *conquest*.

Historical Context

The game will take place in 52 B.C. Italy—centering around historical events that occurred during that time and place.

Setting

The game's setting will be the Ancient Roman Empire

Premise

You are the young, ambitious General Julius Caesar—and you have just crossed the Rubicon River to start a civil war in the greatest empire of all time: Rome. Your hated enemy, Pompey the Great, was given the power to control and protect all of Rome because his troops far outnumber yours. Permission from the Roman Senate backed by numerous legions prove a difficult match for your ambitious nature—but nothing compared to the tide of your destiny.

Backstory

In 71 B.C., Pompey the Great returned victorious to Rome after having put down a threatening rebellion in Spain. At the same time, Marcus Licinius Crassus, a rich patrician, suppressed the slave revolt led by Spartacus. Pompey and Crassus both ran for the consulship—an office held by two men—in 70 B.C. Pompey, who was ineligible for consulship, somehow still managed to win with the help of Julius Caesar. Crassus became the other consul. Ten years later when Caesar returned to Rome, Caesar joined forces with Crassus and Pompey in a three-way alliance known as the First Triumvirate. Caesar gave his daughter, Julia, to Pompey in marriage—an act of goodwill—but soon the Roman Senate became leery of Caesar's lust for power. They sent him to conquer Gaul, thereby keeping him out of Rome and Roman politics. When Crassus was killed in battle in 53 B.C., the Senate instated Pompey the Great to rule all of Rome—an idea that did not sit well with the ambitious Julius Caesar.

Synopsis

On the foggy banks of the Rubicon River, Julius Caesar—formerly one of the three leaders of Rome—keeps watch at the head of his small legion of soldiers. With a single word, he commands the troops across the water and thus hurls the empire into a turbulent civil war while civilization itself hangs in the balance. In order to defeat his enemy, Pompey, Caesar acts swiftly and decisively by placing his men throughout Northern Italy—while Pompey gathers his numerous but far-flung legions. City after city is conquered—town after town falling to Caesar. Many cities fall without resistance until Rome herself lay at risk. Within weeks, the Senate and Pompey evacuate Rome—leaving in their wake the bloody warning that any who stay within the city will be considered Caesar's ally and Pompey's enemy. Pompey's retreat eastward is a strategic one, since his intent is to draw Caesar to Asia where Pompey has many allies in the form of powerful kingdoms. Unfortunately for Pompey, during the scramble to evacuate Rome, he and the senators forget to take the vast amounts of treasure stored under the temple of Saturn. Caesar is quick to discover the plunder, which significantly increases his war purse. For another six months, Caesar relentlessly pursues Pompey, eventually crushing the last of his armies in Spain. The defeated Senate has no choice but to instate Caesar as head consul and dictator of all of Rome.

Levels

Since this game is about the progression of Caesar's attempt to take over Rome, perhaps a more linear progression would help keep the player focused directly toward the goal. As players reach new towns and settlements, they will be able to gather resources either by trade, force, or politics.

Allowing for player choice is essential—so the player should be able to choose whether to play Caesar (with fewer, but consolidated, resources) or Pompey (with greater, but scattered, resources). If the player chooses to play Pompey, gameplay will begin at an entirely different level—and the player will need to work backward to meet Caesar and try to stop him before he has gained too much ground. Again, management of resources and strategically placed troops are all part of the game.

Victory and Loss Conditions

CAESAR
Victory = Gaining control of the empire; Pompey's death
Loss = Death

POMPEY
Victory = Caesar's death
Loss = Losing control of the empire; death

Challenges

1. Build up forces.
2. Acquire more resources.
3. Attack the enemy, attempting to destroy enemy's resources and infrastructure.

Strategies

Now let's look at strategies for the second challenge just listed (acquire more resources):

1. Conquer a town by brute force, but be prepared to meet resistance; perhaps trade soldiers' lives for resources.
2. Cut deals with town officials, promising high positions in government after taking over.
3. Send in a small legion of bandits and steal goods from a town (although this is very un-Roman and would not inspire the respect and awe needed later when winning control of the empire).

Establishing Design Goals

In order to meet the particular limitations of the DS platform, we'll have to change *CQ*'s gameplay significantly from the RTS norm. Many standard RTS interface conventions must be abandoned to suit the platform. On the other hand, having two separate screens will be an asset to an RTS. These types of games often involve a lot of interfaces that aren't part of the action itself—but on a PC or console system, there is a strong desire to minimize the amount of space the interface consumes. For the DS, an entire second screen is available and can house the non-action interface elements.

From the details of how *CQ* will play, you'll note how the interface needs drive the game design. We can simplify the core elements of an RTS to involve:

- Real-time (as opposed to turn-based) combat
- Unit management (control of armies comprised of multiple troops)
- Resource management (armies created through resources that are points of contention among the players)

Caesar Game

Crossing the Rubicon River
Gameplay includes invade northern Italy, dominate small towns, gain their resources from small towns

Gain territory with newfound resources
Trade off resources for gain of land. Nearing Rome. Legions of Pompey show up - Opposes Player and his troops.

Player enters City of Rome
Opposition from Roman guard.

Player finds the Roman treasury
Buys more troops and resources. Pompey leaves the city.

Player pursues Pompey
Player eventually conquers all of Pompey's legions.

Player named Emperor and gains control of the empire.

In *Caesar's Quest*, all the action moves forward in a linear fashion.

The future of game interface design is the removal of the interface. As humans, we interact and 'interface' with the world every day. We turn door knobs to open doors, turn on light switches, look for doors to enter buildings, and look out windows to see outside. In current games, we are often constrained by being presented with the game interface in a way that we have to learn how to use. I think that this artificial way of how an 'interface' is constructed limits us.

—*Joe Maruschak*
(Creative Director, GarageGames)

Whatever changes we make to the typical RTS to create *CQ*, we want to ensure that these elements are still part of the game. Others might define RTSs in some other way (and some of those definitions might even make it impossible to create one for the DS), but this will serve as an RTS's requirements for the purposes of *CQ*'s design.

Throughout the design of *CQ*, the bottom (touch) screen will be referred to as the Primary Screen and the top screen as the Secondary Screen.

Interface First

It may seem strange to attempt to develop a game's interface before understanding details of the game design. Indeed, it is more common in the industry for the game design to be established first and then an interface developed to match it. Then, if the interface doesn't work, its design is improved upon. It is fairly uncommon for the game design to actually be changed due to interface problems. This can be a mistake and can result in a game that doesn't play well because the game design was ill-suited to the interface limitations associated with the platform. Many less-experienced designers view gameplay as the most important aspect of design, without necessarily realizing the critical role that interface has in establishing that particular gameplay. Experienced designers are able to begin with the game design while keeping interface restrictions in mind. Since our focus is on the interface and not game design per se, we'll examine the design from the perspective of interface.

© 2005 Stormregion Ltd.

Codename: Panzers, Phase II displays a side view of units and top-down view of the world.

To limit the scope of this illustration, *CQ* will be made as only a single-player game. *CQ* will utilize a top-down view of the terrain, with units viewed from the side so that they can be easily distinguished. This technique is used commonly in handheld and

Proposed character concepts for *Caesar's Quest* illustrate side views of units.

older games, such as the early Ultima games and Intelligent Systems' *Advance Wars* and *Fire Emblem* series. The reasons are due to a combination of limited processing power and limited screen size.

Mini-Map

The ability to quickly survey the battlefield is a critical element of RTS gameplay. *CQ*'s interface will have to meet this need to at least some extent.

The DS platform will serve *CQ* well, with the Secondary Screen being an obvious option for the mini-map and other supplemental information.

Unit Selection

Obviously, *CQ* must allow the player to select both individual units and groups of units. Double-click selection and box dragging are not practical options for the DS, however, since these are specifically mouse-driven conventions. Having only eight buttons and a D-pad limits *CQ*'s ability to define control groups— but this feature is critical if the player is to control any significant quantity of troops. For brevity, control groups will be referred to as "squads" in *CQ*.

Vivendi Universal Games, Inc.

The mini-map is a key interface component of an RTS such as *Empire Earth II.*

Command Queues and Waypoints

More advanced features such as command queues and waypoints might not be practical for *CQ*. They should be considered—but they are not as important as many of the other features.

chapter 9 Prototype Interface Design: putting it all together

Nintendo

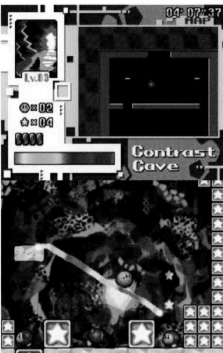

Kirby: Canvas Curse makes excellent use of the DS stylus.

Seeing how some of today's games utilize audio input from the player (shouting objections in *Phoenix Wright: Ace Attorney* or calling your pet in *Nintendogs*) or can be played solely with a stylus (*Kirby Canvas Curse*), a whole new set of interfaces can already make use of unique controllers. I think the future of game interfaces is a progression toward more and more "as soon as you think it, it happens" feedback and design. Anything that allows the player to react at the speed of thought without waiting for the impulse to travel to your finger, hand, or foot is generally a safe bet.

—Chris Avellone
(Chief Creative Officer & Lead
Designer, Obsidian Entertainment)

Static Interface

Recall from the discussion of RTS interfaces in Chapter 5 that a static interface is a common component in an RTS due to the quantity of information that must be conveyed. You've already learned that most RTS games used a horizontally oriented static interface along the bottom of the screen—while some used a vertically oriented one along the right-hand side. What is the best method of designing *CQ's* static interface?

The dual screen has a small viewing area, making it difficult to have a horizontal static interface that is large enough to be serviceable. Also, the 2D gameplay makes a square play area more appealing than a sharply rectangular one. These factors suggest that a *Command & Conquer*-style vertical interface design would be more appropriate. However, since the DS has two screens, we will instead try to keep the entire static interface off of the Primary Screen and on the Secondary Screen. This arrangement not only cleans up the Action Screen, but it also gives us a large amount of space for extra information.

DS-Specific Considerations

One of the innovative features of the DS is the option of using the stylus and touchpad to control the interface. This control scheme can work well for a game such as *Kirby: Canvas Curse,* in which the entire game is played with the stylus.

Art by Ian Robert Vasquez

Proposed main menu for *Caesar's Quest.*

Given the complexity of an RTS, however, it would be difficult to allow all the necessary controls without also using the D-pad and buttons. Using buttons in addition to the stylus can be very awkward because one of the player's hands is dedicated to holding the stylus. Therefore, we will not attempt to incorporate the touchpad and stylus into *CQ*'s interface controls. If we had included portions of the static interface on the touch screen, then we would have had an interesting option available to use: The stylus could be used to press buttons on the static interface itself.

> The future of game interface design involves moving closer and closer to the interfaces that we learn as children: cues tied to the five senses, and an intuitive representation of a phenomenon such as gravity.
>
> —Harvey Smith
> (Studio Creative Director,
> Midway Studios-Austin)

Developing the Control Scheme

The first aspect of the interface that we will examine is the game's control scheme. After establishing the systems and modes the game will use, we will develop the specific controls.

Identifying Systems and Modes

As you learned in Chapter 6, developing a proper control scheme requires an analysis of the interface's control requirements. We'll examine these requirements by outlining the game's systems and modes.

Identify Actions

The first step in this process is to identify the actions that the player can take. For *CQ*, these might include the actions listed in the accompanying diagram.

Notice that this list of actions is much shorter than the one we had for *Fairy Tale* in Chapter 6. There are a few reasons for this:

1. This list is not as detailed, with functions like loading and saving grouped together and various options unspecified. This is done to simplify this example. In general, it is best to break everything down as much as possible. While it may seem unnecessary, remember that eventually a programmer and artist will have to create every aspect of the interface—so detailing each will make their work easier and reduce the chance of error. If you can't specify every detail in documentation, how can you hope to implement completely?

Diagram by Per Olin

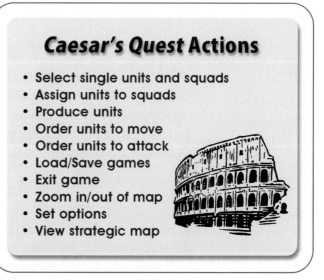

Caesar's Quest Actions

- Select single units and squads
- Assign units to squads
- Produce units
- Order units to move
- Order units to attack
- Load/Save games
- Exit game
- Zoom in/out of map
- Set options
- View strategic map

The actions the player can perform in *Caesar's Quest*.

Diagram by Per Olin

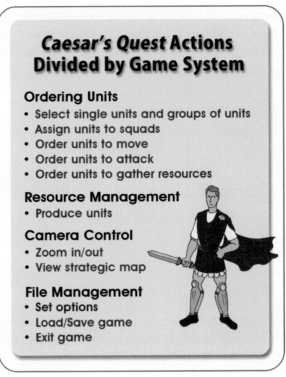

Caesar's Quest Actions Divided by Game System

Ordering Units
- Select single units and groups of units
- Assign units to squads
- Order units to move
- Order units to attack
- Order units to gather resources

Resource Management
- Produce units

Camera Control
- Zoom in/out
- View strategic map

File Management
- Set options
- Load/Save game
- Exit game

Four game systems cover the 11 player actions in *Caesar's Quest*.

2. The combat and movement controls are much simpler because it is a 2D strategy game instead of a 3D action-RPG.
3. The fact that we are designing the game for the DS has led us to a more limited scope, which naturally decreases the actions available.

Organize Actions by System

Now that the actions have been outlined, they should be organized by game system. Recall that each action should belong to only one system. After some consideration, it appears that we have four systems: ordering units, resource management, camera control, and file management. The systems would contain those actions as illustrated in the accompanying diagram.

Identify Modes

Having identified the systems for *CQ*, the next step is to define the game modes. Instead of considering the modes from a global perspective as we did with *Fairy Tale*, it might make sense to look at the modes per screen for this DS game.

Unlike a turn-based strategy game—which will often send players to other screens to help manage their empires—RTS games typically emphasize more action, and they always show the battlefield. *CQ* will follow this design philosophy and have the Primary Screen focus on the action at all times. However, the Secondary Screen will serve multiple purposes. The modes for *CQ* could then be:

Primary Screen:

- Action

Secondary Screen:

- Combat Information
- Administration

With this setup, the Combat Information mode is the equivalent of the Action mode for the Secondary Screen. However, when thinking critically about this arrangement, a problem becomes apparent. Though we are using both screens to provide feedback to the player, we still only have one set of controls. The Administration and Action modes both require the player to be able to provide input to the game. In the Administration mode, the player loads and saves games and sets options—while in the Action mode, the player controls and produces units.

If we use the scheme suggested earlier, then the Action and Administration modes could be in use simultaneously—which either limits the controls (buttons) that can be used for the Action mode or requires the buttons' functions to change when the Administration mode is active. However, neither of these options is desirable!

Let's revisit our plan to keep the Action mode available at all times. Why not consider this scheme:

Primary Screen:

- Action
- Administration

Secondary Screen

- Combat Information

Note that our original idea of considering game modes per screen didn't work. Since both screens share a single control scheme, they must be considered simultaneously when developing that scheme. This reveals a flaw in the process we outlined in Chapter 6. We considered modes for the purposes of control schemes specifically—which isn't really applicable in the case of the DS, where the second screen is often used for feedback only. We'll consider how we'll use the Combat Information mode when we look into the feedback schemes for *CQ*, though we might find that some of the controls should be linked to the Secondary Screen regardless of what mode the Primary Screen is in.

Another arrangement would be to separate ordering units and managing resources into two different modes. The primary advantage to this scheme would be that we could have a more robust resource management aspect to the game. Doing so, however, would require that we take unit control away from the player. Instead, we'll explore a simplified resource management system that can be utilized while still being able to command units from the same mode.

Diagram by Per Olin

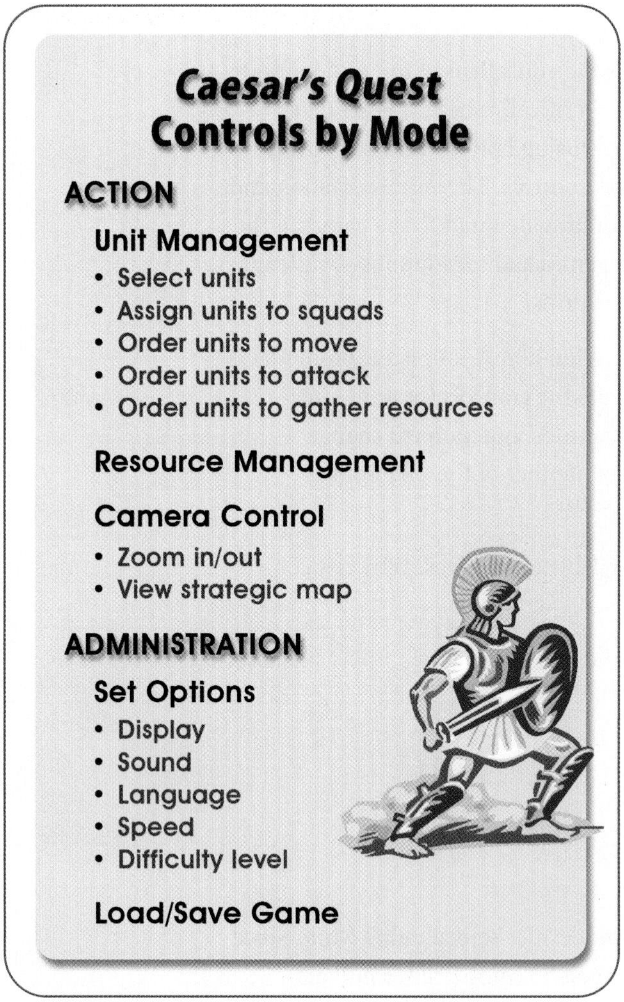

Caesar's Quest Controls by Mode

ACTION

Unit Management
- Select units
- Assign units to squads
- Order units to move
- Order units to attack
- Order units to gather resources

Resource Management

Camera Control
- Zoom in/out
- View strategic map

ADMINISTRATION

Set Options
- Display
- Sound
- Language
- Speed
- Difficulty level

Load/Save Game

Assigning controls to each game mode reveals the requirements of *Caesar's Quest's* interface design.

Organize Modes by System

Combining the last two steps reveals which systems must be covered in each of the game modes that use the Primary Screen. By mode we have the controls listed in the accompanying diagram.

Now that we understand the systems that we must support in each mode, we can begin to assign controls to all of the required functionality. Because we are intentionally designing *CQ* to be a fairly simple game, the number of modes is small. A more complicated game, such as a role-playing game (RPG) or turn-based strategy game (TBS), might have half a dozen modes or more—with each supporting multiple systems.

I nterfaces are becoming more integrated into games, and I think that trend will continue. I've always been interested in seeing more gesture-related interfaces come about. *Black & White* and *Darwina* both have gesture recognition in their interfaces, and I think we'll see more of that in the years to come.

—*Ian Wall*
(Senior Artist, Obsidian Entertainment)

Determining Controls for Action Mode

Looking at the list of actions we've defined for the player in the Action mode, it is clear that some details are left out. While we have identified that the player needs to be able to select units, we haven't established that there is a cursor that the player moves to do so. As we determine the exact controls, we'll develop any of these details that we missed in our first pass.

Navigation in *CQ* is accomplished by moving a cursor with the D-pad. The cursor moves toward the edge of the screen until a certain point and then the terrain scrolls beneath it. This implementation—as opposed to the cursor remaining in the center and the terrain always scrolling— seems best. It allows the players to have their units and enemy units at opposite edges of the screen and then command their units without changing their view of the map.

When nothing is selected, the A button selects the unit or structure underneath the cursor. If a unit is already selected, then pressing A while another unit is under the cursor results in both being selected. When a unit, squad, or build-

ing is selected, the B button unselects it and the A button performs an action. This convention is consistent with the standard for DS games: A triggers an action, and B cancels it.

What we'll see are more uses of advanced technology in game interfaces, such as light controllers and visual capture devices. As the technology evolves, these devices will be able to detect our hand, arm and leg movements more effectively and translate them precisely within a game. Imagine playing a dancing game within an area of colored lights to detect your movements and see yourself controlling the character on the screen using a camera. Pretty neat stuff!

—Aaron Marks
(President, On Your Mark Music Productions)

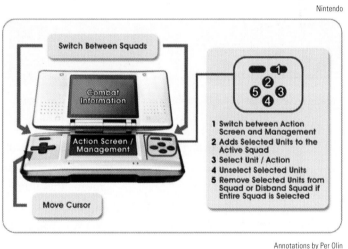

Nintendo

Control scheme for *Caesar's Quest.*

Annotations by Per Olin

Switch Between Squads

Combat Information

Action Screen / Management

Move Cursor

1 Switch between Action Screen and Management
2 Adds Selected Units to the Active Squad
3 Select Unit / Action
4 Unselect Selected Units
5 Remove Selected Units from Squad or Disband Squad if Entire Squad is Selected

I'd like to see more person-to-person gaming where people play together face-to-face in the real world. Right now they have to look at a screen and not at each other. Adding a lot of physical interaction and body movement will also address the sedentary drawbacks of gaming and bring people together rather than isolate them.

—Nicole Lazzaro
(Founder & President, XEODesign, Inc.)

Unit Management

Selection of a group of units is very difficult with the DS platform. Therefore, units will typically be selected and given orders as squads. The player can establish up to five squads at any time. The members of each squad are shown in the Combat Information screen. The player can switch between squads by using the R and L triggers.

Art by Ian Robert Vasquez

Possible contents when in the unit management system in *Caesar's Quest.*

Whenever one or more units are selected, the X button adds it to the current squad and the Y button removes it. If a squad is selected, then the X button absorbs all onscreen units into the active squad. Any units that already belong to another squad are not added to the active one, however, to prevent the player from accidentally dissolving them.

The player would also need some method of emptying a squad. With a squad selected, the Y button disbands it. By itself, this implementation makes it easy for the player to become frustrated through a mistake. Accidentally pressing the Y button could result in a disastrous organizational setback. Therefore, when a squad is disbanded, all of its members will remain currently selected—which means that immediately pressing the X button reforms the squad. To accidentally disband a squad, the player would have to press Y and then B.

> **A**llowing people to select and arrange the UI elements that they find useful will become increasingly important in the future.
>
> —*Stieg Hedlund*
> *(Lead Designer, Perpetual Entertainment)*

Resource Management

One of the more enjoyable features of RTSs for players is the large variety of units. Having many unit types forces the player to predict (or react to) the units enemies are using to create an army that can effectively counter theirs. With only one unit type, an important and interesting decision is not necessary.

CQ should then also allow for a wide variety of units. But how will players select which type he desires? With our limited control options, it quickly becomes clear that we are forced to add a new mode to the game—separating the resource management system into its own mode. Although doing so makes *CQ*'s interface somewhat clumsier, a quick review of PC RTS games reveals that this extra layer of interface is employed there as well! In order to build troops, the player must select the appropriate building and then click on the desired troop. While doing so, units are not selected (since the building is) and both attack and movement orders cannot be issued without first switching back to the unit management system. Even though the Action screen looks very similar in these two systems, it is still distinct.

Note that current PC RTS games include keyboard shortcuts that can allow the player to build units without exiting the unit management system. By moving around some of the controls for *CQ*, this could be accomplished on the DS as well—although the result might not be preferable. For example, only the right trigger might cycle through the squads, while the left trigger is used to build units in some way. This implementation would most likely feel awkward, however, since the two triggers would have very different functionality.

World of Warcraft®, StarCraft®, Diablo®, and Warcraft® images provided Blizzard Entertainment, Inc.

Though most of the game screen in *Warcraft III* still depicts the battlefield, resource management occurs in a system that is distinct from unit management.

If *CQ* did not implement squads, then the X and Y buttons and left and right triggers would be available to issue orders to build troops. We have made the decision, however, that squads are more important for the player than keeping army and resource management in the same mode. Depending upon the development time and resources available, it might be worthwhile to experiment with some of these other options to determine what feels most appropriate for the type of game you are creating.

Synergistic Design of Interface and Gameplay

Suppose that the gameplay of CQ were balanced such that each player only controlled a handful of units. These units engaged each other and died fairly quickly, making deciding which units to build a bigger part of gameplay than moving around large groups of units (because the players generally wouldn't have many units). For this flavor of gameplay, it might be worthwhile to reduce the support for squads and increase support for a more accessible way of building units. This simple example illustrates how the interface can directly support the type of gameplay desired.

Returning to the original problem, how might CQ provide for a large variety of units while maintaining an intuitive and accessible interface? Another issue that has not been addressed is how buildings are created. Both of these problems can be solved with the same design decision—not allowing the player to construct buildings.

Production queues are important in traditional RTS games such as *Command & Conquer: Generals—Zero Hour* because a player might not want to build units constantly.

If creating buildings isn't part of *CQ*, then the player's resources are only available for producing units. Furthermore, if players have only one "factory" that creates units, then they could conceivably issue orders to build units without ever having to select that factory (if we provided a different method of entering the resource management mode).

While in the resource management system, the player does not need to be able to add or remove units from control groups. The X and Y buttons can then change which troops are being created. If players have only one factory, then it isn't necessary to even have a production queue. In other words, if the game knows which unit the player wants to create, it should produce it whenever the player has the necessary resources. In most PC RTS games, the player might be saving resources to build a specific building—but since *CQ* does not allow the player to construct buildings, the game can assume that the player will always build units. (Some RTS games, such as *Battle Realms,* have buildings that do automatically create certain units—so the game does not require players to make this decision.)

> Transparency is the future of interface design. I'd like to see experiences that are so instinctively easy to engage that you are able to immerse yourself more fully into embodied experiences of playing games. It's somewhat analogous to the quality of special effects. The best effects are the ones you don't even notice as effects, but as real sights and sounds. The best interfaces will be the ones you don't even notice as interfaces, but as real actions in space and time.
>
> —*Drew Davidson*
> *(Faculty, Entertainment Technology Center, Carnegie Mellon University)*

Developing the Feedback Scheme

Now that the controls for *CQ* have been outlined, let's determine the feedback scheme. To some degree, this was already done while the controls were decided. However, many details have not yet been established,

> We will see more information displayed directly on the environment or character—similar to the racing game genre where damage to vehicles is shown in the form of scraps, dents, and broken parts.
>
> *Tim Donley*
> *(Lead Artist, Obsidian Entertainment)*

Action Screen Interface Feedback

First, let's consider what feedback we might want for the Action Screen. In addition to the normal sounds and visual cues for when buttons are pressed, we'll want a few more elements. To make the two sides obvious, they'll each use their own color: red for Caesar's troops and blue for Pompey's. (Red and blue are more distinct for most people with color blindness, making these two colors a better choice than, say, red and green.) Furthermore, Caesar's units will face right and Pompey's left. (We'll typically place Caesar's army on the left side of the map during our level design.)

Since *CQ*'s controls revolve around the squad, we should show which squad is currently selected. While this information could be displayed on the Combat Information Screen (the Secondary Screen), it is probably referenced often enough to deserve placement on the Action Screen.

We'll also want health indicators of some sort. While the details could be deferred to the Combat Information Screen, the Action Screen should convey this information to some degree. One option would be to have the units' coloring indicate their health levels. Fully healed units can use the brightest colors, with the coloring dimming to near grey for units that have almost been destroyed. Colorblind players may have difficulty distinguishing almost dead units of each side from each other, but they can also utilize the facing of the units to tell them apart.

> Interfaces of the future might begin to learn the habits or needs of the player and even intelligently configure themselves to meet each individual's play style or patterns.
>
> —*Troy Dunniway*
> *(Lead Game Designer, Midway Los Angeles)*

Combat Information Screen Feedback

The Combat Information Screen exists entirely to provide the player with feedback. What information should we display here to supplement what the Action Screen shows? As you would imagine, the normal components of an RTS should all be present. For *CQ*, we should include:

- Mini-map
- Stats for selected units
- Stats for any unit under the cursor
- Unit construction progress

The details of what information we'll actually display won't become obvious until more of the game has been designed—but these elements are a good starting point.

Art by Ian Robert Vasquez

A sample mock interface for the *Caesar's Quest* Combat Information Screen.

As time passes and the younger generation ages, some ways of interfacing with the world will change as well. When I was growing up, there was no Internet, no TIVO, no Google; the younger generation has never known a world without these things.

—Joe Maruschak
(Creative Director, GarageGames)

Note that the interface design we've proposed here is by no means the only solution. It is one possible interface to achieve specific goals. How well it works depends upon many other aspects of the game.

For example, this interface was designed for a game that emphasizes troop movements and tactics. The player is not able to construct buildings and only possesses a single building. Will it be possible to create a compelling game along these lines? More important, will this game feel like an RTS? Without implementing and playtesting, it is often hard to answer these questions. Game interface design is a complicated field, with many differing opinions. Theory and planning will help you to construct great interfaces—but without rigorous testing, it will often be impossible to determine how strong your designs really are. Keep in mind that interface design is an iterative process and you will rarely, if ever, end up with the perfect interface on your first attempt.

Shawna Olwen on Interfaces for the "Net-Generation"

Shawna Olwen
(President, Digital
Simulation Labs)

Shawna Olwen began in the feature film industry as a specialist in the areas of photorealistic people and clothing. She made significant contributions in modeling and animation to such films as *Titanic, The Mask, The Little Princess,* and *Batman.* Her game industry credits include *Barbie "Cool Looks" Fashion Designer* and Meta4's MMOG technology. Digital Simulation Labs is a company that specializes in the creation of algorithms for the visually realistic deformation of cloth Fabrix™ and animation tools for digital artists. Fabrix was a standard in the feature film industry and is striving toward the goal of real-time cloth simulation for games. Shawna has been guest lecturer at the University of Pennsylvania, Human Visualization Department for Norman Badler, and the Annenberg School of Communication. She was also a guest teacher at the Fashion Institute of Technology and at the New York Chapter of Siggraph, where she discussed design issues affecting computer-generated fabric. Currently, Shawna is a adjunct facilitator for the Art Institute Online in the Game Art and Design program.

A huge portion of gamers now fall into what is dubbed the "net-generation" (1977–1994)—according to Don Tapscott, the chairman of the research think-tank Alliance for Converging Technologies. These players like options, customization, the ability to change their minds, and the ability to "try before you buy." With this generation having upwards of $130 billion of disposable income and influencing their parents' spending of an estimated $500 billion, this extremely computer-literate market segment—which is under 20 years of age and 88 million strong—will have a huge voice in how the video game market formats future game projects.

People within this bracket grew up with technology and demand more from it. For games to compete for this generation's mindshare, interfaces will have to be highly adaptable—not the ordinary forking *path choice= consequence* interactivity, but mutable immersive environments that contain highly customizable characters orchestrated by an artificially intelligent nervous system. This is the generation that I believe will not just want, but demand to be able to create and own their content. Game companies that are aware of how and why technology is a second skin to this generation will strive to include the customer (player) in the content creation process as much as possible.

References: Don Tapscott (http://www.growingupdigital.com) and Lisa Krakowka, "Kaleidoscope: A Swiftly Changing Scene," American Demographics (http://www.findarticles.com/articles/mi_m4021)

[Note: For more information on the "net" generation (also known as the "millennial" generation), see Chapter 2 of Game Development Essentials: An Introduction *by Jeannie Novak.]*

> The future of game interface design is that there will be no interface. The game experience will be so compelling that the interface will melt away.
>
> —John Comes
> (Lead Content Engineer, Gas Powered Games)

In this chapter, you have combined the lessons you have learned throughout this book and have applied them to the design of the interface for an unorthodox game design. Remember: The most important tools at your disposal—whether designing games, game interfaces, or something else entirely—are your creativity and ingenuity. Regardless of what design "rules" you learn, every situation is unique and you need to determine what is best for the specific challenges you face.

After reading this book, you should have a clear understanding of how important interface design is to a game project. Incorporate what you've learned in this book into your original game ideas—and focus on how your interface can truly enhance the game experience!

1. How can you identify both control and feedback schemes within an original interface? Create interfaces for an original game idea. List all elements that convey information to the player and those that empower the player.

2. Choose a genre and platform that are usually not associated with one another, and create hypothetical manual and visual interfaces for this combination. (Your manual interface should consist of an original or "exotic" interface. You might also want to modify the mappings on the controller associated with the platform you chose so that it interfaces with the game in a unique way.)

3. Choose a new platform for the idea discussed in this chapter *(Caesar's Quest)*. Create new manual and visual interfaces for the game based on the platform change.

4. How might story elements affect the design of a game's visual interface? Choose an event in history and list game story elements (e.g., setting, premise, backstory) related to that event. What genre do you think would be most appropriate for a game based on this event? What interface elements would be required in order to convey actions associated with this event?

5. What is the future of game interface design? Discuss whether you agree or disagree with some of the statements made by industry professionals in this chapter. How do you personally see interface design changing? Consider how both hardware and software advances might affect interface design.

Resources

There's a wealth of information on game development and related topics discussed in this book. Here is just a sample list of books, news sites, organizations, and events you should definitely explore!

News

Blues News—www.bluesnews.com

Computer Games Magazine—www.cgonline.com

Game Daily Newsletter—www.gamedaily.com

Game Developer Magazine—www.gdmag.com

Gamers Hell—www.gamershell.com

Game Music Revolution (GMR)—www.gmronline.com

Game Rankings—www.gamerankings.com

GameSlice Weekly—www.gameslice.com

GameSpot—www.gamespot.com

GameSpy—www.gamespy.com

Game Industry News—www.gameindustry.com

GIGnews.com—www.gignews.com

Internet Gaming Network (IGN)—www.ign.com

Machinima.com—www.machinima.com

Music4Games.net—www.music4games.net

1UP—www.1up.com

PC Gamer—www.pcgamer.com

Star Tech Journal [technical side of the coin-op industry]—www.startechjournal.com

UGO Networks (Underground Online)—www.ugo.com

Video Game Music Archive—www.vgmusic.com

Wired Magazine—www.wired.com

Directories & Communities

Apple Developer Connection—developer.apple.com

Betawatcher.com—www.betawatcher.com

Fat Babies.com [game industry gossip]—www.fatbabies.com

Gamasutra—www.gamasutra.com

GameDev.net—www.gamedev.net

Game Development Search Engine—www.gdse.com

Game Music.com—www.gamemusic.com

Game Rankings—www.gamerankings.com

Games Tester—www.gamestester.com

Moby Games—www.mobygames.com

Overclocked Remix—www.overclocked.org

Organizations

Academy of Interactive Arts & Sciences (AIAS)—www.interactive.org

Academy of Machinima Arts & Sciences—www.machinima.org

Association of Computing Machinery (ACM)—www.acm.org

Digital Games Research Association (DiGRA)—www.digra.org

Entertainment Software Association (ESA)—www.theesa.com

Entertainment Software Ratings Board (ESRB)—www.esrb.org

Game Audio Network Guild (GANG)—www.audiogang.org

International Computer Games Association (ICGA)—www.cs.unimaas.nl/icga

International Game Developers Association (IGDA)—www.igda.org

SIGGRAPH—www.siggraph.org

Events

Electronic Entertainment Expo (E3)
May—Los Angeles, CA
www.e3expo.com

Consumer Electronics Show (CES)
January—Las Vegas, NV
www.cesweb.org

Game Developers Conference (GDC)
March—San Jose, CA/San Francisco, CA (cities alternate)
www.gdconf.com

D.I.C.E. Summit
March—Las Vegas, NV
www.interactive.org/dice

SIGGRAPH
Summer—Los Angeles, CA; San Diego, CA; Boston, MA (location varies)
www.siggraph.org

Austin Game Developers Conference
September—Austin, TX
www.gameconference.com

Indie Games Con (IGC)
October—Eugene, OR
www.garagegames.com

Books & Articles

Adams, E. (2003). *Break into the game industry.* McGraw-Hill Osborne Media.

Adams, E. (September 14, 1999). "Designing and developing sports games." *Gamasutra.*

Ahearn, L. & Crooks II, C.E. (2002). *Awesome game creation: No programming required. (2nd ed).* Charles River Media.

Axelrod, R. (1985). *The evolution of cooperation.* Basic Books.

Bates, B. (2002). *Game design: The art & business of creating games.* Premier Press.

Bethke, E. (2003). *Game development and production.* Wordware.

Brin, D. (1998). *The transparent society.* Addison-Wesley.

Broderick, D. (2001). *The spike: How our lives are being transformed by rapidly advancing technologies.* Forge.

Brooks, D. (2001). *Bobos in paradise: The new upper class and how they got there.* Simon & Schuster.

Caminos, R., & Stellmach, T. (March 26, 2004). "Cross-platform user interface design." *Gamasutra.*

Campbell, J. (1972). *The hero with a thousand faces.* Princeton University Press.

Campbell, J. & Moyers, B. (1991). *The power of myth.* Anchor.

Castells, M. (2001). *The Internet galaxy: Reflections on the Internet, business, and society.* Oxford University Press.

Chiarella, T. (1998). *Writing dialogue.* Story Press.

Cooper, A., & Reimann, R. (2003). *About face 2.0: The essentials of interaction design.* Wiley.

Crawford, C. (2003). *Chris Crawford on game design.* New Riders.

Csikszentmihalyi, M. (1991). *Flow: The psychology of optimal experience.* Perennial.

Dalmau, D. (November 8, 1999). "Learn faster to play better: How to shorten the learning cycle." *Gamasutra.*

DeMaria, R. & Wilson, J.L. (2003). *High score!: The illustrated history of electronic games.* McGraw-Hill.

Egri, L. (1946). *The art of dramatic writing: Its basis in the creative interpretation of human motives.* Simon and Schuster.

Evans, A. (2001). *This virtual life: Escapism and simulation in our media world.* Fusion Press.

Fox, B. (2004). *Game interface design.* Thomson Course Technology.

Friedl, M. (2002). *Online game interactivity theory.* Charles River Media.

Fruin, N. & Harringan, P. (Eds.) (2004). *First person: New media as story, performance and game.* MIT Press.

Fullerton, T., Swain, C. & Hoffman, S. (2004). *Game design workshop: Designing, prototyping & playtesting games.* CMP Books.

Galitz, W.O. (2002). *The essential guide to user interface design: An introduction to GUI design principles and techniques.* (2nd ed.). Wiley.

Gardner, J. (1991). *The art of fiction: Notes on craft for young writers.* Vintage Books.

Gershenfeld, A., Loparco, M. & Barajas, C. (2003). *Game plan: The insiders guide to break in and succeeding in the computer and video game business.* Griffin Trade Paperback.

Gladwell, M. (2000). *The tipping point: How little things can make a big difference.* New York, NY: Little Brown & Company.

Gleick, J. (1987). *Chaos: Making a new science.* Viking.

Gleick, J. (1999). *Faster: The acceleration of just about everything.* Vintage Books.

Godin, S. (2003). *Purple cow: Transform your business by being remarkable.* Portfolio.

Hamilton, E. (1940). *Mythology: Timeless tales of gods and heroes.* Mentor.

Heim, M. (1993). *The metaphysics of virtual reality.* Oxford University Press.

Irving, R. (April 12, 2002). "Lost along the way: Design pitfalls on the road from conception to completion." *Gamasutra.*

Johnson, S. (1997). *Interface culture: How new technology transforms the way we create & communicate.* Basic Books.

Jung, C.G. (1969). *Man and his symbols.* Dell Publishing.

Kent, S.L. (2001). *The ultimate history of video games.* Prima.

King, S. (2000). *On writing.* Scribner.

Knoke, W. (1997). *Bold new world: The essential road map to the twenty-first century.* Kodansha International.

Koster, R. (2005). *Theory of fun for game design.* Paraglyph Press.

Krawezyk, M. & Novak, J. (2006). *Game development essentials: Game story and character development.* Thomson Delmar.

Kurzweil, R. (2000). *The age of spiritual machines: When computers exceed human intelligence.* Penguin.

Laramee, F.D. (Ed.) (2005). *Secrets of the game business. (3rd ed).* Charles River Media.

Laramee, F.D. (Ed.) (2002). *Game design perspectives.* Charles River Media.

Laurel, B. (1990). *The art of human-computer interface design.* Pearson Education.

Laurel, B. (Ed.) (2003). *Design research: Methods and perspectives.* MIT Press.

Levy, P. (2001). *Cyberculture.* University of Minnesota Press.

Lewis, M. (2001). *Next: The future just happened.* W.W.Norton & Company.

Mackay, C. (1841). *Extraordinary popular delusions & the madness of crowds.* Three Rivers Press.

MacQueen, D. (November 25, 2002) "Postmortem: The game kitchen's wireless pets." *Gamasutra.*

Marks, A. (2001). *The Complete Guide to Game Audio.* CMP Books.

McConnell, S. (1996). *Rapid development.* Microsoft Press.

Mencher, M. (2002). *Get in the game: Careers in the game industry.* New Riders.

Michael, D. (2003). *The indie game development survival guide.* Charles River Media.

Montfort, N. (2003). *Twisty little passages: An approach to interactive fiction.* MIT Press.

Moravec, H. (2000). *Robot.* Oxford University Press.

Morris, D. & Hartas, L. (2003). *Game art: The graphic art of computer games.* Watson-Guptill Publications

Mulligan, J. & Patrovsky, B. (2003). *Developing online games.* New Riders.

Murray, J. (2001). *Hamlet on the holodeck: The future of narrative in cyberspace.* MIT Press.

Negroponte, N. (1996). *Being digital.* Vintage Books.

Nielsen, J. (1999). *Designing web usability: The practice of simplicity.* New Riders.

Novak, J. (2005). *Game development essentials: An introduction.* Thomson Delmar.

Novak, J. (2003). "MMOGs as online distance learning applications." University of Southern California.

Oram, A. (Ed.) (2001). *Peer-to-peer.* O'Reilly & Associates.

Rheingold, H. (1991). *Virtual reality.* Touchstone.

Rheingold, H. (2000). *Tools for thought: The history and future of mind-expanding technology.* MIT Press.

Rogers, E.M. (1995). *Diffusion of innovations.* Free Press.

Rollings, A. & Morris, D. (2003). *Game architecture & design: A new edition.* New Riders.

Rollings, A. & Adams, E. (2003). *Andrew Rollings & Ernest Adams on Game design.* New Riders.

Rouse III, R. (2001) *Game design: Theory & practice.* Wordware.

Saladino, M. (November 19, 1999). "Postmortem: Star Trek—Hidden Evil." *Gamasutra.*

Salen, K. & Zimmerman, E. (2003). *Rules of play.* MIT Press.

Sanger, G.A. [a.k.a. "The Fat Man"]. (2003). *The Fat Man on Game Audio.* New Riders.

Sellers, J. (2001). *Arcade fever.* Running Press.

Standage, T. (1999). *The Victorian Internet.* New York: Berkley Publishing Group.

Strauss, W. & Howe, N. (1992). *Generations.* Perennial.

Strauss, W. & Howe, N. (1993). *13th gen: Abort, retry, ignore, fail?* Vintage Books.

Strauss, W. & Howe, N. (1998). *The fourth turning.* Broadway Books.

Strauss, W. & Howe, N. (2000). *Millennials rising: The next great generation.* Vintage Books.

Tufte, E.R. (1983). *The visual display of quantitative information.* Graphics Press.

Tufte, E.R. (1990). *Envisioning information.* Graphics Press.

Tufte, E.R. (1997). *Visual explanations.* Graphics Press.

Turkle, S. (1997). *Life on the screen: Identity in the age of the Internet.* Touchstone.

Van Duyne, D.K. et al. (2003). *The design of sites.* Addison-Wesley.

Vogler, C. (1998). *The writer's journey: Mythic structure for writers. (2nd ed).* Michael Wiese Productions.

Williams, J.D. (1954). *The compleat strategyst: Being a primer on the theory of the games of strategy.* McGraw-Hill.

West, N. (May 2005). "Pushing buttons: Intelligent resolutions for ambiguous player controls." *Game Developer,* pp. 19-26.

Wolf, J.P. & Perron, B. (Eds.). (2003). *Video game theory reader.* Routledge.